Educating in Faith

The English Catholic Public School since 1800

— MARK CLEARY —

Sacristy
Press

Sacristy Press
PO Box 612, Durham, DH1 9HT

www.sacristy.co.uk

First published in 2024 by Sacristy Press, Durham

Copyright © Mark Cleary 2024
The moral rights of the author have been asserted.

All rights reserved, no part of this publication may be reproduced or transmitted in any form or by any means, electronic, mechanical photocopying, documentary, film or in any other format without prior written permission of the publisher.

Every reasonable effort has been made to trace the copyright holders of material reproduced in this book, but if any have been inadvertently overlooked the publisher would be glad to hear from them.

Sacristy Limited, registered in England & Wales, number 7565667

British Library Cataloguing-in-Publication Data
A catalogue record for the book is available from the British Library

ISBN 978-1-78959-337-2

Contents

Preface..iv
Acknowledgements..ix
List of illustrations and credits..............................x
List of tables...xii

Introduction: The Catholic public school..........................1

Chapter 1. Education in a missionary country c.1800–1914........18
Chapter 2. A new-found confidence c.1914–40.....................67
Chapter 3. The Last Hurrah! c.1940–70..........................116
Chapter 4. Reinventing the model? c.1975–2010..................149
Chapter 5. A crisis of authority: The schools and child sexual abuse . 182

Conclusion: Contemporary perspectives and looking ahead........210

Bibliography..230
Index..241

Preface

The Catholic public schools in England have a shared history of over 200 years. It was the emancipation of Roman Catholics, beginning in the late eighteenth century, and ending in the Emancipation Act of 1829, which created the conditions in which Catholic public schools could emerge. Taking advantage of a gradual loosening of restrictions on Catholics in society, the earliest public schools were migrants from the Continent—Ampleforth, Stonyhurst, Downside and Ushaw—joining already existing, small schools at Sedgley Park, Oscott and Old Hall (which became St Edmund's). Alongside an expansion of the English public schools more generally, new Catholic establishments at Prior Park, Mount St Mary's, Ratcliffe, the Oratory School, Cotton, Beaumont, Belmont Abbey and Douai were added to the list by the early twentieth century. It is this group of 15 or so major boys' boarding schools that are the chief focus of this book; their history, structures and character encapsulated many of the features that were integral to the shape and direction of Roman Catholic elite education over many decades. Space does not allow the very significant Catholic secondary day schools for boys, and convent schools for girls, to be covered here. They must await their own historians.

These schools, for all their diversity and varying histories, shared a range of characteristics. They were boarding schools for boys only who might spend some two-thirds of their young lives in that environment. They catered almost wholly for a Catholic elite or, in later decades, for a growing upper-middle-class constituency. They were established by different religious groups, who shared a single-minded determination to create an elite section of Catholic society that was well educated, socially well networked, and imbued with a strong sense of the importance of Catholic spirituality, morals and teaching in everyday life. The aspiration to create such an elite was, of course, shared by the growing numbers of Anglican and non-denominational public schools emerging by the end of the nineteenth century. But what made the Catholic public school so distinctive was that it was staffed almost exclusively by priests, monks and lay brothers. Whilst other public schools had, to varying degrees, elements of religious focus and spirituality—a focus which was, in any case, declining in many such schools by the end of the century—the Catholic boarding schools alone were staffed almost entirely by secular priests, members of the religious orders and teaching brothers. It made them unique. That is not to argue that lay teachers were absent. They were an important part of the teaching staff, especially as the numbers of clerical staff began to fall towards the end of the millennium. But the clerical staff were fundamental to the character and ethos of the schools. Every aspect of a boy's education, daily life, military, sporting and cultural activities, and worship was under the control and eye-line of the clerical teachers and authorities in the school. That gave the Catholic public school a unique character which set it apart from the public-school sector as a whole. Whilst the public schools began to retitle themselves as independent schools (largely for marketing reasons) from the late 1970s, for consistency the term "public school" continues to be used here.

Our focus is, in part, on the individual histories of this group of schools. Founded at different times and for different reasons, these histories reveal much about the motivations of the religious authorities controlling the schools, the extent to which these schools sought to model themselves on public schools as a whole, and on the nature of the educational experience they offered. A number of school histories have provided an important source of information and insight for this book. The detail they contain about the nature and development of individual schools has been invaluable. The aim of this book, however, is not to provide a detailed history of every aspect of these schools, but rather to set their individual development within a wider historical, social and political context. Two themes underpin our understanding of how, and why, these distinctive schools emerged and developed as they did.

First, it is important to see the growth of these schools alongside the wider educational activities of the Catholic Church. From Emancipation in 1829, through the educational changes of the early twentieth century, the development of free secondary schooling following the 1944 Education Act, and the educational reorganizations of recent decades, the Catholic Church has consistently devoted huge energy, resources and political influence to seeking to provide an education for all members of its community in order to secure and maintain the strength of the Catholic faith. Put bluntly, schooling, the Church argued, should be within a strong Catholic framework, taught by Catholics and managed by the Church authorities. State support was always welcomed (and fought for), but control must remain with the bishops. The development of free elementary education for a rapidly growing Catholic community in the latter part of the nineteenth century, the expansion of Catholic day schools, public schools and grammar schools, and the growth of secondary schooling in the 1950s and 1960s, all required huge resources to be ploughed into the wider educational mission.

That money came from rich supporters and benefactors on the one hand, and the "penny collections" of countless parishes across the country, on the other. Within this wider context, providing an elite boarding education for a very small segment of young, privileged Catholic boys in the public schools might be seen as somewhat questionable. Why place significant numbers of priests or monks in boarding schools designed to teach a Catholic elite when there were very urgent and pressing needs in the local schools, parish or mission? Why divert resources needed in poor urban parishes in Liverpool or Birmingham, to support a Catholic elite in colleges in the countryside of Yorkshire, Lancashire or the Midlands? It was a tension that was always present, especially within the Benedictine monastic communities who set up many of these schools alongside their missionary work, and which was to become critical and, ultimately, unsustainable, as vocations to the religious life began to decline from the 1960s onwards.

A second important context in the development of these schools was their relationship with English Catholicism as a whole. The establishment of these public schools was, in part at least, a response to the loosening of attitudes towards Catholics in the early nineteenth century, and to the rapid growth in numbers of Catholics in the nineteenth century, due to Irish immigration and converts from the Church of England. The latter, in particular, helped to boost demand for a Catholic public-school education, because they were often aristocratic, wealthy, had attended public schools in their youth, and wanted the same for their offspring.

What John Henry Newman (canonized in 2019) called the "Second Spring" of Catholicism in the 1850s, helped to encourage the emergence of new Catholic public schools and the consolidation of older ones. Newman himself created and ran his own school, the Oratory School in Birmingham, as a fee-paying and elitist public school. A further growth in Catholic numbers and social confidence in the inter-war years of the twentieth century saw a significant strengthening of the public schools, alongside the creation of a number of strong and influential Catholic day grammar schools. The two decades or so following 1945 reinforced what some have called a "fortress Church" and others a "Catholic ghetto", when a kind of Catholic ecosystem of Church, priest, parish, school, and lay organizations might encompass, enclose and direct virtually every aspect of Catholic life. Vocations to the priesthood were high, the prestige and financial position of the public schools was positive, and it was a period of confidence in the future which I have termed the "last hurrah" for the Catholic public school. There was in some circles an almost hubristic faith in the continued presence and importance of public schools in Catholic life. The authority of the Church, the position and status of the priests and monks, and the confidence with which Catholic parents packed their boys off to boarding schools, seemed immutable.

What has changed in recent years? Underlying much of the evolution of these schools in recent decades has been the major fall in vocations to both the priesthood and the consecrated religious life as a whole. In short, that central, defining feature of the Catholic public school, the powerful presence and control exerted by the religious—priests, monks, lay brothers—has gone forever. Greater social liberalism, the growth of secularism, the impact of Vatican II (the Council of the Church from 1962–5 which wrought major changes in the liturgy and character of Catholic life and worship), have all impacted directly or indirectly on the nature and evolution of the schools. How these schools were created, developed and changed over the decades can only be properly understood within the context of strategies of Catholic education, and changes within the Catholic community as a whole. Former boys' schools are now primarily co-educational. Boarding is now for a minority, with day pupils dominating. Non-Catholics outnumber Catholics within many of these schools. Almost the entire teaching, management and governance structures in the schools has been transformed and is now delivered by lay rather than clerical staff. The chapel or Abbey, once such a central part of daily life in schools, now exists primarily to provide a chaplaincy and pastoral service to pupils, together with a convenient assembly hall. That close connection between the religious community—be they monks, priests or brothers—and the everyday life of the school has gone forever. The story of the growth, maturing and transformation of the Catholic public school is the subject of this book.

Acknowledgements

This book arose from an interest in Catholic education in England in the nineteenth and twentieth centuries. Alongside the enormous expansion of Catholic elementary education, these years saw a parallel growth in public schools catering for a new Catholic elite, and their history is traced in this book. A primary debt of thanks is due to those historians who have uncovered the character and ethos of a significant number of individual schools, a body of work which has been very important to this study, and which is gratefully acknowledged here. I would also like to thank those schools who kindly granted permission to use their photographic material in the book.

I am also grateful to a number of people who have offered help and support as the work has progressed. John Brophy, Nigel Cave, Denis Clarke, Paul Holmes, Simon Johnson, Giles Mercer and Mo Glackin all helped at various stages of the book. At home, Marie provided significant help with the text, and Matt and Chris were always helpful and supportive. I was fortunate enough to be able to use the library resources of Downside Abbey in my research, and am grateful to Abbey staff and fellow volunteers for their help in creating a unique working environment. The errors and omissions which undoubtedly remain are, of course, entirely my responsibility.

List of illustrations and credits

1. Hodder Place, Stonyhurst, late nineteenth century. By kind permission of the Governors of Stonyhurst College © Stonyhurst College.
2. Examinations Day Poster, Ampleforth, 1815. © Ampleforth Abbey Trustees, reprinted with kind permission.
3. Prospectus for Prior Park, early twentieth century. By kind permission of Prior Park Foundation.
4. Cotton College Study Place, c.1900. From Frank Roberts, *History of Sedgley Park and Cotton College*.
5. Stonyhurst Study Place, c.1907. By kind permission of the Governors of Stonyhurst College © Stonyhurst College.
6. Mount St Mary's College, front, late nineteenth century. By kind permission of Mount St Mary's College.
7. Beaumont College staff and pupils mourn the death of Queen Victoria, 1903. By kind permission of the Beaumont Union.
8. Prospectus for the Oratory School, 1859. By kind permission of the Oratory School.
9. Downside School and Monastery, c.1916. By kind permission of Downside Abbey General Trust.
10. Prior Park Centenary celebrations, 1930. By kind permission of the Prior Park Foundation.
11. Ampleforth buildings, early twentieth century. © Ampleforth Abbey Trustees, reprinted with kind permission.
12. Cotton College buildings, 1930s. From Canon W. Buscot, *Cotton College*, 1940.
13. Opening of Bickford Wing, St Edmund's College, 1938. By kind permission of St Edmund's College.
14. The Mount Association, 1910. By kind permission of Mount St Mary's College.

15. Corpus Christi Procession, Stonyhurst during the First World War. By kind permission of the Governors of Stonyhurst College © Stonyhurst College.
16. Table of Fees, St Edmund's College, 1921. By kind permission of St Edmund's College.
17. Science Lab and Teacher, St Edmund's College c.1910. By kind permission of St Edmund's College.
18. Talbot House, St Edmund's College, 1926. By kind permission of St Edmund's College.
19. College Captains at Mount St Mary's College, 1926. By kind permission of Mount St Mary's College.
20. The Mendip Hunt meeting in front of Downside School, c. late 1920s. By kind permission of Downside Abbey General Trust.
21. Cross-country running, Stonyhurst, 1950s. By kind permission of the Governors of Stonyhurst © Stonyhurst College.
22. School dormitory, the Oratory School, late 1950s. By kind permission of the Oratory School.
23. School washrooms at the Oratory School, late 1950s. By kind permission of the Oratory School.
24. Archbishop Griffin (an old Cottonian) with pupils at Cotton College, 1946. From Frank Roberts, *Sedgley Park and Cotton College*.
25. Cotton College Bicentenary celebrations, 1963. From Frank Roberts, *Sedgley Park and Cotton College*.
26. Prior Park Alumni, 1947. By kind permission of the Prior Park Foundation.
27. Queen Elizabeth II visiting Beaumont College, 1961. By kind permission of the Beaumont Union.

List of tables

1. Major Catholic public schools c.1900
2. Major alumni associations
3. Catholic Association of Teachers, Schools and Colleges, annual conferences, 1891–1956
4. Roman Catholic demographics, 1939–62
5. Educational background of lay, male entrants in *Who's Who in Catholic Life, 1997*
6. Independent Inquiry into Child Sexual Abuse
7. Educational background of Archbishops of Westminster, 1850–2009
8. Key contemporary Catholic education documents

INTRODUCTION

The Catholic public school

The history of the English public school has elicited a sizeable, entertaining and occasionally illuminating literature. *Tom Brown's Schooldays* still shapes many impressions of the fictionalized horrors of the Victorian public school, whilst a range of autobiographies from all eras fill shelves with accounts of the triumphs and tribulations of the public-school experience. It was an experience which has apparently both enriched and scarred generations of boys (and it is largely, though not entirely, a male rite of passage) over the years.[1]

Alongside this sometimes lurid and sensationalist literature, there are a range of histories of the English public schools, both individually and as a sector, which look at school origins and development, the character and life of the public school, and the place of public schools in the social, economic and political life of the country.[2] The wealth of studies of public

---

[1] For an introduction see V. Ogilvie, *The English Public School* (London: Batsford, 1957); J. Gathorne-Hardy, *The Public School Phenomenon* (London: Hodder & Stoughton, 1977); J. de S. Honey, *Tom Brown's Universe: The Development of the Victorian Public School* (London: Millington, 1977).

[2] See in particular T. Bamford, *The Rise of the Public Schools: A Study of Boys' Public Boarding Schools in England and Wales from 1837 to the Present Day* (London: Nelson, 1967); D. Turner, *The Old Boys: The Decline and Rise of the Public School* (London: Yale University Press, 2016); F. Greene and D. Kynaston, *Engines of Privilege: Britain's Private School Problem* (London: Bloomsbury, 2019); M. Peel, *The New Meritocracy: A History of UK Independent Schools, 1979–2015* (London: Elliot & Thompson, 2015); R. Verkaik, *Posh Boys: How English Public Schools Ruin Britain*, (London: Oneworld, 2018).

schools, especially for boys, much less for girls, is especially striking given that at no time in their history did they ever educate above about 7 per cent of all children, and it is only in recent years that the percentage has been as high as that. Yet the nature of public schools, their educational character, their social composition, and their role in facilitating access to the corridors of power has been a significant issue for many decades, if not centuries.

The development of what have come to be termed public schools dates back to the founding of Winchester in 1382 and Eton in 1440. The term is of course a misnomer: a familiar historical trope has it that the English public school was called English because it taught almost exclusively Latin and Greek, public because it was private and fee-paying, and a school because it devoted itself almost exclusively to beating, fagging and a cult of athleticism! The numbers of pupils at such schools by the mid-nineteenth century was rarely more than a few thousand, based in perhaps 20 or so schools across England.[3] Their status was firmly aristocratic, with the finely tuned differences between schools articulated through snobbery and the ability to secure senior positions in the state and Church for their alumni. Reputationally though, the mid-nineteenth century saw the public-school sector at something of a low point.

It took a government inquiry, the Clarendon Commission, reporting in 1864, to identify many of the weaknesses, and rather fewer of the strengths, of the public schools of the time.[4] Criticism of the curriculum, teaching methods, quality of boarding facilities, the food, and overall management were made, leading to the *Public Schools Act* (1869) which sought to improve the system, and tidy up the mess of charters which had underpinned their creation.[5] How many such schools were there? The

---

[3] Ogilvie, *English Public School*, pp. 8–10 contains a list of the dates of foundation of some 200 public schools.

[4] C. Shrosbee, *Public Schools and Private Education: The Clarendon Commission 1861–4 and the Public Schools Act* (Manchester: Manchester University Press, 1988).

[5] Shrosbee, *Public Schools*, pp. 30–5; S. J. Curtis and M. Boultwood, *An Introductory History of English Education since 1800* (London: University Tutorial Press, 1964), pp. 83–91.

Clarendon Commission focused on just nine schools: Eton, Winchester, Westminster, Charterhouse, St Paul's, Merchant Taylors, Harrow, Rugby and Shrewsbury. These nine henceforth became fossilized as the "original" public schools, against which all other public schools were pejoratively described as but pale imitations by the original group. In reality, there were significantly more (and, in some ways, many more significant) public schools than these.[6] Most, of course, up until the end of the twentieth century, were exclusively for boys. With these broad criteria in mind, one estimate identified around 175 various and varied public schools in operation in 1864.[7] A focus, even obsession, on social class, on connectivity with the higher echelons of government, business and politics and on exclusivity, were integral to most public schools, irrespective of the virtues or deficiencies of the particular schools themselves.

If there is a significant literature on public schools in general, that of the major Catholic public schools in England is tiny by comparison; there is no single recent volume which examines the history of these schools as a whole.[8] But the Catholic Church was very active in establishing, staffing and running public schools for the elite in England from the late

---

[6] Bamford, *Rise of the Public Schools*, pp. 108–10; Gathorne-Hardy, *Public School Phenomenon*, pp. 68–136.

[7] Ogilvie, *English Public School*, pp. 8–10.

[8] Broad accounts of the development of Catholic schools include: A. S. Barnes, *The Catholic Schools of England* (London: Williams & Norgate, 1926); W. J. Battersby, "Secondary Education for Boys", in G. A. Beck (ed.), *The English Catholics: Centenary Essays to Commemorate the Restoration of the Hierarchy of England and Wales* (London: Burns & Oates, 1950), pp. 322–6; A. C. Beales, "The Struggle for the Schools", in G. A. Beck (ed.), *The English Catholics: Centenary Essays to Commemorate the Restoration of the Hierarchy of England and Wales* (London: Burns & Oates, 1950), pp. 365–409; H. O. Evennett, *The Catholic Schools of England and Wales* (Cambridge: Cambridge University Press, 1944); A. B. Morris, *Fifty Years On: The Case for Catholic Schools* (Chelmsford: Matthew James, 2008), pp. 14–32; P. Shrimpton, *A Catholic Eton? Newman's Oratory School* (Leominster: Gracewing, 2005), pp. 10–34.

eighteenth century onwards. Something like a dozen of these schools were operating and thriving by the start of the twentieth century. The development of these public schools can only be fully understood within the context of the much wider efforts by the Church to create a network of schools to serve the growing Catholic population through the nineteenth and twentieth centuries.

Why then did the Church wish to establish their own elite public schools alongside the enormous efforts and resources that were already being devoted to providing a basic, Catholic elementary education for their growing, largely working-class congregations? The origins and early development of Catholic boarding education in England elicits a number of general comments about the Catholic educational mission, especially for the better-off classes who were the key market for all these schools. For the Catholic Church, a set of public schools, whether founded by the diocesan bishops, or by religious orders such as the Jesuits or the Benedictines, were seen as an important means of raising the social standing, authority and influence of Catholicism in the wider world. Better that a Catholic elite be trained in wholly Catholic schools, rather than being "corrupted" through attending one of the Protestant public schools. These public schools then, entirely Catholic in ethos and mission, would be the engine driving the creation of a more confident, assertive and influential Catholic elite. The model for such schools, for better or worse, was the traditional English public school.

The character and standing of the English public schools in the mid-nineteenth century was, however, hardly the most propitious example for the Catholic Church to follow. As we have seen, the Clarendon Commission, in examining the character, curriculum and organization of nine leading public schools was far from flattering, although a range of reforms and reformers (notably Arnold of Rugby and Thring of Uppingham) had, by the late nineteenth century, improved the standing and quality of a growing public-school system. The original nine schools established a Headmasters' Conference (the HMC), which by the end of the nineteenth century had a membership of around 100. Membership of the HMC often served as an indicator of public-school status, and the Fleming Report of 1944 actually ended up defining public schools as those schools in membership of the HMC.

What did these schools look like? Firstly, they were, and are, fee-paying rather than state-funded, and that, by and large, meant they were socially exclusive, although this was mitigated to a very small degree by bursaries and scholarship support. Secondly, they were primarily boarding schools, although, over time, the balance between day and boarding pupils in the public schools shifted with fashion and parental preference. In recent decades, for example, a significant number of former day grammar schools have moved into the public-school sector following shifts in government policy. Thirdly, the focus of the curriculum was historically on the classics; it was not until the twentieth century that the curriculum of many public schools began to embrace science and the wider humanities. Fourthly, many recruited their students at the age of 13 via the Common Entrance examination (introduced by the public schools from 1910), rather than the eleven-plus, which was dominant in the state-funded schooling system until recent decades, and which still survives in some pockets of the country. Many of the pupils going on to public schools at 13 had their early education in the fee-paying preparatory ("prep") schools, and most of the public schools had their own, specific preparatory schools in place by the early decades of the twentieth century.[9] Fifthly, they were socially exclusive, and that whiff (or overpowering smell) of exclusivity was a key marker for all of these schools, and an important differentiator between the schools themselves, with social exclusivity and elitism being the key to their market position and success.

From the foundations of Winchester and Eton, the flourishing of new foundations in the late sixteenth century—for example Shrewsbury (1552), Christ's Hospital (1552), Tonbridge (1553), or Westminster (1560)—to the flurry of Victorian foundations such as Marlborough (1843), Clifton (1862), or Bedales (1893)—the public schools have been important in educating and shaping elite generations of young men. Access to Oxford and Cambridge, the securing of positions in the senior levels of the structures of government, smoothing the path to progression in the Church of England and the professions, training generations for

---

[9] D. Leinster-Mackay, *The Rise of the English Prep School* (London: Falmer Press, 1984).

military or civil leadership in both country and Empire have all, at various times, been defining features of the public schools. They have long been the subject of close, sometimes critical scrutiny.

It is interesting to note that government inquiries into the public schools in the nineteenth century began from the premise that the existing public schools had dismal educational methods, were excessively brutal, and emotionally damaged their pupils in later life. Inquiries also noted how many public schools had consistently betrayed their founding charters by which they were supposed to provide free education for poor pupils, with fee-paying wealthier students only intended to constitute the exception. Their continued existence back in the 1860s was by no means certain, putting some context to the multitude of more recent inquiries and commissions, in which the focus has turned more sharply to issues of social and educational equity, and the role of public schools in perpetuating inequalities in access to positions of power and authority. If the images of barbaric and uncivilized customs and traditions have now been consigned firmly to the realms of fiction, the public schools remain important in debates about inequalities in the English educational system, and their impact on society at large. What, then, of the Catholic public schools?

Prior to the Reformation of course, all existing public schools (and that may have been as many as 20 boarding and day schools) were Catholic; they were public schools in a Catholic country. The Reformation introduced new doctrines, a new liturgy and new church structures. The authority of the pope in Rome, central to the Roman Catholic religion, was abandoned. New Church of England public schools emerged; some, but not as many as had been hoped, were able to use revenues from the dissolution of the monasteries and the chantries to fund their foundations. Existing public schools adapted fairly seamlessly to the new regime and continued to develop and grow. Following the Reformation, Catholic schools were declared illegal and that remained officially the case until the late eighteenth century. There were, however, a number of Catholic schools, both day and boarding, existing in a kind of quasi-legal status in the late seventeenth and eighteenth centuries, but the main subject of our book—the boys', fee-paying, largely boarding school, staffed primarily by Catholic priests, monks and lay brothers—disappeared from England for the 250 years or so from the onset of the Reformation until official toleration of Catholicism developed from the 1790s.

The key change from the Reformation onwards was of course that Roman Catholicism was illegal. Not only were Catholic rituals and practices banned (ranging from the liturgy of the Mass to the use of the rosary, the veneration of relics to the observance of some saints' days and pilgrimages), but Catholic priests could not legally enter the country, and Catholics were subject to prosecutions for treachery because of their stated allegiance in matters spiritual to an outside power, namely Rome. A series of increasingly hostile Recusancy Acts in the late sixteenth and early seventeenth centuries imposed a whole series of fines and imprisonment for those failing to accept the new forms of Church of England worship and the new spiritual authority of the monarch which replaced that of the pope. Fines for non-attendance at church services could bankrupt families. The capture, trial, and, in some cases, execution of Catholic priests, sat alongside huge changes in the material fabric of the Catholic traditions (what Duffy has termed "the stripping of the Altars") in the sixteenth and seventeenth centuries.[10]

As a consequence of these changes, Catholic education went underground and overseas for some two centuries between about 1550 and 1800. The implications for the survival of the religion were very significant, as any kind of Catholic school was banned, and there were, in any case, very few trained Catholic priests in the country to carry out a teaching role. Those members of the gentry and aristocracy who sought to continue as Catholics faced not only significant legal and financial challenges, but also enormous difficulties if they wished to educate their children in the "old Faith". In addition, the education and training of

---

[10] J. Bossy, *The English Catholic Community 1570–1850* (London: Darton, Longman & Todd, 1975); D. Rosman, *The Evolution of the English Churches 1500–2000* (Cambridge: Cambridge University Press, 2003), pp. 117–46; R. Hattersley, *The Catholics* (London: Vintage, 2018); V. A. McClelland and M. Hodgetts (eds), *From Without the Flaminian Gate: 150 Years of Roman Catholicism in England and Wales, 1850–2000* (London: Darton, Longman & Todd, 1999); E. Duffy, *The Stripping of the Altars: Traditional Religion in England 1400–1580* (London: Yale University Press, 1992).

students for the priesthood was also under threat since there were no seminaries (colleges set up to provide priestly training) in the country. The Church of England public schools continued to send their aspirant clergy to the new seminaries beginning to appear in the late sixteenth century, but that door was firmly closed to the Catholic community that had neither schools nor seminaries to provide for their future. Setting up such a system in Catholic continental countries was the only option.

In 1568, William Allen established a small English College and seminary near the new University of Douai, in the Spanish Netherlands, with the avowed intention of creating a cadre of priests to "serve on the English mission" in support of the Catholic population of England. By the end of the sixteenth century, the conjunction of a new religious order—the Jesuits, created by Ignatius Loyola—and the establishment of a number of new "English Colleges" in France, Spain, Italy and Portugal, to educate lay students and train new priests, meant that an English Catholic education survived, but only on the Continent. Those overseas outposts were to provide the important antecedents for many of the Catholic public schools which emerged in England from the late eighteenth and early nineteenth centuries.

Who then were the people that were active in ensuring that English Catholic education and the provision of priests could be both maintained during the period of continental exile, and subsequently developed in England as religious toleration grew? Two groups were especially significant in this work. The first were the priests, monks and friars who lived in semi-autonomous religious communities (usually in monasteries), under the authority of a religious superior (the Prior) and the discipline of a rule (*regula*). They were known as *regulars*. These groups included the Benedictines (under the rule of St Benedict), the Dominicans (rule of St Augustine) and the Franciscans (rule of St Francis), as well as newer groups such as the Jesuits, created in the mid-sixteenth century, and the Rosminians, Passionists and Christian Brothers, who arrived in the mid-nineteenth century. The first of these regulars, the Benedictines, were especially significant in England in the growth of Catholic public schools, but almost all the regulars were active in both missionary and educational work in the resurgent Catholic community of the nineteenth century. The pattern of a monastic community in an

Abbey church, alongside a boys' school, often in a semi-rural location, was to characterize many of the largest and most successful Catholic public schools through to recent decades. Communities such as the Benedictines and Jesuits, whilst owing ultimate allegiance to the pope, could nevertheless exercise a degree of independence of spirit and action with local and national loyalties, and differences in emphasis and tradition. At times, their role and interests might conflict with those of the Church authorities represented by the bishops as, for example, in the balance to be struck between educational work in the schools and work in the missions. The Jesuits, with their sometimes fearsome internal discipline and hierarchy, were at times regarded almost as a Church within a Church, and, for a time in the late eighteenth century, incurred significant pressure to disband. The Benedictines, too, often faced conflicting pressures between a contemplative, monastic life and the demands of education and missionary work.

The second group were those priests working in a defined region (which after 1850 was termed a diocese), under the authority of senior Vicars Apostolic, who took on the designation of bishops after the English Catholic Hierarchy was restored by the Vatican in 1850. They were regarded as "out in the world" (*saeculum*) rather than in a religious community, and were known as *seculars*. As with the regulars, they played a very important role in the survival of Catholicism in England, and in the later expansion of Catholic education of all kinds. They were often educated by the regulars but, rather than moving into perhaps a Benedictine or Jesuit community, they were recruited into work as seculars under a bishop. Existing church hierarchies in England (a pyramid, if you like, with the pope and bishops at the apex and the laity at the base) had disappeared with the Reformation, and the country became, in the terminology of Rome, a "missionary country". Papal authority was thus exercised directly through the *Sacred Congregation de Propaganda Fide* in Rome who played an important part in "managing" Catholic affairs in its missionary territories such as England. Decisions over things like appointments, territories, missionary strategies and the education and training of priests had to be continuously implemented through Propaganda until the start of the twentieth century. The work of the seculars—missionary activity, serving new parishes, establishing new schools—was guided by the Vicars Apostolic and later the bishops, at the head of regional dioceses. They became diocesan priests.

These two key groups, the regulars and seculars, should not be thought of as being in conflict. There were sometimes issues of power and responsibility which arose because the lines of authority could be complex and opaque, but such issues were pretty rare. Recruitment to the regular or secular orders might sometimes create tensions, especially as new colleges and seminaries competed for those lay students who wished to become priests. A Benedictine or Jesuit public school, for example, might well have an interest in steering potential recruits to its own order, whilst the bishops would be most anxious to secure recruits into secular vocations which it could control and allocate more easily. As we will see, schools established by either regulars or seculars might become adept at ensuring that "their" pupils chose a particular route into the priesthood.

As the strength of the old Recusancy laws began to be relaxed from the late eighteenth century, and anti-Catholic outbursts and violence eased somewhat, becoming episodic rather than chronic, the role of the Continental colleges became more, not less, important. Catholic schooling remained effectively illegal through to the closing decades of the eighteenth century, though it survived and was tolerated in some rural, more isolated pockets of the country. Political change in religious toleration was slow and piecemeal, but the first Catholic Relief Act (1778) permitted, for example, the building of Catholic chapels, provided they were not free-standing and did not have a tower or spire to mark them out. Regulations on Catholic marriages and burials were also eased in the early nineteenth century.

Catholic schools enjoyed quasi-legal status and, from 1791, Catholics were permitted to enter the professions. By the start of the nineteenth century, the prohibitions on Catholics sending their children to be educated or trained as priests overseas (prohibitions which had, in any case, long been defied by the old Catholic families) were lifted, and Catholic colleges were legally permitted in England. At the same time, some of the overseas colleges were struggling and found themselves short of both students and money.[11] Somewhat ironically this more benign political environment in England coincided with the French Revolution, and with growing political and religious uncertainty on the Continent. These changes prompted the shift of some overseas colleges back to England. Four of the most famous Catholic public schools—St Edmund's (Diocesan), Ampleforth (Benedictine), Downside (Benedictine), and Stonyhurst (Jesuit)—all arrived back on English soil in this period from their continental homes.

The end of much of the anti-Catholic legislation came with the Emancipation Act of 1829.[12] It was, in part, a consequence of pressure from the old, recusant Catholic aristocracy, together with influential social and political groups such as exiled French clergy and Catholic military who had fought with Wellington against the French, who paved the way for the 1829 Act. Such groups exemplified the traditional "gentry management" of the Church, which was eventually to weaken with the growth and increased centralization of the Church from the mid-nineteenth century. The restoration of the English Catholic Hierarchy by the pope in 1850 established a structure of dioceses across the country, with a bishop for each diocese, and the Archbishop of Westminster at the top of the Hierarchy. Bishops were appointed with very specific territorial titles, designed to clearly differentiate the Catholic bishops from their Church of England counterparts.[13] The whole panoply of customs and traditions that had marked the Church in pre-Reformation and recusancy times were declared "to be abrogated in principle and the new hierarchy was given a free hand to conduct itself with them as

---

[11] Bossy, *English Catholic Community*, pp. 295–332; *Catholic Emancipation 1829–1929: Essays by Various Writers* (London: Green & Co., 1929); E. Norman, *Roman Catholicism in England* (Oxford: Oxford University Press, 1985), pp. 33–82; B. Green, *The English Benedictine Congregation* (London: Catholic Truth Society, 1979), p. 31.

[12] Norman, *Roman Catholicism*, pp. 57–82.

[13] Beck, *The English Catholics: Centenary Essays to Commemorate the Restoration of the Hierarchy of England and Wales* (London: Burns & Oates, 1950), pp. 86–115.

it saw fit".[14] These sets of changes underpinned the creation of a tightly organized, rather rigid and inflexible structure, whose main rationale was adherence to Rome and the papacy at all costs. It has sometimes been termed "ultramontane" (i.e. reinforcing the power of Rome "beyond the mountains" that surrounded the city). "More Roman than Rome" was one of the more charitable epithets used by some to describe the often rather inflexible doctrinal, spiritual and practical character of the emerging Church.[15] That character was to set the tone for the Catholic public schools that developed from the early nineteenth century.

From about 1800, the Catholic public school emerged in England as a distinctive educational institution. We can define it as a fee-paying boarding school for boys, set up and run almost entirely by diocesan authorities or the monastic orders, staffed almost entirely by priests, brothers or monks, and imbued with a powerful sense of Catholic religiosity. That religiosity was expressed through the timetable of the school day, the regularity with which Mass and the sacraments (notably Confession and Communion) were celebrated, and the continual presence of the religious in all aspects of daily life, from pre-breakfast attendance at church, through lessons and sports, to night prayers in the dormitory. The priest or monk was quite literally at the heart of every aspect of the daily lives of boys in these schools. Whilst in the numerous Church of England public schools any strong religious control and oversight had weakened by the end of the nineteenth century (with the exception of a few Nonconformist schools), in the Catholic schools, teaching, management and oversight were firmly in the hands of the dioceses and bishops or the religious orders. We can identify around a dozen or so such schools as constituting the core of this book—those of the Benedictines (Ampleforth, Downside, Douai, Belmont Abbey), the Jesuits (Stonyhurst, Mount St Mary's College, Beaumont), the Diocesan schools (Sedgley Park, St Edmund's, Ushaw, Oscott, Cotton College, Prior Park), the Oratory Fathers (Oratory School), the Rosminians (Ratcliffe), and a number of smaller, sometimes transient institutions,

---

[14] Bossy, *English Catholic Community*, p. 361.
[15] J. D. Holmes, *More Roman than Rome: English Catholicism in the Nineteenth Century* (London: Burns & Oates, 1978).

such as the schools run by the Dominicans (Laxton) and the Franciscans (St Bernardine's). Most of these schools eventually established their own preparatory schools for younger children wishing to progress to the senior school. Some also combined a role as seminaries (training priests) and schools (educating pupils) at various times. Not all have survived through to the present day.

The very important role of female religious communities, and the part they played in creating a network of Catholic day and boarding schools for girls across the country, is important to note. That achievement was remarkable, as was the role of the female religious communities in delivering elementary education through Catholic schools. Recording and celebrating that achievement through a history of the educational role that these female communities played is, unfortunately, beyond the means of this book. It certainly deserves a full and comprehensive study.

It is also worth noting that our focus is on the public schools rather than the seminaries. The seminaries offered a very specific higher education tailored closely to the requirements of the priesthood. There was an ongoing debate within the Catholic Church for much of the nineteenth and early twentieth centuries over whether it was appropriate for candidates for the priesthood to be educated alongside lay pupils. Sometimes the two groups studied together in the same institution; sometimes aspirants for the priesthood were separated into different streams within the same schools; sometimes they were placed within entirely different and separate institutions. In this study, the focus is on the schools, but, on occasion, and for certain periods of time, colleges such as Oscott, Ushaw and St Edmund's taught both "lay boys" and "church boys" together and provided a seminary training for the latter. They were, for a time, both public schools and seminaries. Oscott College in Birmingham, for example, was a distinguished public school and seminary from 1794 until 1889 when the school was closed, and it became effectively a national seminary serving a number of dioceses. It then reverted back in 1911 to functioning as a seminary, primarily for the Birmingham Diocese.[16]

---

[16] J. Champ (ed.), *Oscott College 1838–1988: A Volume of Commemorative Essays* (Oscott: Oscott Publishing, 1988).

It is worth underlining at the outset that the aspiration to create a new Catholic elite that underpinned so many of the newly established schools was inevitably compromised to some extent by what were effectively self-imposed restrictions on Catholics progressing to Oxford and Cambridge University. Whilst in the early part of the nineteenth century, matriculation at Oxford and Cambridge required a religious oath of allegiance, which was clearly problematic for Catholics, those restrictions had largely gone by mid-century (at Oxford, religious tests were abolished in 1854 and at Cambridge two years later). However, right up until the end of the century, pupils from the Catholic schools were barred by the Hierarchy from going to Oxbridge, thus closing off a vital routeway into the Establishment. Driven partly by a fear of the "corrupting vices" of the universities, and partly by a desire to create their own Catholic university in England (which proved a dismal failure), this blocking-off of access to Oxbridge undoubtedly limited the key aspiration of creating a new elite. By the start of the twentieth century, with the lifting of restrictions, the Catholic public schools began to compete with the rest of the public-school sector for sought-after Oxbridge places.

The origins and growth of the Catholic public schools in the nineteenth century is examined in Chapter 1. Some, as we noted earlier, had transferred from continental Europe as the political environment in England became more receptive to Catholics, others grew from missionary activity, and some sprang directly from individual endeavour by particular orders. By the first decades of the twentieth century, these schools had matured, as Chapter 2 shows. Their numbers and reputation grew, they expanded their facilities and academic range, and began to provide the members of a new Catholic Establishment, both aristocratic and upper middle-class, reflecting the changing status and confidence of the Catholic faith in England. Their old-boy networks and alumni activities multiplied. From the 1940s to perhaps the late 1960s and early 1970s, these schools, for all their individuality and differing features, were at their zenith. Catholic numbers, especially in the middle classes, had grown. The number of vocations to the priesthood and monastic orders was high, the Church itself was very self-confident, comfortable and, perhaps, complacent. Chapter 3 provides a picture of the schools in those years. Catholics were numerous, well connected and well represented in the professions. Their public schools reflected this sense of confidence, secure in the religious mission, and assertive in its values.

This seemingly inevitable rise of the Catholic public school was soon to face significant challenge. As Chapter 4 shows, the religious changes of Vatican II in the mid-1960s brought about wide-ranging transformations in the Catholic Church itself. The opening-up, or *aggiornimento* of the Church, which was one of the aims of the Council, meant structural, liturgical and personal change for all members of the Church—priests, monks, leaders and the laity alike. Those changes, together with the social and political turmoil of the 1960s, had significant consequences for their public schools. Vocations fell, sometimes dramatically, some priests left their orders, and Catholic parents experienced periods of major change, challenge and doubt about the best place to educate their children. Whilst Vatican II was by no means solely responsible for these changes, and the process itself was drawn out, things, quite simply, were never the same again. In the schools, lay teachers swiftly increased in numbers as both trainee priests (an important teaching resource in the schools) and ordained priest numbers fell.

These shifts meant that the school environment, characterized by close, continual control and oversight by priests, monks and brothers of so many aspects of the personal and academic life of their pupils, was weakened; the clerics were no longer there, and the boys and their parents were no longer automatically accepting of clerical authority as wider religious and social changes took place. In addition, the economic model which sustained many of the schools was threatened: the "free" labour of religious communities working in the schools was increasingly replaced by salaried lay staff. By the late 1980s and early 1990s, lay influence was greatly increased. Lay teachers and housemasters, lay headteachers, and governing bodies with significant lay membership were becoming the norm. Two key changes within the schools also led to fundamental alterations in the school environment. Co-education grew, and by the late 1980s almost all the schools in our study, as with most of the wider public-school network, had significant percentages of girls at all levels. The decision to accept girls was financial, not ideological or moral, and was facilitated by, and helped to contribute to, the precipitate collapse of many boarding convent schools for girls at around the same time.

A second feature was the arrival of ever-larger numbers of day pupils. For many generations, schools had stressed the virtues of the closed, all-male boarding environment in inculcating a strong sense of Catholic religiosity and values amongst pupils. The virtues of that close, almost 24/7 intimacy of the all-male boarding environment now suddenly gave way to a school prospectus extolling the clear and self-evident benefits of co-education, and of a system which encouraged day pupils. These changes, again driven by financial rather than ideological rationales, fundamentally altered the Catholic public school.

The impact of those wider changes within the school environment was to be seriously, near-fatally, damaged by issues of clerical abuse. Chapter 5 examines the nature and impact of this abuse in Catholic public schools which was to have a near-catastrophic impact on some schools. The emergence of accounts of significant historic clerical abuse within a number of Catholic boarding schools fundamentally undermined the core character and characteristics of the schools. The inquiries into safeguarding issues in Catholic boarding and day schools, and, in particular, the government inquiry, led by Professor Jay, which reported between 2018 and 2022 (the Independent Inquiry into Child Sexual Abuse or IICSA), and which focused in particular on the Benedictine boarding schools, served to highlight the ways in which so many of the features of the schools which persisted until the 1970s—all-male environments; the overwhelming and sometimes suffocating power of priests, monks and brothers; the lack of appropriate governance and safeguarding—contributed to an environment in which abuse might emerge. The intertwined everyday intimacies that were characteristic of the Catholic boarding school could, in the wrong hands, be personally and socially damaging for pupils. The model was greatly compromised, not just as a result of a collapse in vocations, or of wider social change, but because without a serious engagement with child safeguarding issues, the school environment potentially exposed pupils to significant damage. A changed model and restructured schools were, and remain, the only option.

Whilst there have been school closures, most of the Catholic public schools, however, have weathered these storms. They continue to recruit, to develop, to invest and to compete. As I argue in the Conclusion, their structures, staffing, governance, openness to the outside world and the expectations of pupils and their parents are now very different. Has their fundamental religious character changed, as diversity in pupils and staff has grown? They are now mainstream public schools with a Catholic ethos, although quite what constitutes "Catholic" in a changed environment is a matter of some debate. What is clear is that the days of the traditional Catholic public school of 30 or 40 years ago, based on strong clerical input into teaching, leadership and governance, and on an overwhelmingly Catholic, male pupil intake, have long gone. The Catholic public school must now shape its own identity in a very competitive and diverse market.

1

Education in a missionary country c.1800–1914

The emerging Catholic public schools at the beginning of the nineteenth century developed within an increasingly tolerant political environment, which saw the steady withdrawal of many of the restrictions on Catholic education and practice, and by a period of demographic change. The Catholic population of England expanded significantly in the nineteenth century. The 1851 Religious Census, which was the first, and indeed last, of its kind in the country, estimated the Catholic population at around 600,000, based on attendance figures at Sunday Mass. By 1900, it had more than doubled to reach some 1.3 million, and by 1914 it stood at about 1.8 million. The number of priests had also grown from perhaps 700 in the 1820s to almost 2,000 in 1880, and 2,856 in 1900.[1] From being a somewhat hidden, discreet and geographically isolated religious group, Catholicism had emerged as a very visible, growing and increasingly confident community. That growth reflected a number of factors.

The in-migration of individuals and families from Ireland lay behind much of the increase in Catholic numbers, beginning in the 1830s, and not tailing off until the end of the century, when the United States took on more importance as a destination for Irish emigrants. Driven by endemic poverty, oppression and famine, most of the new migrants were poor, rural labourers who sought a new life in the growing urban-industrial cities of the north of England, finding work in the factories

---

[1] D. Gwynn, "Growth of the Catholic Community", in G. A. Beck (ed.), *The English Catholics: Centenary Essays to Commemorate the Restoration of the Hierarchy of England and Wales* (London: Burns & Oates, 1950), pp. 410–30.

and workshops that underpinned Britain's industrial revolution. They were also almost all Catholic, at least by baptism, and cities such as Manchester, Birmingham and, especially, Liverpool became important centres for the new Catholic communities.[2]

The rising numbers of "missions"—the term used to describe what became parishes in the early twentieth century—reflected efforts by the Catholic Church to serve this growing population; the 2,000 such missions in 1880 had doubled to 4,000 by 1910 in an effort to provide for the religious, educational and social needs of this new Catholic population.[3] Whilst London remained the political hub of the faith, Liverpool and Lancashire were the demographic centres of gravity. Elsewhere, the end of the century saw the emergence of larger Catholic communities in cities such as Bradford, Birmingham and Wolverhampton. In the Birmingham diocese, for example, the number of Catholics more than doubled between 1850 and 1900. The number of missions and parishes grew from around 70 in 1850 to 136 some 50 years later. Even in less urbanized dioceses such as Clifton, the estimated Catholic population grew significantly in the same period.[4]

Irish immigration was undoubtedly important, but its role should not be exaggerated. Whilst the new arrivals were overwhelmingly baptized as Catholics, their observance of the faith (such as attendance at Sunday Mass or at Confession and Communion) was often found wanting. Many would be seen only at key family events—baptisms, marriages and funerals—so that, ironically, parish priests often spent much of their time and effort "reconverting" these groups to a full and active membership

---

[2] Gwynn, "Growth of the Catholic Community", pp. 436–41; see also K. Snell and P. Ell, *Rival Jerusalems: The Geography of Victorian Religion* (Cambridge: Cambridge University Press, 2000).

[3] S. Gilley, "The Roman Catholic Church and the Nineteenth Century Irish Diaspora", *Journal of Ecclesiastical History* 35:2 (1984), pp. 188–207.

[4] J. J. Scarisbrick (ed.), *History of the Diocese of Birmingham, 1850–2000* (Strasbourg: Editions du Signe, 2008), pp. 11–15; data compiled from J. A. Harding, *The Diocese of Clifton 1850–2000* (Clifton: Clifton Catholic Diocesan Trustees, 1999).

of their parishes.⁵ They were also very poor and largely remained so through the century, further exacerbating the already stretched resources of the Church.

Converts to Roman Catholicism were a second major source of new recruits. The most important, with a significance far beyond their actual numbers, were those who moved from Anglicanism to the Roman Catholic Church as a result of the so-called "Oxford Movement" in the 1830s and 1840s. John Henry Newman was the most significant of these converts, along with important and influential religious personalities such as William Lockhart, Ambrose Phillips de Lisle and Frederick Faber. What especially marked them out was that they were almost all well-educated (ironically most with the Oxbridge degrees denied to Catholics by their bishops), and socially and politically very well connected. They often had wealthy backgrounds too. Many had been educated in the public schools and this group often lent vocal support to the expansion of a Catholic public-school system. They helped to transform the image and influence of Roman Catholicism, though not without controversy, both within and outside the Church. One survey in 1910 identified at least 2,000 very influential individuals who moved over to Catholicism during this phase of what Newman termed the "second spring" of the Church. Of this group, some 600 were clergy, 29 peers of the realm, 53 peeresses of the realm, and over 400 members of the nobility. Their influence and very public espousal of Roman Catholicism were enormously important in moving the Church from being a marginal, politically suspect faith, to one which was increasingly acknowledged and accepted within the Establishment.⁶

The third element in the Catholic "mix" were the old, recusant families who had helped keep the faith alive in the pre-Emancipation era. They were often socially conservative and of aristocratic or gentry lineage. Their feelings about the new, growing and very public and

---

5   G. Connolly, "The transubstantiation of myth: towards a new popular history of nineteenth-century Catholicism in England", *Journal of Ecclesiastical History* 35 (1984), pp. 78–104.

6   D. Mathew, "Old Catholics and Converts", in G. A. Beck (ed.), *The English Catholics: Centenary Essays to Commemorate the Restoration of the Hierarchy of England and Wales* (London: Burns & Oates, 1950), pp. 223–42.

visible faith could be equivocal. Historically accustomed to a degree of control over "their" clergy (after all, in recusant times, many chapels and their priests only survived within the physical confines of the Catholic country house), they were sometimes ambivalent towards the centralized and controlling tendencies of the new Catholic Hierarchy established after 1850. Used to a faith which was discreet, undemonstrative and "English", they sometimes bridled against new "Romish" innovations and directions which were an integral part of some of the new orders arriving from overseas, especially from Italy, to "re-Catholicize" England. Pilgrimages, public processions, parish and mission retreats, ever-more ostentatious Gothic chapels, churches and liturgical clothes (especially from the architect of the new faith, the convert Augustus Welby Pugin), and even the public wearing of black clerical garb and the Roman biretta, sometimes posed a challenge to this very important sector of the Catholic population. Undoubtedly their numbers and influence tailed off through the century, but, for many of these families, the Catholic public school continued to be seen as important in educating their sons.

Educating the masses

Education was of primary importance to the Church and was at the very heart of its mission. The development of the Catholic public school, important in itself, does need to be set within the context of the much wider and more demanding efforts made by the Church to educate all of its members. The dozen or so public schools established in this period for the upper classes were actually only a very small fraction of the huge network of elementary schools set up to serve the growing Catholic population through the nineteenth and into the twentieth century. As we have seen, the nineteenth century witnessed a remarkable growth in the numbers of Catholics in England whose children needed an elementary education that the state was unable or unwilling to provide. Whether a poor urban proletariat, a growing middle class, or an aristocratic elite, all required an education which was Catholic in character and intent. The resource challenges of providing that education were huge, and the efforts needed to establish elementary education in particular dwarfed whatever efforts were invested in developing an influential public-school network. If the public schools were seen by some as marking the pinnacle of Catholic educational efforts, a far greater achievement was the extensive network of elementary schools set up and funded largely by the Catholic Church by the end of the century. It is worth reflecting on the enormity of those challenges.

From the outset, the aim of the Church was to secure a Catholic education, taught by Catholics within schools which were firmly under the control of the Hierarchy. There were Catholic schools, both elementary and secondary, prior to Emancipation, but numbers were very small, and they were isolated. An 1835 Select Committee reported a total of around 80 Catholic schools in England. By the 1830s and 1840s, the State was, albeit reluctantly, becoming increasingly involved in the development and funding of new elementary schools, and had begun to provide some capital and revenue funds for them. The needs of the rapidly growing Catholic population were not considered the responsibility of the state. As numbers grew, the creation of elementary Catholic schools was prioritized by the Hierarchy and became the overwhelming educational focus. "Better to build a single school than ten new churches because the school represented the future!" was a common theme.[7]

The newly emergent Hierarchy from 1850 was, not unnaturally, anxious to secure access to any government funding it could for its elementary schools and, in particular, sought equitable treatment for Catholic schools alongside other non-conformist ones. At the same time, it was adamant in resisting any state interference in the management, staffing and curriculum of the nascent Catholic school sector. Demanding funding without any interference from the funder was not always the most persuasive position to adopt towards government.

In 1847, the Catholic Poor School Committee was established with the aim of trying to secure some share of pretty meagre government

---

[7] H. O. Evennett, *The Catholic Schools of England and Wales* (Cambridge: Cambridge University Press, 1944), pp. 16–20; A. C. Beales, "The Struggle for the Schools", in G. A. Beck (ed.), *The English Catholics: Centenary Essays to Commemorate the Restoration of the Hierarchy of England and Wales* (London: Burns & Oates, 1950), pp. 365–409.

expenditure on schools for the Catholic populations. The committee became a key vehicle for Church authorities to press for funding for the growing elementary school sector for over 50 years.[8] Not only was the state reluctant to sanction any kind of public monies for schools in general, but it argued that specific religious education was a matter for the denominations themselves and should be funded by them. Changing such positions required increasing political involvement for the Catholic elite in matters of state and, as the new-found confidence of the Church grew in the latter decades of the century, so its ability to win the argument to secure state funding was enhanced. That funding was essential if only to loosen some of the enormous pressures on what were often very poor parishes to fund adequate school provision. It was a slow process but was vital for a Church eager to cater for the growing numbers of Catholic children, rich and poor, and to ensure that there was no "leakage" of Catholics towards non-denominational schooling. For the Hierarchy, "the education of the higher as well as of the lowest of our people is a part of the cure of souls for which we must give account. Every baptized soul, whether of the rich or the poor, has a right to a Catholic education.[9]

The 1870 Forster Act saw the state begin to provide at least some supplementary funds for Catholic elementary schools and, according to Evennett, "marked the point at which the independence and vigour of the Catholic school policy began to emerge".[10] Manning, who succeeded Wiseman as Archbishop of Westminster in 1857, was especially focused on growing Catholic elementary schools and argued forcefully with the government that Catholic elementary schools needed proper, secure funding, a strategy that at least partially succeeded with the passing of the

---

[8] *100 years of Catholic Emancipation 1829–1929* (London: Longmans Green, 1929), pp. 50–1.

[9] J. Gilbert, "The Catholic Church and Education", in D. Gwynn (ed.), *100 Years of Catholic Emancipation 1829–1929* (London: Longmans Green, 1929), pp. 47–76; J. T. Smith, "The Priest and the Elementary School in the second half of the nineteenth century", *Recusant History* 25:3 (2001), p. 533; E. Tenbus, *English Catholics and the Education of the Poor, 1847–1902* (London: Pickering Chatto, 2010).

[10] Evennett, *Catholic Schools*, p. 18.

1870 Education Act. The number of places in Catholic schools quadrupled between 1870 and 1902 at a time when the non-denominational "Board Schools" were both better placed and more securely funded to grow their numbers at the expense of the Catholic schools. Catholic schools continued to expand and resisted the temptation to become better-funded but non-denominational institutions. They also produced better academic results. The financial sacrifices for the community were huge, with parish collections being integral to the financial survival of the Catholic elementary school sector. Between 1870 and 1890, the number of Catholic schools grew from 350 to 946.[11] The Church Hierarchy retained tight control over staffing, management and the curriculum, despite the financial costs to priests, parishes, parishioners and the religious orders. The role of the female religious orders in staffing elementary schools was hugely important to their survival. Many religious sisters spent their whole lives working and teaching in often very difficult circumstances. Not one of the Catholic schools opted to become a "Board" school whose financial conditions were much less challenging but which, importantly, were outside Church control.[12]

The 1902 Education Act, which led to the creation of Local Education Authorities, provided the elements for a marginally improved situation for the Catholic sector. Better capital provision, and funding towards running costs, provided some relief for Catholic schools, along with better salaries for teachers. By the start of the twentieth century, the Catholic Church had established a country-wide network of elementary schools which were especially important in the larger urban centres—Liverpool, Salford, Preston and Birmingham—where the growth of the Catholic community had been so substantial. It is an impressive story and a tribute to the growing political confidence of the Catholic Hierarchy, the dedication of countless local parish priests and nuns, and the monies raised from the richer members of the community in support of their elementary schools.

In the Birmingham diocese, for example, parish schools in the diocese had doubled between 1860 and 1880, requiring a prodigious effort on behalf of priests, parishioners and the diocese to create this network of

---

[11] Beck, *English Catholics*, pp. 378–89.
[12] Gilbert, "The Catholic Church and Education", p. 55.

schools from scratch. The 1870 Act encouraged the emergence of new Board schools across the city taking advantage of better funding (both capital and recurrent) than was the case for existing Catholic schools. Between 1870 and 1900, some 87 new, non-denominational Board schools were established across the city; only three brand-new Catholic elementary schools could be funded in that period. Whilst many other denominational schools (such as the Methodist and Baptist schools) were soon transferred into Board control, the Catholic schools remained defiantly outside the mainstream, and were largely funded by the local parish and the diocese. It was a desperate financial struggle. Money from the collection plate, the role of wealthy benefactors and in particular, the work of the newly arrived orders of nuns—the Sisters of Mercy, Sisters of Joseph and the Sisters of Charity of St Paul—were instrumental in this struggle. The priority—a Catholic elementary education run by the Hierarchy—was costly of time and resources, and required enormous effort on the part of the diocese for its maintenance and consolidation.[13]

The position of secondary education was equally challenging. There were of course significant numbers of independent grammar schools. Some dated back many hundreds of years, but in the mid-nineteenth century their role and effectiveness was somewhat in doubt, whilst others were small, often hampered by their foundation charters, and few had any significant numbers of Catholic pupils. Not until the late nineteenth century, most notably after the 1870s, were these charters regularized and a "free" grammar school system began to take shape. The emergence of a number of significant Catholic day schools for secondary pupils, founded by both Diocesan authorities and orders such as the Jesuits, was a feature of these years. There were also numerous private schools which were commercially run enterprises which waxed and waned, depending on the drive and personality of the individual school heads.

The origins of a state-funded secondary school system dated from the 1902 Education Act. The Act gave the Local Education Authorities responsibility for developing systems of "higher education" (which in 1902 meant secondary schooling) in their areas. What those newly established authorities did was constrained by both finance and individual

---

[13] Scarisbrick, *Diocese of Birmingham*, pp. 44–54.

temperament. Funding of secondary schools was not compulsory, and in some areas the very notion of state or local funding for Catholic secondary schools was decried as facilitating "Rome on the Rates". The Free Place System, begun in 1907, was one important outcome, which helped to provide some funding for Catholic secondary schools who were able to take poorer pupils. They began to provide an alternative, cheaper destination for Catholic boys, unable to afford public or grammar school fees. Many new foundations emerged with both male and female religious orders playing an important role in founding and running these new day secondary schools which, unlike the public schools, were in receipt of some government funding. The proportion of funding granted was a matter of long and continued debate right through to the last decades of the twentieth century. A remarkable growth of these schools took place in the inter-war years just at the time, as we will see later, when the Catholic public schools were likewise growing in both numbers and confidence.[14]

Given this context of a massive, far-reaching expansion of elementary schooling, coupled with the growth of secondary schools for Catholic boys and girls, what role might the newly emergent Catholic public schools have played in the educational and political strategies of the Church? It is appropriate to question why the post-Emancipation Church, and its secular and regular clergy, placed such a premium on creating what were expensive, socially elite and tradition-bound public schools, when the model that they often explicitly emulated was hardly a paragon of educational excellence. As we have seen, the reputation of the public school in the nineteenth century was far from exalted, with the curriculum, discipline systems and standards of individual care subject to significant public and parliamentary criticism. Given the enormous resources that a far from wealthy Church was pouring into the elementary schools of the period, why would such faith have been placed in an educational model which was recognized at the time as somewhat flawed? One possible explanation was that the Church clung on to the models it inherited when the great Catholic schools, seminaries and religious communities, which had existed for some 200 years on the Continent, returned to England in the early years of the nineteenth

---

[14] Evennett, *Catholic Schools*, pp. 44–54.

century. Perhaps an inbuilt conservatism was transferred with them? An excessive respect for tradition? A failure to recognize the new social environment within which they were now placed? Arguably, the need to create its "own" social elite to storm the bastions of the Establishment might well have been a key factor, given the success of the existing public schools in placing their alumni in positions of power and influence. If you can't beat them ...

One should perhaps not overestimate the importance of the secular authorities in encouraging the growth of the new public schools. For the periods of both Cardinals Wiseman (1850-65) and Manning (1865-92), the priority was always on growing the elementary Catholic schools given the huge influx of poor, largely Irish, urban immigrants into the community. By contrast, the importance of educating a Catholic middle class was seen as a lower priority, and there were sometimes differences between the bishops and the regular orders, such as the Benedictines and the Jesuits, over where the major educational effort should be focused. The differences between the secular authorities and the Jesuits over school development were perhaps the best example of what might be politely termed "differences of opinion". Cardinal Manning in particular had a long-standing mistrust of the Jesuit educational mission and, for example, sought to oppose the creation of Jesuit day schools for the upper classes, especially in Manchester. For Manning, the establishment of secondary education for the growing middle classes was seen as more important than catering for the aristocratic and gentry elite, and he was not always convinced that the education provided by the Jesuits and Benedictines in their public schools was appropriate for the mission of the Church. Such conflicts reappeared from time to time, exacerbated by the fact that bishops sometimes felt unable to control the "independent" regulars, at least until changes in ecclesiastical laws at the end of the nineteenth century gave the bishops more clarity over input into decisions involving those groups.[15]

---

[15] I. D. Roberts, "Jesuit Collegiate Education in England, 1794-1914", MEd Thesis, University of Durham (1986), p. 100, 241; V. A. McClelland, *Cardinal Manning: His Public Life and Influence 1865-1892* (London: Oxford University Press, 1962), pp. 87-128.

A second question concerns the human resources needed to sustain this new Catholic public-school network. Both the seculars and the regulars were active in education, but it was the regulars who were the most important in stimulating the emergence and growth of the Catholic public schools. Education was a key part of their role, especially for the Benedictines. Alongside their missionary activities in the parishes, the regulars played a very important role in the boarding schools. This was at a time when there were huge demands on priests, monks and brothers in servicing the new parishes and missions of a growing Church. Substantial growth in the Catholic population, especially within the poorer communities of the urban centres, placed significant demands on Catholic priests and monks to establish a network of churches and elementary schools, and to help alleviate poverty in the poor urban parishes that were at the core of the Catholic community. There was a balancing act to be performed in those religious orders heavily engaged in staffing the public schools. It is perhaps instructive to compare how male religious and seculars readily embraced the creation of new boarding schools, often in rather pleasant rural locations, with the single-minded focus of their female counterparts, whose burgeoning religious communities in the nineteenth century were centred much more heavily on staffing and supporting the elementary schools in the poorest and most challenging urban parishes.

It might be argued that for the bishops and their diocesan priests, or for religious communities such as the Benedictines or Jesuits, a Catholic boarding school designed to educate a Catholic elite was something of a luxury (perhaps not the word the pupils would have used ...) which risked drawing resources away from a primary missionary role which was at the heart of both regulars and seculars. For the regulars, however, the creation of a network of such colleges may well have been informed by the need to ensure a steady supply of new recruits to their orders. Certainly the Jesuit and Benedictine schools were very adept at directing those of their pupils who wished to become priests or monks into their own orders. The colleges were thus both an educational resource and a recruitment platform. It is not surprising, therefore, to see some members of the Hierarchy expressing concerns at the possible dangers of a private, elite school system which might "siphon off" new recruits into the religious orders, rather than into becoming the parish priests that were greatly needed by the Church and the dioceses for the core mission of conversion.[16]

A final tension evident in the early history of the public schools was between their broader educational mission, and their role as seminaries for training new recruits to the priesthood. As we noted earlier, some colleges educated "lay" boys alongside "church" boys destined for the priesthood. That, indeed, had been the historic pattern in many of the overseas colleges prior to their return to England. Bishops at various times were both receptive to this pattern of mixing and, at other times, hostile. Might not "lay" boys corrupt the morals and morale of those "church" boys set on a vocation to the priesthood? And might not a "church" boy educated by, say, the Jesuits or Benedictines, see their vocation with those regular orders, rather than with the bishops who were in constant need of new recruits? For many of the new bishops, the pattern of individual diocesan seminaries laid down in the Council of Trent in the sixteenth century became the model for training priests. By the middle of the nineteenth century, the three major seminaries in England—St Cuthbert's (Ushaw), St Mary's (Oscott) and St Edmund's (Ware)—were all mixed, educating lay and church students together. That pattern, by and large, did not persist. For some, the answer was to create either diocesan seminaries on their own, diocesan colleges which mixed lay and church boys, or, more ambitiously, a national seminary for training all church boys for priesthood with the seculars. The latter, perhaps the most sensible solution, never happened.[17] These interrelated

---

[16] V. A. McClelland and M. Hodgetts (eds), *From Without the Flaminian Gate: 150 Years of Roman Catholicism in England and Wales, 1850–2000* (London: Darton, Longman & Todd, 1999), pp. 30–5; P. Doyle, "The Education and Training of Roman Catholic Priests in nineteenth-century England", *Journal of Ecclesiastical History* 35:2 (1984), pp. 208–19.

[17] M. Williams, "Seminaries and Priestly Formation", in V. A. McClelland and M. Hodgetts (eds), *From Without the Flaminian Gate: 150 Years of Roman Catholicism in England and Wales, 1850–2000* (London: Darton, Longman & Todd, 1999), pp. 62–83.

issues will colour our account of the emergence and growth of the Catholic public schools in the nineteenth century.

Migrants from the Continent

The end of the eighteenth century saw many of the overseas teaching colleges and communities deciding, sometimes reluctantly, to return to England. The "push" of continental warfare and unrest, coupled with the "pull" of a more benign political environment in England, eventually told on many communities. The Jesuits moved to establish Stonyhurst in Lancashire, whilst the two major Benedictine communities of St Gregory and St Laurence eventually shifted their establishments to Downside in Somerset and Ampleforth in Yorkshire. The seculars established colleges at St Edmund's Ware in Hertfordshire and Ushaw near Durham to cater for students and seminarians disrupted by the closure of the English College at Douai. Together with a small number of existing colleges, these shifts marked the first steps in creating a new network of English Catholic public schools in the early nineteenth century.

The Jesuits had played a vital part in serving the English Catholic community when the recusancy laws and persecution were at their most pressing in the late sixteenth and seventeenth centuries. As missionaries, they were especially active in England, and counted over 20 English martyrs in that period. The order played a key role in providing both a general Catholic education and the training of priests through the college they had established at St Omers in France in 1593. The college grew rapidly and followed the educational structure and ethos that had been set down by the founder of the order, St Ignatius Loyola. It introduced many educational innovations. The curriculum followed the Jesuit *Ratio Studiorum* which laid down the organization of lessons in the fields of Rhetoric, Poetry and Grammar drawing heavily from the classics, together with spiritual and religious readings. It was, noted one historian, a Renaissance education with the Protestant detonators removed.¹⁸ College numbers and financial stability inevitably fluctuated in response to conditions in England, the degree of political instability on the Continent, and competition with some of the colleges established by other religious orders. Numbers rarely fell below 100 between the early seventeenth and late eighteenth centuries; financial stability reflected fluctuating fee income as well as the general lack of sufficient endowment income. The level of fees (around £25 p.a. for much of its history) meant that the intake was very much orientated to the gentry and aristocracy. A range of tuition in fields such as riding, dancing and fencing suggest a clear gentlemanly orientation, a kind of continental religious finishing school for upper-class Catholics from the recusant community.¹⁹

Alongside this training in the ways of a Catholic gentleman, was the central, vitally important role in training boys for the priesthood. For much of its early history the term seminary, rather than college, was used to describe St Omers, whose key role was to supply sufficient suitable candidates to receive their final training and ordination in one of the main overseas seminaries at Valladolid, Lisbon, Douai, or at the English College in Rome. At times, difficulties arose over the final destinations of aspirant priests with the secular authorities anxious to ensure that as many candidates as possible chose the secular rather than regular routes to the priesthood. Not unnaturally, St Omers was equally keen to ensure its seminarians chose to become Jesuits.

At the end of the eighteenth century, the college faced significant challenges as both political and religious difficulties led to the college having to relocate. The Jesuits themselves encountered hostility in France, and in 1762 all the French Jesuit houses were ordered to be closed. The college sought the support of the local administration to help it survive, without success. The college staff and students migrated to set up a new college in Bruges, whilst the existing buildings were taken over by the seculars who established a small college of some 50 students. A further migration to Liège followed as both papal hostility—the Jesuits were suppressed by Pope Clement XIV in 1773 and not fully re-established

---

¹⁸ See T. E. Muir, *Stonyhurst College 1593–1993* (Cirencester: St Omers Press, revised edition, 2006), pp. 25–39.

¹⁹ Muir, *Stonyhurst*, pp. 62–4.

until 1829—and political uncertainty dogged the development of the college. Finally, as the shock waves of the French Revolution further compromised matters, the decision was made to re-found the college on English soil and, after brief interludes in various locations, set up in 1794 at Stonyhurst in rural Lancashire.

Stonyhurst was a large mansion belonging to a prominent Catholic, Thomas Weld. It had been largely uninhabited for some 40 years, as the Welds lived at Lulworth in Dorset, and when the party of three priests, four church students and twelve boys arrived at Stonyhurst in August 1794, they began the task of establishing the first Jesuit boarding school in England. As well as the house, which was to become the core of the new college, a significant (and prosperous) farm and estate was also bequeathed to the Jesuits which helped to provide an important source of income when times were challenging. The change of location also meant a change in temperament, noted Muir: set in an urban environment, St Omers had represented "an isolated, introverted community"; by contrast, Stonyhurst was "English, rural and shaped by the gradual integration of Catholics into the mainstream of British society".[20] It marked an important chapter in the history of the Catholic public school in England.

At Stonyhurst, as with most other such schools, numbers fluctuated depending on fee levels, the character of individual heads (all of course Jesuits), and wider changes in the community. The early growth in numbers was impressive and clearly established the school well above its competitors. From around 40 students in 1798, numbers were over 200 in 1812, not only the largest such Catholic school, but significant too when set alongside the wider public-school sector. Fees were higher than was the case in some of the other colleges founded in this period, but by the 1830s all the main Catholic colleges had fees at roughly the same level of between £40 and £50 p.a., comparable to the better public schools of the time. In these early decades, the school began to cement a reputation for attracting pupils from higher status social groups. One analysis of intakes suggests that between 1794 and 1825, boys from families with a hereditary title or from higher gentry backgrounds were about six times

---

[20] Muir, *Stonyhurst*, p. 69.

more numerous than those of upper middle-class backgrounds.[21] But a series of disputes relating to the status of the Jesuits in England and, in particular, the ability of Stonyhurst to present its candidates for ordination, created significant disturbance in the college and led to tensions in the relationships between the regulars and the seculars. The reassertion of authority by the bishops and diocesan authorities in 1818 led to a fall in college confidence. As Muir notes, "the younger teachers did not know whether they were proper Jesuits or not; the Hodder novitiate became virtually extinct; while parents, sensing a fall in standards and discipline, declined to send their children".[22]

Recovery was slow and not helped by a drift by the middle classes towards independent day rather than boarding colleges in the 1820s and 1830s. Numbers halved to under 100, and whilst the situation regarding the Jesuit order had been regularized by 1829, it took until the 1840s for numbers to get back to around 200. The lack of Jesuit teachers meant that at an early stage the college was required to employ significant (and costly) numbers of lay teachers and secular priests until the numbers of Jesuits rose again. For a time, the novitiate (the training school for potential members of the order) at Stonyhurst was virtually empty, and it was not until mid-century that historical prejudices against the order receded and new ordinations recovered. The boys, notes Roberts, "were educated in a religious and highly moral environment but not primarily for the religious life".[23] The curriculum was broad: science was included as well as the classics, mathematics, history and geography.

The college was swift to engage with the new external examination structures such as the University of London matriculation, which were beginning to emerge from mid-century, and the college was the only Catholic institution visited as part of the Clarendon Commission on public schools in 1864. Its academic performance against the other "top nine" schools was certainly creditable and placed Stonyhurst as the best of the Catholic public schools at this time. The student body was focused on the gentry and aristocracy, although increasingly, middle-class parents

---

[21] Roberts, "Jesuit Collegiate Education", pp. 37–40.

[22] Muir, *Stonyhurst*, p. 96.

[23] Roberts, "Jesuit Collegiate Education", p. 33.

Figure 1: Hodder Place, Stonyhurst, late nineteenth century.

also sent their boys to the school. The Jesuit authorities also adopted the Oxford and Cambridge Board exams in the 1870s and 1880s. This was in contrast to the position of the Hierarchy who, sticking to their general distrust of Oxbridge, did not encourage such engagement. The bishops in 1881 were grudging over these new external exams: "We cannot sanction" (they noted) "and can only unwillingly tolerate, the subjection of Catholic youth of either sex to the Oxford and Cambridge Local Examinations, even in secular subjects."[24]

The curriculum was designed for the new competitive entrance examination for the Indian Civil Service and Sandhurst, success in which were increasingly important markers for all public schools. Its most senior group, the Philosophers, studied to what was effectively degree level with the University of London. Entrance to Oxford and Cambridge Universities, the *raison d'être* of so many public schools, was effectively barred to the Catholic public schools until that ban was lifted in the 1890s.

The most striking impact of the growth of Stonyhurst was in the development of the buildings. Large amounts of capital, sourced from private donations and from Jesuit resources, were sunk in projects ranging from gyms and a swimming pool, through to the remarkable 560ft long south front of the college, built in the late 1870s, and designed to symbolize the position of Stonyhurst as the leading Catholic public school in the country. By the end of the century, its 200 pupils and Jesuit teaching staff would be regarded, and would certainly have regarded themselves, as being at the pinnacle of Catholic public-school education in England.

Alongside the Jesuits, the Benedictine community was to play a very important role in establishing Catholic public schools in the nineteenth century. After the Reformation, the Benedictines had established communities in Lorraine (St Laurence's, Dieulouard, 1608), Flanders (St Gregory's, Douai, 1607) and Hanover (St Hadrian and Dionysius, Lamspringe, 1643). All three of these institutions were generally smaller than the Jesuit school at St Omers, but the pattern of a church, monastery and school on the same site was set in place. Numbers at Lamspringe

---

[24] Roberts, "Jesuit Collegiate Education", p. 235.

in the late eighteenth century ranged from around ten to 50, whilst St Laurence numbers at Dieulouard were even smaller. On the eve of having to leave the Continent, all three schools were functioning and offered a similar education to the Jesuits at St Omers.

At St Gregory's (Douai), the monastic community had begun to take fee-paying boys into a school in the seventeenth century and had high academic standards. Boys were seemingly well fed, dressed in cassock and gown and with a curriculum founded on the classics and philosophy. New building projects in the 1780s included a large main school building and a range of walkways and walls to facilitate games. Numbers grew as did the reputation of St Gregory's for scholarship; it recruited well, charged high fees, sought the children of well-connected families, and arguably offered a wider curriculum and better pedagogic methods than their Protestant public school counterparts in England.

St Laurence at Dieulouard was not dissimilar. Numbers were always relatively small and most of the pupils enrolled in the hope of becoming priests. The curriculum, as with St Gregory's, was wider than that of traditional English public schools with history, mathematics, philosophy and physical education being part of the teaching. There was regular testing of pupils. But it seems that the existence of a school as opposed to a seminary was episodic.

As with the Jesuits, the political turmoil of the French Revolution, combined with an easing in the legal position of Catholic schools in England, brought about a shift in Benedictine interest from the Continent back to England. The two communities of St Gregory and St Laurence, faced with growing hostility on the Continent, were effectively forced to relocate to England. The communities initially moved together to Acton Burnell in Shropshire in 1795, a property belonging to Sir Edward Smythe, an old boy of St Gregory's, but eventually each community chose to establish separate monasteries and schools. After searching across the north for several years trying to find a suitable home, the St Laurence community eventually settled in a property at Ampleforth in north Yorkshire in 1802. The closure of St Hadrian and Dionysius at Lamspringe by the Prussian government meant that the first pupils to arrive at what became Ampleforth were from Lamspringe. In 1803, the school at Ampleforth was founded. Some ten years later, in 1814, having debated over whether a return to a now-pacified Douai might be possible, the community of St Gregory eventually set up a school at a new permanent home at Stratton-on-the-Fosse in Somerset, which was to become Downside. In the first two decades of the nineteenth century, these schools were very small (often only ten to 20 boys) and often in buildings that needed major renovation and expansion. The curriculum was cursory and the living conditions spartan. These were the often unprepossessing beginnings of what were to become two of the most important Catholic public schools in England.

At Ampleforth, early numbers were rarely above 50 pupils and were subject to significant fluctuations. The closure of the Benedictine school and community of Lamspringe near Hanover in 1803 led to the arrival of new priests and pupils at the College together with its first teaching resources—Latin and Greek grammars and a range of devotional books. As Galliver noted, perhaps the most signal arrival was a pupil, Peter Baines, who was later to become hugely important in Ampleforth's early history.[25] Once ordained, he helped to improve the curriculum by adopting the then famous "memory exercises" of a Professor Feinaigle and broadening the range of subjects taught at the college. The teaching of history, geography, arithmetic and geometry at the school contrasted with the teaching at many public schools of the time, constrained as they were within an all-dominant Classics culture. The Clarendon Commission had been especially scathing of the neglect by the traditional public schools of mathematics and science, so it is revealing to see evidence of a rather wider curriculum in some of the emergent Catholic public schools.

By the early 1830s, Ampleforth had around 80 pupils. Its curriculum and teaching methods were successful in attracting students, and Peter Baines was a powerful factor in that success. But he departed to become Vicar Apostolic for the Western District and, in the late 1820s, sought to establish a new school at Prior Park, an extravagant Palladian mansion near Bath. As part of the plan, he had hoped that the Benedictines at nearby Downside might abandon their school, leave the field open to

---

[25] P. Galliver, *Ampleforth College: The Emergence of Ampleforth College as the 'Catholic Eton'* (Leominster: Gracewing, 2019), p. 20; P. Galliver, "The Early Ampleforth College", *Recusant History* 28:4 (2007), pp. 511–25.

A PROSPECTUS

OF THE

Examination of Studies,

IN THE

COLLEGE, AT AMPLEFORTH,

FOR THE YEAR 1815,

On WEDNESDAY and THURSDAY, the 21st and 22d of June,

AT TEN O'CLOCK, A. M.

THE NAMES AND ORDER OF THE STUDENTS.

1 Master Tho. Fairclough	12 Master Richd. Prest	22 Master George Kelly	32 Master Richd. Tyrer
2 .... John Prest	13 .... Jas. Smith	23 .... John Du Vivier	33 .... Chas. Gastaldi
3 .... Ralph Cooper	14 .... Jas. Orrell	24 .... Mich. Delaunay	34 Hon. Charles Stourton
4 .... Robt. Allanson	15 .... John Clarkson	25 .... John Sanderson	35 Master Thos. Buckle
5 .... Edmd. Curr	16 .... W. Greenough	26 .... Daniel Kelly	36 .... Francis Buckle
6 .... Edmd. Kelly	17 .... Peter Allanson	27 .... Nic Cespedes	37 .... Tuke Smelter
7 .... Robt. Nihell	18 .... J. Shuttleworth	28 Hon. Edward Clifford	38 .... Robt. Roskell
8 .... Wm. Smelter	19 .... Pet. Greenough	29 Master Robert Rose	39 .... George Henry
9 .... Wm. Hall	20 .... Mar. Langdale	30 .... John Orrell	40 .... Henry Flinn
10 .... Wm. Hampson	21 .... Walter Kelly	31 .... Jas. Parsons	41 .... Wm. Hutton
11 .... Christr. Shann			

HEBREW.

The *First Class*, 1, 2, 3, will explain the Book of Isaiah.

GREEK.

The *First Class*, 1, 2, 3, will explain the 1st Book of Homer's Iliad.
The *Second Class*, 9, 10, 11, 12, 13, 14, 15, 16, 17, will explain part of the 3d Book of Xenophon's Cyropædia, and answer to the Grammar and Syntax.

LATIN.

The *First Class*, 1, 2, 3, 4, 5, 6, 7, 8, will explain the 1st Book of Virgil's Æneid, and some of his Eclogues.
The *Second Class*, 9, 10, 11, 12, 13, 14, 15, 16, 17, 18, 19, 20, will explain the 1st Book of Valpy's Cicero's Epistles.
The *Third Class*, 21, 22, 23, 24, 25, 26, 27, 28, 29, 30, 31, 32, will explain some short passages from Pliny's Natural History, and answer to the Grammar and Syntax.
The *Fourth Class*, 35, 36, 37, 38, will answer to the Grammar, Rules of Genders, &c.

FRENCH.

The *First Class*, 1, 2, 3, 4, 6, 7, 8, 9, will explain part of Bossuet's Histoire Universelle and Telemaque.
The *Second Class*, 10, 13, 15, will explain the 1st Book of Telemaque, and answer to the Grammar and Syntax.

GENERAL HISTORY.

The *First Class*, 1, 2, 3, 9, 10, 13, 15, 20, will answer to General History from the creation of the world, to the reign of Charlemagne in the year 800.
The *Second Class*, 5, 6, 8, will answer to the same History from the commencement of the Christian era to the reign of Charlemagne.
The *Third Class*, 7, 11, 12, 14, 16, 17, 18, 19, will answer to General History from the creation of the world, to the birth of Christ.
The *Fourth* and *Fifth Classes*, from 21 to 39, will give a short sketch of ancient History till Christ.

Figure 2: Examinations Day Poster, Ampleforth, 1815.

Prior Park and, instead, establish a diocesan seminary at Downside in place of the school. His plans (and financial commitments) were huge, and he anticipated staff and students flowing from Downside. But Baines was no diplomat. The community at Downside was less than keen to work with him on his new, grandiose project. They turned him down, and so he sought to persuade the Ampleforth community (where he had been both a pupil and teacher), to move lock, stock and barrel to his new Prior Park school. Determined to develop his new project Baines almost succeeded in shifting spirits at Ampleforth, but eventually the community said no. But three priests and some 30 boys did leave Ampleforth for Prior Park in 1830.[26]

Ampleforth remained in business, just, but the episode damaged all parties. School numbers fell to some 30 students and remained "bumping along the bottom" until at least mid-century. Very rarely did numbers exceed 100 (reaching a peak of 120 in 1895), despite the growth of the public schools generally in the second half of the nineteenth century.[27] By 1903, the college was both small and quiet with some 100 students and little engagement with the world of external examinations and assessment. It was, noted Galliver, nothing more than "a small, somewhat obscure, northern school".[28] The authorities feared not just falling behind its Catholic rivals, especially Stonyhurst and Downside, but also behind the growing non-Catholic public-school sector.

The picture at Downside was not dissimilar in that fluctuations in fortune were integral to its history. From its establishment in 1814, growth was spasmodic, and had reached around 60 students in 1830. A programme of building was begun in the early 1830s, but the establishment of nearby Prior Park, a few miles away on the edge of

---

[26] Galliver, *Ampleforth*, pp. 36–8; A. Cramer, *Ampleforth: The Story of St Laurence's Abbey and College* (Ampleforth Abbey, 2001); On Bishop Baines, see J. S. Roche, *A History of Prior Park and its founder Bishop Baines* (London: Burns, Oates & Washbourne, 1931).

[27] A. Marett-Crosby, *A School of the Lord's Service: A History of Ampleforth* (London: James & James, 2002), p. 20; J. McCann and C. Cary-Elwes (eds), *Ampleforth and its Origins* (London: Burns, Oates & Washbourne, 1952).

[28] Galliver, *Ampleforth*, p. 73.

Bath, did damage Downside as well as Ampleforth, especially amongst Irish boys, who were an important component of these newly emergent Catholic boarding schools, and who shifted to Prior Park in some numbers.[29] Once the furore over Prior Park had died down there was steady, if unspectacular, growth. The architect Augustus Pugin laid out plans for an ambitious redevelopment of both school and monastery in the early 1840s, with the monks envisaging a school of around 200 pupils. In the end, a more modest programme was adopted with further building and planned expansion in the 1870s. The curriculum in the 1870s and 1880s was diverse, including history, geography and mathematics and the school engaged with the University of London External Examinations as a means of testing how well boys were performing. As at Ampleforth, an annual Exam Day (or Exhibition Day) saw all the pupils examined together at the end of the academic year in July, with both written and oral examinations. Downside recovered and numbers had grown to 100 by the 1880s. By the end of the century, the school was in a stable and sustainable position alongside its main competitors, Ampleforth and Stonyhurst.[30] The school was at times innovative in encouraging debate and drama on a significant scale. One of its former pupils and teachers, Lord William Petre, was influential in shaping the curriculum and encouraging reflection amongst pupils. He was opposed to external examinations being used to judge pupil performance arguing they brought nothing except "contracted brains". By the 1880s, he was still critical seeing "the rough, untrained silly boys produced by the Catholic schools". His own attempt to establish a boarding college at Woburn Park in 1877 on principles of greater pupil involvement and responsibility failed and it closed with financial difficulties in 1884.[31]

---

[29] D. N. Birt, *Downside: The History of St. Gregory's School from its commencement at Douay to the Present Time* (London: Kegan Paul & Co., 1902), pp. 195–7; Abbot Snow, *Sketches of Old Downside* (London: Sands & Co., 1903), p. 61.

[30] H. van Zeller, *Downside By and Large* (London: Sheed & Ward, 1954), pp. 23–6.; Snow, *Sketches of Old Downside*, p. 311.

[31] S. Foster, "Monseigneur Lord William Petre (1847–1903): A Pillar of Downside", *Recusant History* 22:1 (1994), pp. 88–101.

Prior Park itself, after the controversy over its foundation and early staffing, began to grow in numbers and reputation from the mid-1830s. There was naturally a Benedictine influence which had always been very significant in the West Country, but it was clearly a secular college under Baines and the Western District (later the Clifton Diocese). Baines had very ambitious plans for Prior Park, and at an early stage he brought in members of the new Rosminian order from Italy to help shape the college. Fr Gentili, the Rosminian leader, worked hard to establish a new, somewhat austere, religious and educational ethos. Gentili, a remarkable figure, saw his role as conversion and coercion. The regime was not always attractive to pupils or their parents, and numbers declined. Baines and the Rosminians soon fell out and the latter departed to Leicestershire for pastures new and a new college at Ratcliffe.[32]

A major fire in 1836 and the death of Baines in 1842 led to a rapid decline in the fortunes of the college. The diocese of Clifton was not rich, and the new bishop, Ullathorne, decided he could not afford to bail out the college, which closed in 1856 with the buildings sold. It eventually re-emerged in much more modest form in 1867, when the diocese bought back the buildings. By the end of the century, finances forced the diocese to look for an order to take over the running of the school, and the Irish Christian Brothers, already active in the diocese, agreed to take it on. But lack of numbers and the failure of the diocese to support the Brothers meant closure again in 1904.[33]

Life at these schools was governed by routines which hardly changed over the century. At Prior Park, a rigorous religious regime was established by the Rosminians. Sundays were observed with a "Trappist severity". Pupils rose at 6 a.m. with Mass at 6.30 followed by pious readings in unheated rooms until High Mass in the late morning and Vespers in the afternoon. Catechism took up the hours of 5 p.m. to 7 p.m. On weekdays

---

[32] J. Cashman, "Old Prior Park—the final years 1843–1856", *Recusant History* 23 (1996), pp. 79–106.

[33] Roche, *Prior Park*; P. Cornwell, *Prior Park College: The Phoenix* (Tiverton: Halsgrove Press, 2005, revised with additional material by D. Clarke, 2018), pp. 43–60; Champ, *William Bernard Ullathorne 1806–1889: A Different Kind of Monk*, (Leominster: Gracewing, 2006), pp. 128–33.

Prior Park Bath

Colleges of SS. Peter and Paul.

CONDUCTED BY THE CHRISTIAN BROTHERS,

UNDER THE PATRONAGE OF THE

RIGHT REV. WILLIAM ROBERT BROWNLOW,

BISHOP OF CLIFTON.

PRESIDENT :—REV. BR. J. J. STRAHAN.

Figure 3: Prospectus for Prior Park, early twentieth century.

at Downside in the 1850s, boys rose at 5.20 a.m. with study and classes until breakfast at 8.30. Mass was celebrated at 9 with study following until dinner at 1 p.m. Study followed until 3 with classes, then supper at 7, night prayers and lights out at 8.30. The month of July was the only extended holiday period, with boys generally remaining at the school over Christmas and Easter for religious devotions and celebrations. Not until the end of the century was the pattern of three annual holidays at home established. Food seemed remarkably good. There were two meat courses at dinner, and twice a week boys could purchase extra food. Beer in copious amounts, presumably very light and hopefully watered down, was the staple drink.[34] Facilities were primitive at all the schools. Inadequate buildings, a lack of proper washing facilities, water and windows that froze over in the winter, all characterized the early years of these colleges as their numbers, facilities and reputation slowly grew over the century.

Alongside the transfer of Jesuit and Benedictine educational establishments from the Continent, a third component was the transfer of the English College at Douai to a new, merged college, St Edmund's College, under the aegis of the seculars of the London District. The English College at Douai, founded in 1568 by William Allen, had long functioned as a kind of combined university, school and seminary run by the seculars, and, whilst subject to the habitual financial and political upheavals of the other continental colleges, it had a very distinguished educational and theological history. By the 1780s, there were as many as 160 students enrolled at the college. The revolutionary turmoil of the 1790s was to have a profound effect on the structure and finances of the college. Although it claimed immunity from a range of revolutionary edicts on the grounds that it was British rather than French property, conditions eventually became intolerable with the declaration of war between France and Britain in 1793. Armed guards arrived at the college, and for at least a year staff and students were secretly moved from one location to another before finally departing Douai in February 1795, crossing from Calais to Dover on an American ship.

---

[34] van Zeller, *Downside*, pp. 40–1; Birt, *Downside*, pp. 208–11. Cornwell, *Prior Park*, pp. 25–8.

After some significant debate, a major portion of the returning staff and students were relocated to an existing small Catholic school at Old Hall Green Academy in Hertfordshire which was to be merged into the new St Edmund's College. Old Hall Green had been established in 1749 with the strong support of Richard Challoner, then co-adjutator to the Vicar Apostolic of London, as a boarding college. The college, unlike its other continental "migrants" Stonyhurst, Ampleforth and Downside, who answered ultimately to the superiors of their respective orders, was under the control of the secular authorities through the Vicar Apostolic of London.[35]

Not all the parties were content to relocate to Old Hall. At the same time as St Edmund's was being merged with Old Hall Academy—no mean task with a range of internal arguments between staff and pupils—fresh efforts were made to relocate some of the pupils, staff and ethos of Douai to a new northern hub. The reasoning was sound because the north was a very important Catholic region, which, it was argued, needed both a seminary and a college to ensure the large Catholic population could be well served. The closure of the college and seminary at Douai created issues for the training of priests in England. In northern England, historically far and away the centre for the Catholic faith in England, the important seminary and college of Ushaw near Durham was established. Whilst at the outset the college was primarily for training priests, Ushaw soon recruited a range of pupils some of whom were not intended for the priesthood. Milburn's account of the origins of Ushaw College emphasized the size and vibrancy of the Catholic population in northern England in the early nineteenth century with both regulars (Jesuits, Benedictines, Franciscans and Dominicans) and seculars very active in missionary work across the region.[36] The two northern bishops, Douglass and Gibson, were keen to create a seminary-college which would be run through the cooperation of several regions and bishops, rather than the concern of a single diocese.

---

[35] N. Schofield, *The History of St Edmund's College* (Ware: The Edmundian Association, 2013), pp. 6–34.

[36] D. Milburn, *A History of Ushaw College* (Durham: Ushaw College, 1964).

In 1804, work began on the building of the new college. Bishop Gibson sought the advice of contemporaries at St Edmund's College on the nature and costs of construction that they had encountered and set about fundraising. By 1810, Ushaw was functioning as both a boarding school and a seminary. Like St Edmund's, it was a diocesan venture; unlike St Edmund's, its affairs were the concern of more than one diocese. Numbers were very buoyant in such a Catholic region, growing quickly to around 150 in the first half of the century and reaching a peak of over 350 by 1900, making it probably the largest of the Catholic public schools at the time, although that number included significant numbers of seminary pupils. The building of a new Exhibition Hall in 1849 accommodating 300 students emphasized school growth. A chapel designed by Pugin was eventually demolished in the 1880s, because it was too small. Its president for some 25 years, Mgr Charles Newsham, "set about replacing the drab Douai-rooted devotional life of the college by the flamboyant devotions sweeping across Catholic England from Rome" and was keen to engage with the University of London external degrees before establishing links with the University of Durham at the end of the century.

Ushaw faced a variety of "political" pressures as it developed from mid-century, as balancing the needs of a number of different dioceses was not always easy. As Milburn diplomatically noted, managing a series of, to put it politely, "challenging" bishops created an interesting dynamic at the college. It prospered, however, and had some very distinguished alumni. In the nineteenth century, they included two cardinals, three archbishops and 21 bishops, including Cardinal Wiseman, the first Archbishop of Westminster.[37]

The newly arrived community at St Edmund's faced a multitude of challenges as it sought to become effectively the "new Douai" on English soil, albeit on a much more modest scale. The school was successful in attracting a Catholic gentry elite in the early years, but amalgamating with another school posed a particular set of problems and the college experienced an early student revolt in 1809 (the so-called "Great Affair") over discipline, resources and, most probably, food! One of the expelled

---

[37] Milburn, *Ushaw*, pp. 363–6; quotation in W. J. Campbell (ed.), *Ushaw College 1808–2008: A Celebration* (Keighley: PBK Publishing, 2008), p. 18.

revolutionaries was the future Earl of Shrewsbury, who was to become a very important leader, and huge benefactor, of the Catholic community in the middle decades of the century, responsible for helping to fund many of the new Catholic churches built by Pugin in the 1830s and 1840s.[38] The college provided both lay education and trained boys for the priesthood (the group were termed the "Divines" within the school), but in the early years, the numbers entering the priesthood were very small, and for a few years St Edmund's was briefly lay only, church boys only, and, finally, a mix of the two by 1819. That remained the case until 1869 when the church boys left for seminary study in London. Augustus Pugin played a part in important building work between 1845–53 with a significant Gothic chapel taking a central place at St Edmund's. By the end of the century, numbers had stabilized at around 100 following the loss of the seminary students. The school by century-end was, argued Badhern, characterized by "tranquillity, meditation, conversation and spiritual reflection certainly quite different from the ethos of competition, physical courage and manliness; the college was a conservative institution, delighting in its recusant tradition and its Gothic style crowned by Pugin's chapel".[39]

The "English" colleges

Alongside St Edmund's, the Hierarchy in England had also begun to establish a network of college-seminaries to educate Catholics and secure a stream of new priests to serve the growing Catholic population. Unlike Downside, Stonyhurst, St Edmund's and Ampleforth, these were not continental "migrants" but were established independently of continental traditions. The oldest of these was the school at Sedgley Park near Wolverhampton, which, with St Edmund's, might well lay claim to being the oldest Catholic public boarding school in England. It

---

[38] Schofield, *St Edmund's College*, pp. 43–6, 85.

[39] J. R. Badhern, "The symbolic landscapes of nineteenth and early-twentieth century English Catholic Public Schools", unpublished MA Thesis, Faculty of Environment and Leisure, University of Gloucestershire, 2004, p. 77.

was Richard Challoner, the Vicar-Apostolic of London, who played an important role in helping to support the school at a time when, in theory at least, its existence was illegal. The building and grounds were leased from an influential and friendly local landowner by Richard Errington who became the first head, and the first boarding students arrived in 1763. Between then and 1781, some 780 boys went through the college of whom over 70 became priests. It continued to recruit strongly (well over 100 students in the 1780s), and in 1781, the Midland District took it over as a secular college.[40]

Sedgley Park concentrated in the main on lay education but always sent a good proportion of its students to seminaries to train for the priesthood. It constituted one of the largest Catholic boarding schools in the country in the early decades of the nineteenth century with around 200 students in 1810, much larger than some of the rather better-known nascent "continental" colleges of the religious orders.[41] Religious instruction, the reading of sacred texts, and daily Mass and prayers were integral to the life of the school. The curriculum was varied and in the mid-nineteenth century consisted of reading, grammar, arithmetic, geography, dictation and English composition. For those boys wishing to progress to a commercial career, book-keeping, land-surveying and geometry were taught. Interestingly, at this time only a small proportion of boys studied Latin or Greek, a contrast with the other Catholic colleges. Sedgley Park had always drawn both on fee-paying lay students wanting a Catholic boarding education and church boys planning for the priesthood who were often funded by their diocese. By mid-century numbers were around 150, and in the 1860s, driven partly by the lack of secure leases for the school, plans were begun to move the college to a more spacious site at Cotton in north Staffordshire.

The buildings there had originally been given to John Henry Newman and the Oratory Fathers by the Earl of Shrewsbury, a powerful and generous benefactor of the Church, as a potential home. The Oratory

---

[40] F. Roberts (with N. Henshaw), *A History of Sedgley Park and Cotton College* (Privately published, 1985); Canon W. Buscot, *The History of Cotton College at Sedgley Park 1763–1873* (London: Burns, Oates & Washbourne, 1940).

[41] Roberts and Henshaw, *Sedgley Park and Cotton College*, p. 59.

Fathers found the site too remote and rural and decided to move back to Birmingham. By the late 1860s, however, a preparatory school had been established there and, in 1873, the Sedgley Park school moved from Wolverhampton to the new site to become Cotton College.[42] Numbers attending rarely fell below 100 and had reached 125 by the start of the twentieth century. The college was largely staffed by secular priests and trained both church and lay boys reaching high standards in the external Oxford local exams the college used. Church boys generally moved for their final training to Oscott College, the diocesan seminary in Birmingham.

Oscott College itself was opened in 1794 by a group of "liberal" Catholic laymen who sought to establish a school with a strong lay influence in combination and collaboration with the Church authorities. Located at Maryvale in Sutton Coldfield, its early years were dogged by financial difficulties, and there were rarely more than 20 or 30 boys in any year. In 1808, it was taken over by the Birmingham Vicar Apostolic, Milner, and continued to educate both lay and church boys. The cramped site, coupled with growing numbers, meant that plans were drawn up to move to a large purpose-built site a couple of miles from Maryvale. The move took place in 1835.

In its day, the college was one of the most celebrated of the Catholic schools and seminaries of England. Augustus Pugin was appointed to the college as Professor of Antiquities in 1837 and, with the support of the Rector, Nicholas Wiseman, later the first Archbishop of Westminster, took over the building projects for the college from the original architect, Joseph Potter. The opening of the chapel in 1838 was celebrated as a kind of "coming of age" for the new "Romantic Catholic" community. There were 68 robed clergy of all ranks processing at the opening with "the gorgeous number and richness of official dresses flickering with gold, contrasting with purple and the altar lit up with its massy candlesticks".[43]

In the 1840s, under the presidency of Wiseman, the college was at the heart of the Catholic revival and, especially, of the Oxford Movement

---

[42] Roberts and Henshaw, *Sedgley Park and Cotton College*, pp. 60–3.

[43] Quoted in R. Hill, *God's Architect: Pugin and the Building of Romantic Britain* (London: Penguin, 2008), pp. 196–7.

Figure 4: Cotton College Study Place, *c*.1900.

Figure 5: Stonyhurst Study Place, *c*.1907.

converts. The college attracted new recruits with its intellectual traditions and ultramontane devotions, such as the Stations of the Cross and Benediction. It was at Oscott that Newman preached his famous "second spring" sermon in 1852. In the 1860s, the school was at its zenith with an Oxford convert, Northcote, as its head and around 100 boys most years, and was favoured by the sons of local aristocracy and gentry from the supposedly "best" Catholic families of the region. Compared with some of its competitors, there was less engagement with external examinations, and the college seemed comfortable with sending its old boys into business, the services, the Foreign Office and, of course, the Church.[44]

The combination of a seminary and a college, the pattern of Oscott for the best part of a century, was not always a comfortable one. Some observers found the atmosphere too bustling, busy, chaotic and focused on external connections, an environment not always conducive to priestly training. Bishop Ullathorne decided in 1873 to create a new, separate diocesan seminary at Olton. For a decade or so afterwards, the lay college at Oscott continued, whilst priests were trained at both Oscott and Olton. In 1881, Bishop Ilsley, Ullathorne's successor, decided it was unsustainable to run two seminaries in the diocese and closed Olton, concentrating seminary work back at Oscott. In 1889, the decision was made to close the school at Oscott and use it solely as a large seminary. It was a controversial decision for the college was successful, well regarded and financially solvent. The president, Mgr Souter, opposed the decision, as did the Oscotian Society, but Bishop Ilsley was determined that a college and seminary could not co-exist on the same site. Perhaps, as Champ noted, the heyday of the school for the sons of gentlemen was long past and its lustre was fading. The opening of Cotton College in the Birmingham diocese undoubtedly precipitated the decision to close the school at Oscott, which between 1892 and 1909 became effectively a national seminary used by numerous dioceses before reverting back to a single diocesan role.[45]

---

[44] Scarisbrick, *Diocese of Birmingham*, pp. 13–14; J. Champ, *Oscott*, pp. 18–19; *The Oscotian: 1888 Jubilee Edition*, pp. 76–99

[45] M. Williams, "Seminaries and Priestly Formation", pp. 72–4; see also J. Champ, *Ullathorne*, pp. 396–407.

A final example was the seminary college of St Joseph's at Upholland near Wigan, created in 1883 by the Liverpool diocese, and established primarily as a junior and senior seminary, solely for the training of priests from the age of around 11 or 12 rather than a "general purpose" school and seminary which, in their early incarnations, was the model pursued by Ushaw and Oscott. The powerful Liverpool diocese funded the establishment of the college in its entirety, and it had some 40 or so students in its early years. By the end of the century, it became the sole junior and senior seminary for the diocese. It remained solely for church boys intending to train for the priesthood.[46]

Expanding the sector

From mid-century, the numbers enrolled in Catholic boarding schools were increased by several new schools whose creation came at a time when new, non-Catholic, public schools were also springing up across the country. Nationally some 30 new public schools were set up between 1845 and 1875, and Catholics had some share, albeit a small one, in this expansion.

One of the colleges appearing in mid-century was Ratcliffe College near Leicester. It was founded by a new Italian missionary order which had become increasingly active in England, the Rosminians of the Institute of Charity. The Institute was established by Antonio Rosmini in 1828. It was a small order, very "Roman" in its style, and with a missionary zeal to work in England through one of its most active members, Luigi Gentili. The first three Rosminians came to England in 1835 and, as we noted earlier, were invited by Bishop Baines to work at his newly established Prior Park School near Bath. Gentili eventually

---

[46] For Upholland, see D. Atherton and M. Peyton, *St Joseph's College, Upholland: One of the Glories of Catholicism in England. Its rise and fall*. Unpublished (2013), <https://www.academia.edu/48825759/St_Joseph_s_College_Upholland_One_of_the_glories_of_Catholicism_in_England_Its_rise_and_fall_Revised_and_Updated>, accessed on 17 August 2023.

became Regent of the school, and the new arrivals had a big impact on the curriculum and reputation. With the death of Baines in 1843 came a series of difficult challenges both financial and political, and the order left for Loughborough where they had a sizeable mission.[47] That mission had a big impact on the small mining communities around Loughborough where they worked. It was based at Grace Dieu Manor, a faux-medieval house built for Ambrose Phillips de Lisle, which had been extended by Pugin in the 1830s. Ambrose Phillips was a recent convert who represented "a particular type of convert from the gentry (with) a messianic faith in the conversion of England to Catholicism".[48] He was part of an increasingly influential group of converts to Catholicism from the Oxford Movement.

The order was active in missions throughout the east Midlands, ruffling traditional recusant feathers with a vigorous programme of Masses, retreats, pilgrimages and public processions in the area. Angelo Rinolfi, one of the most active members of the order, along with the indefatigable Gentili (who died of typhus whilst on a mission to Ireland in 1848), ran a whole series of retreats and preaching missions across the country in churches, missions and Catholic public schools including Oscott, Ampleforth and Ushaw.[49] For many traditionalists, such missions, retreats and public displays, replete with black garb, cloaks and biretta, brought a new, and sometimes unwelcome, "Roman" atmosphere to a faith accustomed to a lack of display and a low profile. The order established a mission and an order of nuns in Loughborough whose house was funded by Lady Mary Arundell, a local benefactor and friend of Ambrose Phillips. When the Rosminians decided to establish a new college in the area they chose a greenfield site at Ratcliffe-on-the-Wreake, a few miles from Loughborough and not far from Grace Dieu Manor.[50]

---

[47] J. M. Hill, *The Rosminian Mission* (Leominster: Gracewing, 2017).

[48] J. Bossy, *The English Catholic Community 1570–1850* (London: Darton, Longman & Todd, 1975), p. 387.

[49] J. M. Hill, *Angelo Rinolfi: The Preacher* (Leominster: Gracewing, 2021) contains listings of the many missions undertaken across England, Wales and Ireland by Rinolfi.

[50] Hill, *Rosminian Mission*, p. 88.

Donations from a number of benefactors, especially from new converts from the Oxford Movement, were important; William Lockhart in particular made a substantial donation towards the building costs.[51]

The location was a judicious one—close enough to the Rosminian missions in the east Midlands, yet sufficiently far away from the seminary/college of the Birmingham diocese at Oscott, to avoid accusations of poaching either pupils or potential diocesan priests. Ambrose Phillips persuaded Gentili and the Rosminians to employ Augustus Pugin to build the Gothic front of the seminary school which opened in 1844. It looked impressive from the outside, but the accommodation was small and cramped and increasingly inadequate. The story may be apocryphal, but Gentili was said to be keen on dismantling the building brick by brick and starting over again.[52]

The first boys and seminarians for the college arrived in 1847. There were 30 boys a couple of years later. In 1852, it was decided to separate the seminary and college with the former moving to Rugby, precipitating a crisis, because so many seminarians were now lost to the teaching staff by the move. At one point, the order contemplated selling the nascent college and moving to London, where Cardinal Wiseman was keen for the Rosminians to establish a new school. A Belgian also visited the school with well-advanced plans to convert it to a lunatic asylum! But the college survived, and by the 1860s had a regular roll of between 90 and 100 students. As with so many such colleges, fluctuations in numbers and finances were a constant challenge. A new chapel was opened in 1867, and the Golden Jubilee of the College in 1894 was celebrated with a cricket match, theatrical performances and a High Mass conducted by the Bishop of Nottingham. Numbers, however, had fallen dramatically to only 39 by the mid-1890s. By century-end, they stabilized at between 60 and 70. The college, according to the Catholic Directory of 1900, was "the most central Catholic College in England ... imparting a thorough religious and secular education at a moderate charge ... of late years great improvements regarding the boys' accommodation and comforts

---

[51] N. Schofield, *William Lockhart: First Fruits of the Oxford Movement* (Leominster: Gracewing, 2011), pp. 47-8.

[52] Hill, *Rosminian Mission*, p. 288.

have been undertaken".[53] As with many of our schools, numbers had recovered to around 100 boys by 1910. Better qualified teachers were being employed to improve exam results, the financial position was improving, and a range of new buildings were begun in 1911.[54]

Alongside the enormous efforts of the Church to provide mass schooling, especially at elementary level, sat a system of secondary schooling for boys provided by the smaller colleges, and it is here that we can see the creation and development of colleges such as Ratcliffe and nearby Mount St Mary's. For Battersby, "the emergence of a new middle-class, coupled with the growing number of middle and upper-class converts into the church created new demands and brought about the emergence of a type of high school for boys of middle-class families, which had hitherto been a feature lacking in the Catholic system of education and we find a new impetus being given to the . . . colleges".[55]

The Jesuits, building on the success of Stonyhurst, established a new boarding college, Mount St Mary's in north Derbyshire, in 1852, with some 70 pupils, four priests and five lay masters on the first rolls. The location reflected a connection with the Pole family, a strong Jesuit family over several generations, who bequeathed buildings and land to help start the college.

It may well be that the Jesuits, who were keen to grow their educational mission in England, sought specifically to establish a school to appeal to a growing middle class in contrast to the "mother college" at Stonyhurst, which had a much more aristocratic clientele and tone. The *Catholic Directory* of 1843 described Mount St Mary's as seeking "to provide a liberal course of education conducted on a plan sufficiently economical to place it within reach of persons of large families or of small fortunes . . . to do away with the necessity of a variety of charges usually put down under the name of extras, a fixed sum will be charged as the annual pension".[56]

---

[53] *Catholic Directory*, 1900.

[54] C. R. Leetham, *Ratcliffe College 1847–1947* (Leicester: Ratcliffian Association 1950), pp. 64–5, 76.

[55] W. J. Battersby, "Secondary Education for Boys", p. 322.

[56] *Catholic Directory*, 1843.

Figure 6: Mount St Mary's College, front, late nineteenth century.

This might be described as either socially responsible or clever marketing, but it seemed to work. Certainly the traditional public schools usually inflicted a whole host of charges for anything from sport to music to haircuts and additional food. Fees were initially set at £35 p.a. in contrast to the £50 p.a. at Stonyhurst. Roberts has drawn some interesting parallels between the Jesuit educational strategy of developing a range of schools, from strong day schools through to middle-class boarding and upper-class boarding schools, and the emerging Woodard schools which similarly and explicitly sought to cater for different classes within the same group of colleges. For Woodard, Lancing College, founded in 1848, was at the apex of the structure, with Hurstpierpoint (1849) and Ardingley (1858) as part of the same group but catering for a different demographic.[57] Part of the Jesuit strategy, contrasting perhaps with the more individualistic focus of the Benedictine schools, may have been to connect up these different segments of the market into an overall Jesuit educational mission.

The core of Mount St Mary's, the Pole building, was described as a plain and modest affair, gaunt and red brick. It was formally opened in September 1842 in a separate building, because the Pole house was being converted. Within a few years numbers had grown to 60 boys, and in 1845, the first Rector commissioned the architect Hansom to build a new chapel and carry out a range of other work. He was an experienced builder, sometimes described as a low-cost version of Pugin, and had worked at other schools including Downside. A house for the Jesuit community was built in 1859, and numbers had reached a celebratory 100 by 1872. The college also benefited from its own railway halt "Spinkhill for Mt St Mary", and a strong building programme in the 1870s and 1880s ensured that numbers remained at around 100 by the end of the century.[58] The lifestyle at the Mount at this time was, to say the least, challenging: straw mattresses, washing in cold water, no showers and restricted holidays with a Christmas break being established only in the 1890s. But the Mount continued to perform well in external

---

[57] Roberts, "Jesuit Collegiate Education", pp. 89–91.
[58] M. Beattie, *Portrait of our College: Mount St Mary and Barlborough Hall, 1842–2017* (London: Society of Jesus, 2017), pp. 45–54.

examinations, without reaching the exalted heights of its parent school, Stonyhurst.[59]

Beaumont provides a further example of a new Jesuit creation looking to a particular social group. Set up initially as a Jesuit novitiate in 1854, the creation of a new novitiate at Roehampton meant that it became a lay college in 1861. Established not far from Windsor, the property was an eighteenth-century country house with extensive grounds and views of the castle. For the poet Peter Levi, its creation epitomized a kind of "southern drift" of the Jesuits, seeking a "bite of the Establishment" in the south to mirror the importance of Stonyhurst in the north.[60] It also explicitly sought a much more aristocratic, international and socially influential clientele than was the case with either Mount St Mary's or Ratcliffe, established at around the same time. It had attained a school roll of around 130 by the 1860s and had become a fashionable school for the aristocracy and moneyed classes around London by the end of the nineteenth century. It also attracted some well-connected foreign pupils. Alongside the traditional Jesuit curriculum and class organization, tuition in fencing, horse-riding and dancing served to attract a gentlemanly clientele. The proximity of the wealth of London, the royal connections at neighbouring Windsor, and interaction with neighbouring schools such as Eton, set the tone for the school. Levi makes much of this focus on attracting a "better class" of pupils, both through the teaching and by the provision of an environment conducive to that kind of constituency. Arguably, pressure for the kind of adjustment evident at Beaumont came from some of the new aristocratic, well-connected and affluent converts coming into the Church who found existing provision "ungentle, un-English and out of date".[61]

By the start of the twentieth century, newer schools, such as Douai (1903) and St Bernardine's, Buckingham (1896), were adding to a sizeable group of Catholic boarding schools catering primarily for the growing Catholic middle classes. Interestingly, one of the reasons that Bishop Browning asked the Christian Brothers to take on Prior Park in 1895 was

---

[59] Roberts, "Jesuit Collegiate Education", p. 227, 276.

[60] P. Levi, *Beaumont 1861–1961* (London: André Deutsch, 1961).

[61] Levi, *Beaumont*, p. 17.

precisely to make the school more attractive to a middle-class clientele which, he argued, wanted a more commercial ethos in the tone and curriculum of the school. That shift did not initially work in the case of Prior Park, but for other schools, notably Ratcliffe and Mount St Mary's, it did. This varied group of schools were to prosper significantly in the new century.

Nowhere was this search for a marriage between a resurgent Catholicism and the public-school tradition better articulated than at the Oratory School, established in Edgbaston, Birmingham under the guiding hand of John Henry Newman. It was Newman, and fellow members of the Oratory order (the Oratory of St Philip Neri which Newman had joined on his conversion), who drove the creation of the new school in 1859.

The school explicitly sought to create an education ideally suited to the new upper-class convert population. That class drew from the very core of the Establishment, many of whom were dissatisfied with the nature and "tone" of existing schools such as Ampleforth and Downside which, as we have seen, were perhaps more rooted in the experience of the old, recusant Catholic community who were more comfortable with a Catholic boarding education built on the traditions of the old "overseas" colleges. The creators of the Oratory School were clear as to their purpose: "the establishment and formation of a school for lay boys of the upper classes, of the nature of such public schools as Winchester and Eton".[62]

It is worth reflecting a little on that aspiration. The discussions around the establishment of the Oratory School were especially critical of existing Catholic public schools (diplomatically never named), which, argued Newman and his supporters, were too wedded to a traditional view of Catholicism and were not attractive to the new class of educated, professional converts to Catholicism. The Oratory School sought to recreate a traditional boarding school experience but with a powerful

---

[62] P. Shrimpton, *A Catholic Eton? Newman's Oratory School* (Leominster: Gracewing, 2005), p. 70; see also T. Tinkell, *Cardinal Newman's School: 150 years of the Oratory School* (London: Third Millenium Publishing, 2009); J. Cornwell, *Newman's Unquiet Grave: The Reluctant Saint* (London: Continuum, 2011), pp. 148–50.

Figure 7: Beaumont College staff and pupils mourn the death of Queen Victoria, 1903.

School of the Oratory, Edgbaston.

INSTITUTED IN 1859.

Circumstances having suddenly made it necessary to re-arrange the educational staff of the School, it has been thought respectful to the Parents and Friends of the Pupils to issue a list of Masters, &c., as they stand at present.

PREFECT OF STUDIES AND DISCIPLINE—FR. J. H. NEWMAN, D.D.

PREFECT OF DORMITORIES AND PLAYGROUND—FR. WM. NEVILLE, B.A., of Winchester School, and Trinity College, Oxford.

SPIRITUAL DIRECTORS—FR. STANISLAS FLANAGAN and FR. HENRY BITTLESTON.

FIRST MASTER— PROFESSOR ARNOLD, M.A., of Rugby and Winchester Schools; late Fellow of University College, Oxford.

SECOND MASTER—RICHARD POPE, ESQ., late Vice-Principal of St. Bernard's College, Gibraltar.

THIRD MASTER—M. L'ABBÉ ROUGEMONT, B.A., of the University of Paris.

Assisted by Two Tutors, Members of Universities; and by French, Music, Drawing, and Drill Masters.

A Lady, who has had great experience in the care of young persons, and is well known to the friends of the Fathers, takes charge of the House, lately occupied by Miss French.

The Term commences on the 24th of this month.

JOHN H. NEWMAN.

January 13, 1862.

Figure 8: Prospectus for the Oratory School, 1859.

patina of Catholicism. The curriculum was focused on the classics (the classical authors rather than the Church Fathers), and an embryonic house system was established with boys boarding in houses around the school site, with a Dame looking after them as had traditionally occurred at Eton. Corporal punishment was frequent (as in all other public schools) and sport, especially cricket, became a central part of activities. The cult of athleticism, an important part of the public-school ethos, was central. Interestingly the key fixture in the calendar was against Beaumont which, alone amongst the Catholic public schools, it regarded as the Oratory's social equal. Numbers always remained small, arguably a deliberate intent on the part of its founders. The Oratorian Fathers maintained a degree of control and ownership of the school, but lay teachers taught alongside clerical ones from the outset. Periodic financial and domestic crises marked the history of the school for much of the nineteenth century with key constraints of small numbers and a cramped, piecemeal site along the Hagley Road in Birmingham.

But how appropriate was such a social and educational aspiration for the school? We have seen the stringent criticisms of public schools in the 1860s which had recommended wholesale reforms of discipline, facilities and curriculum. Such was the system that the Oratory and Beaumont sought explicitly to emulate, albeit with a wholesale infusion of Catholic values and spirit. Keeping numbers small, a strong religious ethos, the use of lay alongside clerical teaching staff, and improvements in the level of care for pupils especially, as at the Oratory, by employing important female matrons to care for the boys, were designed to create a different atmosphere and level of care. That at least was the theory, but whether they compensated for what was sometimes a slavish adoption of traditional public-school mores and practice is perhaps rather doubtful. Perhaps the end, a new and powerfully connected Catholic Establishment, justified the means?

The Benedictine order established two further public schools at the beginning of the twentieth century. Leaving Douai in France in 1903 amidst significant pressures arising from the legislation on religious orders (part of the separation of Church and State in France), some 30 Benedictine monks and 65 boys arrived in England and amalgamated with St Mary's College, a small college-seminary which was part of the Portsmouth diocese at Woolhampton. The core of the new school had emerged within a few years, and the pattern of a school, monastic community and Abbey church, common to Ampleforth and Downside, was soon established. The merging of the St Mary's and the Douai community eventually created a school of around 100 pupils with, as always, significant pressures on accommodation and resources.[63]

The order was also active in Scotland and, in 1878, established a new monastery (part of the English Benedictine Congregation) at Fort Augustus in the Highlands in a military building and barracks given by the Marquess of Bute. Alongside the monastery, a school was established for the sons of gentlemen combining "the refining influences of home life with the manly and invigorating spirit of a public school". The school did not last, closing in 1894 because of falling rolls. It reopened in 1920 with the help of teaching staff from Ampleforth and with a less aristocratic remit than the previous school. Interestingly, the Benedictine educational mission also extended to Ireland, when Downside Abbey was granted permission to establish a school in the diocese of Ferns. The school at Gorey, Co. Wexford was set up by Fr John Sweetman. It was eccentric to say the least and, as Brunning notes, was something of a thorn in the side of the Downside community, especially during the Irish Civil War, when Sweetman took a strongly pro-Republican line. The Benedictines at Downside eventually managed to close the school in 1925.[64]

The major Catholic public schools are listed in Table 1. Some of the schools such as Prior Park had a somewhat chequered history and were re-founded at various points. Others such as Oscott shifted to become seminaries at the end of the nineteenth century.

---

[63] G. Scott (ed.), *The English Benedictine Community of St Edmund, King and Martyr: Paris 1615/ Douai 1818/Woolhampton 1903–2003* (Stanbrook Abbey, 2003).

[64] D. Brunning, "You collared a Maiden Young Ireland in this House": The patriotism of Don Francis Sweetman and his school, Mount St Benedict, Gorey, Co. Wexford", *Downside Review* 22:140 (2) (2022), pp. 59–81; M. Turnbull, *Abbey Boys: Fort Augustus Abbey Schools* (Perth: corbie.com, 2000).

Table 1: Major Catholic boarding schools

School	Founding order	Foundation	Approximate number of pupils c.1900
Sedgley Park/ Cotton College	Secular	1762/1873	125
St Edmund's	Secular	1793	100
Stonyhurst	Jesuit	1794	200
Oscott	Secular	1794–1890	c.50
Ampleforth	Benedictine	1802	100–120
Ushaw	Secular	1804	350
Downside	Benedictine	1814	120
Prior Park	Secular	1830–56; 1867–1904	No data
Mount St Mary's	Jesuit	1842	80–100
Ratcliffe	Rosminian	1844	60–70
Oratory	Oratorian Fathers (Birmingham)	1859	No data
Beaumont	Jesuit	1861	80
Douai	Benedictine	1903	100

The growing number of pupils in these schools came from a variety of sources—old, recusant families, new converts to Catholicism, the nascent middle classes and an international clientele as well. The Irish constituted an important component in the increase of pupils towards the end of the century. An 1872 committee estimated there were around 250 Irish boys enrolled in these public schools. At some schools, their numbers were very significant. O'Neill's study, based on a set of some 1,300 pupils between about 1850 and 1900 suggests that around 30 per cent of pupils at Downside in this period were Irish, and in the sector as a whole, the figure may have been as high as 20 per cent. At some schools—Stonyhurst was one—special provision and facilities were provided for Irish boys. Elsewhere they may have been less visible but were significant nonetheless.[65]

What then was life like for the pupils studying and living in these schools? All of them shared in what were perhaps typical conditions of the public schools more generally. Discipline was strict and corporal punishment frequent, although in most cases such punishment was the domain of the teaching staff rather than the senior pupils or monitors, and "fagging" was infrequent. Conditions were universally cramped— long rows of dormitory beds, primitive washing facilities, generally poor food, tight control over free time, compulsory sports activities. Many of the individual school histories convey something of the "joys" of the happiest days of the pupils' lives. At Stonyhurst, for example, the delights of the menu included hashed sheep's head and liver, stewed hare, rice soup and flabby salmon. Complaints about the quality and quantity of food in this period (as in all periods) were chronic. The daily schedule in the early years of the college left little free time: rising at 5.30 a.m., morning prayers were at 6; 6.20 Mass; 6.45 studies; 7.40 breakfast; 8–11 study; 11.10 wash; 11.30 dinner; 12 recreation etc. The regime was not dissimilar elsewhere. Daily Mass and morning and night prayers featured everywhere. Codes of behaviour were also widely employed.

At Ratcliffe, for example, the Rosminians enforced strict controls over deportment in church. Proper genuflections, the use of the college prayer book, ensuring that arms were not rested on the rails in front of them, were all part of the daily experience of regular visits to the chapel. A set of "Rules on Morality", "Rules respecting Study" and "Rules for the dormitory and refectory" sat heavy alongside schoolbooks and papers through the century.[66] At Ushaw, days were equally fully occupied. Rising at 6 a.m., the students went straight to Mass and spiritual meditation, after which there was study until breakfast at 8.45. Classes were from 9.30 a.m. until 1 p.m., when dinner occupied an hour. A period of recreation until 3 girded the loins for a four-hour study block, with one short break

---

[65] C. O'Neill, *Catholics of Consequence: Transnational Education, Social Mobility and the Irish Catholic Elite, 1850–1900* (Oxford: Oxford University Press, 2014), esp. p. 75, 81, 92.

[66] Leetham, *Ratcliffe College*, pp. 49–50.

until prayers at 7 p.m., and supper at 7.30. Second prayers closed the day at 9.15. Sunday was equally full, with spiritual readings from 9 to 10.15 a.m., High Mass at 10.30 and Catechism from 12 to 1 p.m. Vespers were sung, and Benediction was at 3 p.m. At 6 p.m., there was study until 7.30 and second prayers at 9.15 p.m.[67]

Music and drama were an important component of school life from an early date. At the Oratory, for example, the tradition of performing the Latin Play each year began in 1865 with the performance being given on the feast of St Philip in May. At Mount St Mary's, drama was also important, as it was at the "mother college" Stonyhurst. There, drama constituted an important part of school life. A new stage was built in 1837 and proceedings became highly formalized and controlled. Female roles were removed (Lady Macbeth was replaced by Macbeth's son Donald), and sometimes plays were kept secret until the day of the performance. Plays were produced by particular years and were apparently the highlight of the Christmas season which boys spent at school, not at home. At Mount St Mary's, drama and elocution were integral to the curriculum. At Christmas, a tragedy, a comedy and two farces were usually performed and sometimes "there were several productions of the same play", whether the audience liked them or not![68] Almost all the schools established drama as an important part of school life. Music too, both sacred and secular, was integral to school life in all of our schools. At the Oratory, Newman had emphasized how "music is an important part of education ... it is a great resource (and) a great point for a boy to escape from himself, and music enables him".[69] Tuition in musical instruments and, more especially, the role of music and singing in the panoply of religious celebrations was common to all the Catholic schools, large and small, socially elite or middle-class.

Much the same could be said for sport, which early on was recognized as both an important outlet for boys' energy and a means of inculcating competition and loyalty within the school. Most of our schools had their own particular sports which became part of the fabric of school life early

---

[67] Milburn, *Ushaw*, p. 139.
[68] Beattie, *Mount St Mary*, p. 29.
[69] Shrimpton, *A Catholic Eton?*, p. 200.

on. At Stonyhurst, a particular form of cricket, which bore little relation to today's game, survived until mid-century, whilst football might embrace teams of unlimited size on a pitch of unlimited width with a complex array of rules making today's offside rule a paragon of simplicity. Other "school-specific" sports included "bandy", a form of ball game, battledore, trap and handball. All our schools played more regular forms of cricket and football from the end of the century. Rugby didn't arrive until the new century.

The extent to which some of the more "gentlemanly pursuits" were available depended on the social tone and aspirations of the schools. For some, horse-riding, rowing and fencing were on offer. Beaumont regularly attended Henley Regatta by century-end. Boxing was an attractive option at many schools. Elocution, dancing and lessons in deportment might also be available, though extra costs would be incurred. Association with the local gentry through hunting was encouraged in almost all our schools, especially the more rural ones. At Mount St Mary's, the hunts at Barlborough Hall and Renishaw Hall were followed by the boys, whilst at Ratcliffe the Quorn Hunt was a regular visitor for over a century. Beagling was from an early date part and parcel of Ampleforth life.

The patterns of our schools were beginning to appear—curriculum, external examinations, a dominant spirituality, an ever-present religious community, houses and prefects, an increased emphasis on sport—and were to become ever more characteristic into the new century. The foundations for twentieth-century expansion were securely laid.

2

A new-found confidence c.1914–40

By the first decades of the new century, all the Catholic public schools had begun to grow in numbers and esteem. In many ways, this new spirit reflected the position of Catholicism in England at this time. The earlier, sometimes fervent, sense of a missionary faith, had perhaps elided to a more secure, confident, even quiescent period in the history of the Church. Gilley, reviewing the period 1892 to 1943, termed them the "years of equipoise", an "era of steady expansion largely untroubled by internal dissent".[1] In formal terms at least, England was no longer a missionary country, with overall supervision of Catholic affairs being transferred from *Propaganda Fide* to the Church Hierarchy at the beginning of the century. The Catholic Church in England, and its public schools, had come of age.

The Catholic population of England continued to grow steadily over these years. There were around 1.8 million Catholics in 1911, rising to around 2.2 million in 1932, and 2.3 million by 1939. Those figures may well underestimate the actual numbers, especially when data from conversions, baptisms and Catholic marriages are considered.[2] The geography of Catholicism remained characterized by a strong

---

[1] S. Gilley, "The Age of Equipoise, 1892–1943", in V. A. McClelland and M. Hodgetts (eds), *From Without the Flaminian Gate: 150 Years of Roman Catholicism in England and Wales, 1850–2000* (London: Darton, Longman & Todd, 1999), p. 21; see also A. Hastings, *A History of English Christianity 1920–2000* (London: SPCK, 2001), pp. 131–55.

[2] D. Gwynn, "Growth of the Catholic Community", in G. A. Beck (ed.), *The English Catholics: Centenary Essays to Commemorate the Restoration of the Hierarchy of England and Wales* (London: Burns & Oates, 1950), pp. 422–5.

concentration in the large urban conurbations—London, Birmingham, Manchester, Newcastle and Liverpool. One of the more interesting geographical characteristics of the pattern of Catholic support in these years, and one which certainly had an impact on educational issues, was the growing suburbanization of the inter-war years. In many urban dioceses, this period saw a significant expansion of suburban parishes. The outer districts of London and Birmingham, for example, saw a rapid growth in Catholic parishes and churches, as a more middle-class population abandoned the crowded inner-city districts. That increased affluence and mobility undoubtedly impacted on the demand for secondary Catholic schooling, whether through day schools or the boarding public schools.

There was also a continued growth in the number of ordinations during this period. The number of Catholic priests in England and Wales grew from around 3,800 in 1912, to just under 4,000 in 1922, and had reached over 5,600 by 1939.[3] Whilst the dioceses were never able to properly work together to create a genuinely national seminary for priestly training, Oscott, Wonersh and Upholland (seminaries only), and Ushaw and St Edmund's (mixed seminaries and lay colleges) were foremost in training the diocesan priests of the inter-war years and beyond. The continental seminaries also continued to train significant numbers of priests. Much the same applied to the regulars, with growing numbers of priests drawn to the Jesuit and Benedictine orders whose schools were very important nurseries for boys wishing to join the order. Whilst the most famous of the Jesuit schools, Stonyhurst, produced a steady flow of new recruits, Mount St Mary's was equally important. The college historian noted that in one year, virtually a whole senior class of one particular teacher, Fr Helsham, went on to become members of the Jesuit order.[4]

---

[3] Data from Faith Survey (University of Roehampton, 2018). Annual *Catholic Directories* have information on priest numbers, baptisms, conversions and marriages.

[4] M. Beattie, *Portrait of our College: Mount St Mary and Barlborough Hall, 1842–2017* (London: Society of Jesus, 2017), p. 49.

The demands on this steadily growing number of priests were certainly significant. For the seculars, the increasing suburbanization of the Catholic population meant a growth in churches and parishes had to be met. In the Birmingham diocese, for example, there were some 58 new churches opened between about 1910 and 1940, the majority of them outside the main urban centres.[5] Similar growth was taking place across the country. Between 1914 and 1949 the number of churches grew from 105 to 151 in the Northampton diocese and from 129 to 175 in the diocese of Nottingham.[6] The resources needed to sustain the building, funding and maintenance of parish life were enormous. Whilst the regulars were important in contributing to this manpower, and had responsibility for a significant number of parishes, much of the growing pressure fell on the secular priests.

It is important to note that these years saw significant changes in Catholic secondary education which had their impact on the public schools. As we saw in the last chapter, the Education Act of 1902 had altered the position of Catholic secondary schools in allowing such schools access to some discretionary public funding through the newly created Local Education Authorities. Whilst that support was mixed both in terms of geography and size, the new conditions did help to underpin a growth in secondary schools, many of which were created and run by both seculars and regulars, and by the growing female religious orders. These years, then, saw the secondary schools mirroring the enormous efforts made by the Church to develop elementary education in the latter part of the nineteenth century. New minimum standards of buildings, together with legislation on pensions and minimum salaries for teachers, also put further financial pressure on parishes and dioceses in the inter-war years.

Catholic day secondary schools grew substantially in this period. By the late 1920s, there were 486 Catholic secondaries educating around 54,000 pupils. As Evennett pointed out, the overwhelming success story was the flourishing of female secondary education, driven almost entirely

---

[5] J. J. Scarisbrick (ed.), *History of the Diocese of Birmingham, 1850–2000* (Strasbourg: Editions du Signe, 2008), pp. 70–192.

[6] Gwynn, "Growth of the Catholic Community", pp. 427–31.

through the work of the religious orders of nuns. There were some 276 members of the Association of Convent Schools by the late 1920s, largely day schools with very low fees. As he suggests, "the educational work of the nuns, operating at all social levels, is by far the largest and in some ways the most effective part of the whole Catholic educational effort".[7]

The work of the regular orders was certainly instrumental in delivering growth in the boys' secondary sector in these years. In the inter-war years, there were around 40 new Catholic day schools set up, the majority of them delivered through the regular orders. Some of these orders—the Jesuits, Benedictines, and Dominicans—saw education as part of a wider set of activities; others such as the Christian Brothers de la Salle, the Xaverians, the Salesians and the Christian Brothers (Ireland) were founded with very specific educational remits. Whilst some of these schools—St Francis Xavier in Liverpool, St Bede's in Manchester, or St Phillip's in Birmingham—had a long and very distinguished pedigree, others were more recent, and their creation reflected the growing Catholic demand for such schools. A review of school foundation dates for these schools shows that of the 50 schools listed by Battersby, 31 had been founded after 1900 and 24 of those first opened their doors in the inter-war years.[8] It was an impressive achievement at a significant cost in human and financial resources. Evennett estimated that there were some 13,000 boys at these new schools by the end of the 1930s.[9] What then of the Catholic public schools?

---

[7] H. O. Evennett, *The Catholic Schools of England and Wales* (Cambridge: Cambridge University Press, 1944), pp. 38–40, 43.

[8] W. J. Battersby, "Secondary Education for Boys", in G. A. Beck (ed.), *The English Catholics: Centenary Essays to Commemorate the Restoration of the Hierarchy of England and Wales* (London: Burns & Oates, 1950), pp. 331–4.

[9] Evennett, *Catholic Schools*, p. 53.

Growth and consolidation

The public-school sector as a whole, and the Catholic public schools in particular, continued to develop in the early decades of the century. Increased numbers, the growing use of public examinations against which to test the qualities of their students, and the continued development of buildings and facilities, suggest a period of much greater confidence and security in Catholic public schools. Downside, to take one example, began to be transformed under the leadership of Dom Leander Ramsay who became headmaster in 1907 and began a process of rebuilding the physical, intellectual and reputational capital of every aspect of the school. For Barnes, writing in 1926, "the last twenty years has absolutely transformed the school of Downside".[10] Numbers grew from 100 at the turn of the century to 150 in 1910 and 200 in 1914. Expanded buildings, a new Junior House and the development of a prefect system were begun.[11]

Elsewhere, the pre-war years heralded something of a change in pace which was to be consolidated after 1918. A new sports hall at Beaumont (1911), continued building and renovation at Ampleforth, new dormitories and kitchens at Ratcliffe (1913) and major refurbishments at St Edmund's (1896–1913), exemplified this period of growth in the decade or so before 1914. All of the schools experienced significant losses amongst their ex-pupils during the Great War, attested to in the early 1920s by the construction of many memorial buildings, chapels and sporting facilities, and bursaries developed with monies raised by the schools and their alumni associations.

The climate for much of the inter-war period then was a positive one. The sector as a whole saw most public schools increasing their numbers in these years. As David Turner noted, "the boarding schools thrived in the years after the First World War despite the caustic comments

---

[10] A. S. Barnes, *The Catholic Schools of England* (London: Williams & Norgate, 1926), p. 207.

[11] H. van Zeller, *Downside By and Large* (London: Sheed & Ward, 1954), pp. 64–6.

Figure 9: Downside School and Monastery, *c.*1916.

of government reports".[12] There were new foundations and sustained growth in most parts of the sector and most parts of the country. The Catholic sector undoubtedly took a good share of that growth.

There were some new establishments created in this period. As we noted in the last chapter, the Benedictine community at Douai relocated back to England following political pressures in France and merged with St Mary's School at Woolhampton to establish Douai in 1903. It was small but very successful with around 150 boys by the late 1930s.[13] The Benedictines, as well as having a new foothold at Fort William in Scotland, also established a new boarding school at Belmont Abbey in Herefordshire in 1926, and the Dominicans opened a small boarding school at Laxton Hall in Nottinghamshire in 1924. The Franciscans also expanded their small college and seminary of St Bernardine's in Buckingham and built two new wings to the college in the late 1930s to allow for further growth.

The Oratory School faced some difficult decisions in the early decades of the new century. The school, run by the Birmingham Oratorian Fathers, had always been deliberately kept small and exclusive which created significant financial difficulties. The physical site of the school at Edgbaston, in the heart of an expanding and busy city, was not seen as ideal for expansion. In 1921, the decision was made to move the school to a new site at Caversham Park, near Reading. It was a difficult and controversial decision, driven in part at least by the lack of land for development in rapidly expanding Birmingham and by the financial difficulties the school faced. Old Oratorians were not impressed by the decision, and the Birmingham Fathers themselves were not always happy that the day-to-day running of their school was no longer as easy as it had been. Though the move was driven, in part at least, by a need to expand, the Oratory nonetheless remained a deliberately small school of around

---

[12] D. Turner, *The Old Boys: The Decline and Rise of the Public School* (London: Yale University Press, 2016), p. 178.

[13] G. Scott (ed.), *The English Benedictine Community of St Edmund, King and Martyr: Paris 1615/Douai 1818/Woolhampton 1903-2003* (Worcester: Stanbrook Abbey Press, 2003), pp. 19-23.

75 boys, still notionally under the control of the Birmingham Oratorians, and with a high reputation and social standing.[14]

Prior Park near Bath also re-emerged. Established with much pomp and ceremony by Bishop Baines in the 1830s and closed by the 1860s, it was revived by the diocese and at the end of the century run by the Irish Christian Brothers, who were active in educational provision in the Clifton Diocese. The school, beset by financial problems, closed yet again in 1904, taking on a life as the headquarters of the Holy Ghost Fathers, as a War Office rest home and a state-run Industrial School before the Christian Brothers again took it over as a boarding school from 1924 onwards.[15] A "muscular" and Irish ethos imbued every aspect of the school which catered for a largely middle-class rather than aristocratic clientele. The involvement of the Christian Brothers was a challenge. Their interests had primarily been in the provision of education for the working classes, and their involvement in the "rebirth" of Prior Park was not universally welcomed. The school, it was felt, had moved down the social pecking-order. Nonetheless it recruited well and, most importantly, was solvent and successful. For the head, writing in 1937, social tone was of no great concern:

> We have not here a goody-goody set of hothouse plants, but a spirited lot that can tackle vigorously on the rugby ground, work hard in class and are yet amenable to College discipline.[16]

The poet Peter Levi has given us an interesting pupil's view! He penned some memorable descriptions of the nine years he spent as a pupil there from the late 1930s, before transferring to Beaumont and, eventually, the priesthood as a Jesuit. Why Prior Park?

---

[14] T. Tinkell, *Cardinal Newman's School: 150 years of the Oratory School* (London: Third Millenium Publishing, 2009), pp. 47–58.

[15] P. Cornwell, *Prior Park College: The Phoenix* (Tiverton: Halsgrove Press, 2005, revised with additional material by D. Clarke, 2018), pp. 51–74.

[16] Cornwell, *Prior Park*, p. 68.

> My father thought that Stonyhurst looked like a prison and drove away without going in. Beaumont was ruled out because of some cousins who were said to have taken to drink there as schoolboys.

Bullied, beaten and totally philistine were some of his descriptions of life there—the wonderful Palladian mansion the scene of schoolboy desolation!

> The smell of unhappiness is the smell of the boot room at Prior Park in the 1940s.[17]

After nine years at Prior Park, Beaumont was a rest and a time of pleasure!

Almost all the Catholic schools moved from a position of fluctuating numbers and sustainability in the early part of the century, to more secure, steady growth. Ampleforth numbers were rarely over 100 until after the war. By 1919, there were around 200 boys at the school, and the numbers of prep and main school boys grew to 250 in 1924 and had doubled to a celebratory 500 by 1939.[18]

The head, Fr Paul Neville, was hugely important in this recovery of numbers and influence. Downside too continued to expand, albeit at a slower rate than Ampleforth. The detailed plans drawn up by the school after the war anticipated building requirements for some 350 boys.[19] Stonyhurst, the largest of the Catholic boarding schools in the early years of the new century (209 boys in 1905) had grown to a school of almost 350 by 1912. Unusually, numbers fell to around 200, but by the mid-1930s were back up close to the 300 mark. At Douai, numbers were kept deliberately low in this period at between 120 and 150 boys. Belmont Abbey School, established partly at least to provide greater

---

[17] P. Levi, *The Flutes of Autumn* (London: Arena, 1985), pp. 35–42.
[18] A. Marrett-Crosby, *A School of the Lord's Service: A History of Ampleforth* (London: James & James, 2002), p. 60.
[19] D. A. Bellenger (ed.), *Downside Abbey: An Architectural History* (London: Merrell, 2011), pp. 45–9.

Figure 10: Prior Park Centenary celebrations, 1930.

Figure 11: Ampleforth buildings, early twentieth century.

Figure 12: Cotton College buildings, 1930s.

financial security for the monastic community, remained small with around 50 boys in the 1930s.[20]

Elsewhere it was a similar picture. Numbers at St Edmund's were always smaller than the "big three" and fluctuated around 100 boys, although overall numbers were swollen by seminarians training for the priesthood. In the three Midland colleges, Cotton, Ratcliffe and Mount St Mary's, the growth in numbers largely reflected the increasing Catholic professional middle class around Birmingham, Nottingham, Leicester and Sheffield. At Ratcliffe, numbers rose from about 100 in 1913 to 140 in 1921 and had reached 170 by 1938, whilst Cotton saw numbers of around 75 on the eve of the war increase to 115 in 1929 and 150 by 1940.

Ushaw, which like Cotton educated both lay students and candidates for the priesthood, saw numbers fluctuate at around 300 or so in this period, though the numbers of lay students began to tail off quite rapidly in the 1920s; the 100 or so lay students in 1920 had fallen to just 30 by the late 1930s with church boys training for the priesthood becoming dominant.[21]

The growing numbers enrolled in the Catholic boarding schools reflected a number of factors. Certainly they were able to share in the larger market that seemed to be available for a boarding education in these years. In addition, of course, the business model of these Catholic schools was helped by the growing numbers of priests and lay brothers being trained in the seminaries. Often returning to their *alma mater*, they constituted a "free" labour force to teach in both the religious and secular schools. Whilst the costs of accommodation and provision for old age had to be met, overall costs were undoubtedly less than was the case for lay teachers. Many were well qualified, and schools often sought to provide

---

[20] T. E. Muir, *Stonyhurst College 1593–1993* (Cirencester: St Omers Press, revised edition, 2006), pp. 150–1; Scott, *The English Benedictine Community of St Edmund*, p. 21; Belmont Association, <https://www.cyberarc.co.uk/belmontabbey/index.php>, accessed 17 August 2023.

[21] D. Milburn, *A History of Ushaw College* (Durham: Ushaw College, 1964), p. 366; F. Roberts (with N. Henshaw), *A History of Sedgley Park and Cotton College* (Privately published, 1985), p. 163, 205; C. R. Leetham, *Ratcliffe College 1847–1947* (Leicester: Ratcliffian Association, 1950), pp. 83–5.

additional training for their religious staff. Undergraduate and Doctoral degrees amongst the religious undoubtedly expanded and created an intellectual capital in the schools which enhanced their reputation. Staff at both Ampleforth and Downside, for example, had high academic reputations. Their journals, the *Ampleforth Journal* and the *Downside Review*, were an important part of the growing intellectual reputation of both Abbey and school.

This model also meant that there was a ready supply of younger trainee priests and brothers returning to their schools, helping to develop and renew the wider sporting and cultural activities (from rugby and athletics to drama and music), which were increasingly an expected and key part of school activity. It is certainly the case that lay teachers were ever-present on staff lists in these years but were usually only a small proportion of the overall staff. By contrast, in the wider public-school sector, lay teachers had largely replaced religious staff well before the end of the nineteenth century. For those colleges geared primarily to the middle classes, such as Ratcliffe or Mount St Mary's, the availability of "free" teaching resources was important in maintaining fees at relatively low levels. For the secular colleges, run by the dioceses, the economic calculation was a little different because placing a priest or brother to teach in a boarding college meant one less person set to work in the parish, where there remained very significant demands, especially in the growing suburban districts. These differences may help to explain the significant reputational advances of schools run by the regulars (Jesuit and Benedictines) in these years compared to the secular schools where resource pressures may have been greater.

The consolidation of the influence and reputation of the Benedictine schools in particular was not without its own challenges. Not all members of the Benedictine communities necessarily saw education work as their prime aim. Education, missionary work in the parishes and a contemplative role within the monastery competed for space and resource, especially as schools such as Ampleforth and Downside consolidated their position as the top Catholic public schools. The progress made in the inter-war years led to internal debate within the monastic community about the true purpose of a monastic vocation and, at both Downside and Ampleforth, this period did see a degree of questioning and dispute within the community. The school leaders, Fr Neville at Ampleforth and Dom Ramsay at Downside, had to work hard to persuade their communities to commit huge resources to their public schools. Both communities reduced the number of parishes they served in the 1930s, and some members of the community did question whether educating an upper-class clientele was the most appropriate way to fulfil their monastic vows and vocation. The tension between the desire for the quiet, contemplative internal life, and the busy teaching and missionary external activities of the order was a constant.

Capturing the market? Prep schools and the old boys' network

One of the distinctive features of these years was the establishment of preparatory schools, linked to the colleges, to act as "nurseries" for future growth. The public-school sector as a whole had always relied on recruiting from a range of prep schools which traditionally fed into their own establishments. By the end of the nineteenth century, many public schools started to establish their own prep schools, rather than relying on pupils from a range of other establishments.[22] By the early twentieth century, the Catholic schools began to do likewise. Some predated this period. The prep school at St Edmund's (St Hugh's), for example, had been established as far back as 1874. The creation of a prep school reflected a wish to ensure greater sustainability and suitability of pupils moving into the senior school. We have seen the extent to which numbers of entrants had fluctuated wildly for some schools, and the creation of a prep school, which could provide a steady supply of appropriate entrants, was an attractive proposition. It did involve risk in terms of the capital costs of establishing a school for pupils aged between about 8 and 13, but the long-term benefits were clear. In addition, it was argued, the prep schools would be instrumental in developing the "right" kind of pupil for the senior school—familiar with the academic, religious and sporting

---

[22] D. Leinster-Mackay, *The Rise of the English Prep School* (London: Falmer Press, 1984) pp. 231–59.

culture that was required, and ensuring a seamless transition at the age of 13 to the senior school.

Ampleforth opened a prep school in 1913 with the first pupils arriving in 1916. It was a success, and the community debated whether to create a new prep school in either Oxford or Malvern during the 1920s, in the hope of attracting a more southerly clientele. It decided instead, in 1929, to buy nearby Gilling Castle which became the main site for the prep school.[23] Downside also made the decision to move what had been the Junior House from Downside to its daughter priory at Worth in Sussex in 1932. The move not only provided for larger numbers of boys to be educated in the prep school, but also released space at Downside itself for a number of building projects.[24]

Other schools catering for the middle classes did likewise. At Ratcliffe, a decision was made in 1933 to open a prep school, and the college was able to lease Grace Dieu Manor, some ten miles from Ratcliffe, and once the home of one of the early college benefactors, Ambrose Phillips de Lisle, as the location for the prep school. It was a financially risky project, but within a few years it paid dividends. Around half of all entrants to Ratcliffe by the late 1930s were progressing to the senior school directly from Grace Dieu, and expansion of the buildings on the eve of the war meant that around 80 to 90 boys attended the school. An additional advantage was that the curriculum, cultural activities and sport could easily be mapped from junior to senior schools, making, in theory, for a smooth transition of boys upwards.[25] At Mount St Mary's, the decision to create a new prep school was made in 1939, when Barlborough Hall was bought, in part at least because of recruitment difficulties at the main school. Despite the challenges of opening during the war years, it was eventually making a major contribution to new intakes of pupils at the Mount.[26]

---

[23] Marrett-Crosby, *School of the Lord's Service*, p. 68; A. Cramer, *Ampleforth: The Story of St Laurence's Abbey and College* (Ampleforth Abbey, 2001), pp. 148–50.

[24] van Zeller, *Downside*, pp. 130–1.

[25] Leetham, *Ratcliffe College*, pp. 119–24.

[26] Beattie, *Mount St Mary*, pp. 93–7.

As well as securing a supply of new arrivals at the senior school, from the late nineteenth century schools began to coordinate the activities of old boys with the creation of a number of alumni associations. Their role was varied. The maintenance of a network of old boys was primarily seen as helping to enhance the reputation and influence of the school. Networking was important in helping ex-pupils into the "right" kind of employment and, eventually, into positions of social and political influence. As Table 2 shows, almost all the schools had alumni associations in operation by the 1870s. For some, a key role was also to provide additional funding for capital projects in schools through fundraising. Annual dinners, both regionally and especially in London, were an important part of the social calendar, and were an opportunity for heads to outline the progress and growing social cachet of their schools and to appeal for funds. For the big northern schools such as Ampleforth and Stonyhurst, London events were an important vehicle for demonstrating the breadth of networks and influence that former pupils had achieved. They were a key part of enhancing reputation and demonstrating the strength of their connections into academia, the business world and government. Smoothing the way for former pupils to progress into the Establishment was a vital role for these associations.

Table 2: Alumni/Old boys' associations

School	Alumni association	Founding year
Sedgley Park/ Cotton College	St Wilfrid's and Parkers'	1839
St Edmund's College	Edmundian Association	1853
Ratcliffe College	Ratcliffian Association	1865
Downside	Gregorian Society	Early 1870s
Oratory School	Old Oratorians	1874
Ampleforth	Ampleforth Society	1875
Beaumont	Beaumont Union	1877
Douai	Douai Society	1903
Prior Park	Prior Park Association	c.1900

Figure 13: Opening of Bickford Wing, St Edmund's College, 1938.

Figure 14: The Mount Association, 1910.

These associations played an increasingly important academic, sporting and networking role. A number of them had begun to make annual awards available to pupils progressing to Oxbridge, which had become the "gold standard" for schools, especially the smaller ones, by the first decades of the twentieth century. Sporting awards were also important, as were features such as the annual Past v Present cricket and rugby matches that were a central feature of so many Exhibition Days at all the schools, a tradition that remains strong today.

The financial contributions of these varied associations were not insignificant. At Ratcliffe, for example, not a rich school, the association in the inter-war years helped provide bursaries for the sons of Ratcliffians killed in the First World War, a number of University Scholarships, the funds for a major land purchase, which allowed for an expansion of the school footprint, and the creation of the Emery Library at the school. The Annual London Dinner was replicated in the 1920s at Nottingham, Cardiff, Manchester and Liverpool. There were also weekly Ratcliffian Masses held at St Ethelreda's, Ely Place, followed by lunch at the Café Royal. For neighbouring Mount St Mary's, the association was important in both maintaining links with ex-pupils and providing support through bursaries and educational grants. At the Mount Association annual dinner in 1939 at the Waldorf Hotel in London, the members were told that "there are many schools, perhaps better known than the Mount, and one might justly ask if it did not want shoring up a bit . . . he did not claim for the Mount that it has a monopoly of educational virtues but . . . it yielded to none in instilling into boys the sense of their stewardship . . . of things that are eternal".[27]

The pattern of regular meetings, fundraising and the provision of bursaries and scholarships was common to all of our schools. For the larger schools, overseas events also became more important in these years, emphasizing the increasingly international nature of recruitment, especially for schools such as Beaumont within the orbit of London.

---

[27] Leetham, *Ratcliffe College*, pp. 132–3; Beattie, *Mount St Mary*, p. 56.

School spirituality

The *raison d'être* of the schools was to provide a superior Catholic education. That education placed the Catholic faith at its heart, though quite what that meant was not always explicit. For Evennett, a Catholic education was inherently holistic, because "it is indissolubly bound up with the organic life of the Catholic Church ... in an experience of the Church's sacramental and corporate life, lived in common and shared in common by pupils and teachers alike".[28]

It was this ethos which had underpinned the enormous investment made by the Church in the development of elementary and secondary education from the mid-nineteenth century onwards. It is worth emphasizing, however, that for most Catholics, children and parents alike, that education took place within the family and the parish, not the boarding school. It was through the parish priest and parish church, coupled with the emergent local Catholic elementary and secondary schools, that the core elements of a Catholic education were delivered. We have already seen how school provision, outside of the public schools, grew in the 1920s and 1930s. The school developed alongside a range of parish individuals and organizations seeking to provide this inherently indivisible and holistic education.

Much of the educational focus had traditionally been on the poorer, urban communities where the Catholic faith was concentrated. Within those communities the chief instruments of the faith—the Sunday High Mass, regular Confession and Communion, daily Mass, the recital of the rosary, evening Benediction—sat alongside the faith inculcated through the school. A key task of the parish priest was to help oversee the education of the children of his parishioners through regular visits to test young schoolchildren on the principles expounded in the catechism, which was an important part of the domestic and school environment of most Catholic families. The diocese and the bishop were at the apex of this pyramid tying together (in theory at least) child, family, parish priest and school.

---

[28] Evennett, *Catholic Schools*, p. 3.

In some ways the development of the Catholic boarding school created new and sometimes conflicting tensions in this structure. The close connection between family, parish and child, for example, was liable to be broken with a boarding child absent from home and parish for some three quarters of the year. The boarding school, *in loco parentis*, thus became increasingly the focus for both their educational experience and their spiritual and religious development, features consistently celebrated by boarding school leaders. The role of both parents and the parish priest in the spiritual development of children was now supplemented, if not replaced, by the work of the priests and monks who ran the boarding schools. Parental involvement in parish life might also be expected to alter somewhat, especially as the Catholic middle classes became increasingly aware of the range of educational opportunities available to their children in the boarding schools. If their children were now spending a large part of their lives away at school, parents might understandably shift some of their focus, energies and resources away from the parish. The way in which the public school might weaken the link between child, family, priest and parish—a link at the heart of Catholic religious, social and educational policy—remains something of a paradox.

A final factor concerned the issue of vocations. The growth and consolidation of our schools in these years may well have had the effect of diverting vocations from the secular to the regular orders who dominated the boarding sector. As Gilley noted, "increasingly, both Benedictines and Jesuits were to turn their private schools into ... recruiting grounds for themselves". Such recruits were by and large lost to the secular, diocesan system, although some may have gone on to work in parishes served by the regulars.[29]

What then of the spiritual dimension of the boarding schools? In the first place, religious ritual, observance and celebration were an integral part of the daily life of the pupils. The intellectual and moral dimensions of a "true" Catholic education were inseparable according to many advocates. For Newman, for example, in setting up the Oratory School in the 1860s, a "proper" Catholic public school was to be far more than simply a classic public school with the addition of some Catholic

---

[29] Gilley, "The Age of Equipoise, 1892–1943", p. 30.

spirituality: his "harmonious synthesis of the secular and religious in education" was designed, to quote Newman, "to fit men for this world while it trained them for another".[30] The church or chapel was at the heart of the daily lives of the boys. Daily Mass was an important, and, in these years, almost always compulsory part of the timetable along with prayers at various points during the day. At Cotton, for example, in the 1920s, the boys rose at 6.30 with compulsory Mass at 6.55. On Sundays, boys attended two Masses in the morning and Benediction at 6.30 in the evening.[31]

High Mass on Sundays was a key event in the life of all the schools, celebrated with much pomp and ceremony, as were the major college feast days such as the Immaculate Conception (Ratcliffe, Mount St Mary's), St Francis (St Bernardine's College), St Laurence (Ampleforth), or St Edmund (St Edmund's). Major feast days saw high ceremonial in all of the colleges. At Stonyhurst, Corpus Christi celebrations were a key event for both school and community.

At the Oratory School, the annual Corpus Christi celebrations crowned a true Church militant. At the sung High Mass, just before the moment of consecration, a guard of honour from the Officer Training Corps with ceremonial swords, rifles with fixed bayonets and military dress, marched into the chapel and up to the altar rails. At the sacred moment of the elevation of the Host, they presented arms, gave the Royal Salute and marched out again![32]

Probably the most fundamental characteristic which marked out a Catholic boarding environment was the ever-present, close relationship between priest, teacher and pupil, which was far more pervasive and all-embracing, not to say claustrophobic, than was the case in any of the day schools. As we have seen, in most cases, the religious members of the community were numerically far more important than lay staff in running the school. That is not to say that there were no lay teachers.

---

[30] P. Shrimpton, *A Catholic Eton? Newman's Oratory School* (Leominster: Gracewing, 2005), p. 263; See also, C. Butler, 'Newman and Modern Education', *Downside Review* 221 (1952), pp. 259–74.

[31] Roberts and Henshaw, *Sedgley Park and Cotton College*, pp. 199–219.

[32] Tinkell, *Newman's School*, p. 76.

Figure 15: Corpus Christi Procession,
Stonyhurst during the First World War.

All of the colleges had a number of lay teachers in these years, but, as a percentage of all teachers, they were relatively small, although their importance should not be underestimated. In all of the schools, however, the key positions such as the head and the housemasters, who played an important pastoral and spiritual role in the daily life of the boys, were always held by priests or monks. For most boys then, priest and teacher were almost always the same person. The bulk of their schooling was carried out by priests and members of the religious orders, and those same people catered for the religious and spiritual education of the boys under their charge. Lessons, sporting activity, supervision in play areas, monitoring dormitories at night, celebrating Mass (served by the boys), hearing confession, organizing outside activities, were all done by the religious.

Almost every aspect of the education, disciplining, personal development, emotional support and religious activity of the boys fell to the religious, whether diocesan priests or members of the religious orders. A sense of religion and religious authority enveloping all aspects of their daily lives was a commonplace experience. The structures were so pervasive as to be almost invisible and, whilst there were differences between colleges (the Jesuit tradition of close supervision at all times being perhaps at one end of the spectrum), the overall sense of authority, power and control were similar and could be both claustrophobic and overpowering. A boy might serve at Mass in the early morning, have a physics lesson, take part in rugby training, attend Benediction or Confession, and be supervised in the dormitory, all with the same priest or monk. This was a system wholly different from the experience of boys in the parish and local Catholic school, as well as from boys in the wider public-school sector. As we shall see in a later chapter, it created a closeness and intimacy which in some instances could ultimately prove damaging.

The boarding colleges also provided a fuller experience of Catholic ritual and liturgy than the parish. Crichton has argued that the rapid growth of the Church in the inter-war period, and especially the immense demands on the Church as it expanded into the suburbs, meant that developments in the liturgical practices of many parish churches could be very limited: "The staple diet of most Catholics was the Low Mass, said without any music at all, often near-inaudible and sometimes (in the neo-Gothic churches) hardly visible."³³

Most of the Catholic boarding colleges were an exception to this pattern, giving their boys a very different experience of the same ceremonies. Singing is but one example. All of the schools had very active choirs working within the school and taking part in external events. At Ampleforth, for example, the involvement of the boys in singing at Mass and other services had been introduced by the early 1920s, and at Cotton College by 1923 this was also common practice. By the end of the decade, sung Mass and the importance of the school choir in the liturgy of the Church was common to most of the public schools.

Alongside such innovations, many of the schools were swift to adopt practices such as Marian devotions, especially through the rosary. The Catholic Evidence Guild, devoted to helping young Catholics understand and thereby proselytize their faith, was influential from the 1920s with Douai (1921), Ratcliffe (1925) and Downside (1926) amongst schools establishing their own guilds. The Guild of the Blessed Sacrament, which encouraged more intense devotional exercises, also had an influence in some schools. At Ratcliffe, the Guild was established in 1925 at the same time as a cinema, though presumably the events were unconnected. The school magazine noted that "most of the boys now make daily, in their free time, a five-minute visit to the Blessed Sacrament and keep a record of the number of visits made". We don't know whether the authorities kept a tally of these visits as well!³⁴

The issue of spirituality was a significant one for many of the orders engaged in school work. That the tension between the needs of the school, missionary work in the parishes and the monastic, contemplative life noted earlier, made itself felt in these years is evident from a number of examples. At Douai, the Benedictine community was exercised by tensions between missionary work in the parishes and servicing the school. As Scott noted, "the community was small, young and untrained

---

³³ J. D. Crichton, "1920–1940 The Dawn of a Liturgical Movement", in J. D. Crichton, H. Winstone and J. Ainslie (eds), *English Catholic Worship* (London: Chapman, 1979), p. 21.

³⁴ *The Ratcliffian* (1926).

and there was little money", so that trying to both grow the school and maintain parish missions was a challenge. By 1929, the Douai community (24 monks in the early 1920s and 42 monks by 1939) was serving both the school and as many as 34 parishes in a range of different dioceses across the country. For some in the community, missionary work in the parishes needed to be prioritized; for others work in the school, educating a new Catholic elite, was an appropriate core activity.[35] Those tensions existed in most of the schools, religious or secular, as school staff were relocated on a regular basis to work in the parishes and vice versa. Benedictine and Jesuit school heads would often leave at short notice to take up national roles with their orders, whilst secular heads might be required, sometimes at short notice, to take up senior diocesan roles.

The growth of the schools was clearly affected by this tension. For the monastic orders, notably the Benedictines, the significant expansion of their schools at Ampleforth and Downside in these years served in some ways to disguise underlying tensions in the work of the orders. At Downside, for example, the issue of resourcing the work of the order was largely resolved by returning a significant number of parishes to the dioceses in the late 1920s and early 1930s, and concentrating resources on the school. Such a strategic shift was not always popular, with a tension between the contemplative, meditative life sought by some in the community and the outward-looking, busy, educational involvement of others. At Downside, a group of monks led by Dom David Knowles had sought to establish a new community in the early 1930s which would not involve itself in running the school. It was not successful (Knowles eventually left the order and became a distinguished historian), but the episode served to illustrate the tensions that school expansion in this period could produce. Ampleforth experienced similar pressures with a programme to expand the school in the 1930s being approved by the monastic chapter only after significant debate and dissent. The intermingling of school and monastery, which was such a fundamental feature of the Benedictine schools, also led to stresses within the monastic community: there was "always a tension present between a monk's, and

---

[35] Scott, *The English Benedictine Community of St Edmund*, p. 33.

especially a junior monk's, responsibilities in the monastery and in the school".[36]

Academic life

Rather like their rivals in parts of the public-school system, the Catholic schools in the late nineteenth century had seemed little persuaded of the merits of external examinations and comparisons. Indeed Marrett-Crosby noted that at Ampleforth in 1903 not a single one of the 78 students enrolled had even taken, let alone passed, a public examination of any kind.[37] That may be exceptional, or even apocryphal, but it underlines just how slow many schools were to adopt public examinations of their pupils' qualities. The University of London had begun to offer degree-level qualifications to the Catholic public schools from the late 1860s, and some schools had looked to public examinations and had entered boys for the Oxford Local examinations from the 1880s, and Higher Certificate from the 1890s. It may well be that the Jesuit schools—Stonyhurst, Beaumont and Mount St Mary's—were more comfortable with such external judging because they formed part of a wider Jesuit educational network alongside a number of successful day schools. It was perhaps a useful way of comparing the performance of schools under their control.[38]

By the inter-war years, however, all of the schools began to seriously explore entering their boys for external examinations under two sets of pressures. First, parental pressures were evident, especially as school numbers and fees began to grow and schools had to compete more overtly with each other. Competition with the wider non-Catholic public schools was less challenging than it might have been because of the significant pressures from the Hierarchy to ensure that parents sent their children to Catholic rather than non-Catholic schools. That prohibition meant that

---

[36] Scott, *The English Benedictine Community of St Edmund*, p. 23.

[37] Marrett-Crosby, *School of the Lord's Service*, p. 50.

[38] I. D. Roberts, "Jesuit Collegiate Education in England, 1794–1914", MEd Thesis, University of Durham (1986), p. 227, 276.

our schools were less exposed to the challenges of the market than they might have been. Nonetheless, parents increasingly wanted to know what they were getting for their money, and increased recourse to external examinations meant that, if results were good, there were marketing opportunities. Certainly by the 1920s, all of our schools were engaging in the process of external exams, and the joint Oxford and Cambridge Examinations Board had become pre-eminent in the public schools by the early 1930s.

A second pressure came from the opening up of opportunities for entering boys for Oxford and Cambridge. The Hierarchy had effectively prohibited Catholic students entering these universities (though not others such as London or Manchester), because of a perceived danger to morals resulting from what was thought to be an alien intellectual and social atmosphere. That prohibition was also tied in with the attempts by the Hierarchy to create a distinctive and separate Catholic University in London. The project eventually collapsed in the early 1880s, and whilst students certainly could and did enter Oxbridge before the admonition was formally lifted in 1895 (one estimate has some 50 Catholic students at Oxbridge on the eve of the lifting of the ban), it was not with the approval of the Hierarchy. Catholic students also had the opportunity of studying at Catholic universities and colleges in Europe.[39]

The lifting of the ban at the end of the nineteenth century was quickly seized upon, especially by the larger schools such as Ampleforth, Stonyhurst and Downside, who sought to establish "homes" at Oxford and Cambridge within which students successful in the entrance examinations to the University could be based and through which, in theory at least, their "moral education" could be supervised and safeguarded. The "houses" also provided a convenient opportunity for school religious staff to upgrade their qualifications. The Jesuits established Campion Hall in Oxford in 1896 as a "safe haven" for those students who had won places from their boarding or day schools. Similarly St Edmund's College set up St Edmund's House in Cambridge for its students and secular priests. The new institution was intended to be "clerical in nature", and "Rome

---

[39] V. A. McClelland, *Cardinal Manning: His Public Life and Influence 1865–1892* (London: Oxford University Press, 1962), pp. 87–128.

St. EDMUND'S COLLEGE,

Old Hall, Near Ware, Herts.

1921.

FEES.

ENTRANCE FEE.—Five Guineas (in lieu of plate and linen).

PENSION.—At the College the annual Pension is **£100**, payable in advance at the beginning of each term.

At St. Hugh's Preparatory School the annual Pension is **£90**.

EXTRAS.—College Books and other School requisites, including Laboratory Charges, **£2** per term, payable in advance.

Medical Fee, including Doctor, Trained Nurse and Medicines, and use of Infirmary, **£1** per term, payable in advance.

Laundry, Mending, and Repairs in Wardrobe, **£1 5s. 0d.** per term, payable in advance.

INCIDENTAL EXPENSES.—(*Not* payable in advance).

Music Lessons (piano) when required are charged for at three guineas per term.

Each boy will be charged **5/-** a term subscription to the Public Games for the Autumn and Spring Terms, and **8/-** for the Summer Term.

College Cadet Corps.—Entrance Fee, **£1 10s. 0d.** Subscription per term, **12/6**.

St. Hugh's Boy Scouts.—Entrance Fee, **£1**, Subscription **2/6** per term.

College Magazine.—Subscription **2/-** per term.

Haircutter.—**1/6** per term.

Tailoring Repairs and Boot Repairs are charged for as incurred at low rates.

A FULL TERM'S NOTICE IS REQUIRED FOR THE REMOVAL OF A STUDENT FAILING WHICH ONE TERM'S FEES WILL BE CHARGED.

Figure 16: Table of Fees, St Edmund's College, 1921.

stressed that students should follow literary or scientific subjects with a view to a qualification in education".[40] The project was bankrolled by the college and the Duke of Norfolk and reflected the importance that St Edmund's attached to a Cambridge degree. Downside established a similar house, Benet House in Cambridge, which became instrumental in the flourishing and distinguished intellectual tradition of Downside scholars and teachers from the 1920s onwards, although the house was largely for monks studying for degrees. Not to be outdone, Ampleforth established their own St Benet's Hall at Oxford in 1897.[41]

The speed with which these three major schools sought to facilitate the progress of their students reflected the increasing importance of an Oxbridge degree for Catholic parents in the inter-war years. Here, at last, was the opportunity for a Catholic elite to secure access, through Oxbridge, to the Establishment. School histories, annual reports, marketing literature—the *Annual Catholic Directories* provide an insight into how the competing schools viewed themselves—increasingly focused on the twin achievements of Oxbridge entry and strong performance in external exams, which now sat alongside the social cachet of a school in determining growth and sustainability. Not surprisingly it was these larger schools—Stonyhurst, Ampleforth, Downside, and St Edmund's— that began to set in train a curriculum and support system both at the school and through personal networks into Oxbridge colleges, that would deliver significant Oxbridge places and, in particular, the prestigious open scholarships and exhibitions, in the inter-war years. But numbers were always relatively small, especially in relation to the larger, non-Catholic public schools who so dominated Oxbridge numbers through both open and closed scholarships. One estimate suggests there were around 200 Oxbridge students from the Catholic public schools by 1914 and some 300 in 1939 so growth was fairly slow.[42] Other, smaller colleges, were also adept in focusing on Oxbridge entrance. Beaumont,

---

[40] N. Schofield, *The History of St Edmund's College* (Ware: The Edmundian Association, 2013), p. 106.

[41] Marrett-Crosby, *School of the Lord's Service*, pp. 40–1; Cramer, *Ampleforth*, pp. 106–9.

[42] Evennett, *Catholic Schools*, pp. 97–8.

for example, achieved its first open scholarship (in mathematics) in 1906 and Mount St Mary's was sending pupils to Campion Hall in Oxford by 1914. Ratcliffe too had achieved open scholarships by the early 1930s and set up bursaries to support entry to Oxbridge.

These twin imperatives—external exam success and Oxbridge entry—wrought a number of changes in both curriculum and school organization. The Jesuit schools (Stonyhurst and Mount St Mary's) had historically followed the *Ratio Studiorum* which laid down the principles of timetable and curriculum. It was structured around the four key areas of Rhetoric, Poetry, Upper Grammar and Middle Grammar and, within these areas, largely dictated a particular set of texts and exercises which were to form the core of the teaching. Public presentations (the "exhibitions" dating back to the early nineteenth century), and examinations together with debate and discussion, provided the opportunities for personal development. The class names themselves were drawn from the continental experience—Lower Syntax, Upper Syntax, Poetry, Philosophy—and set the Jesuit schools apart from the rest. It is a moot point whether such structures were sufficiently flexible into the twentieth century. For Muir, a growing involvement with external examinations was the trojan horse bringing about the downfall of this system. Once Stonyhurst made the switch to the Higher and Lower Certificate exams and to broader public examination systems, "almost without realizing it, the College abandoned the academic curriculum laid down by the *Ratio Studiorum* and started to compete directly with the major public schools. Jesuits found that they had tied themselves to the chariot wheels of government educational policy."[43]

Classics—written, translated, declaimed—continued to dominate the curriculum of most public schools, Catholic and non-Catholic alike. Latin and Greek were fundamental to most curriculums at the start of the century with a canon of standard texts common to many of our schools. A refocus towards some of the biblical and religious texts perhaps distinguished the Catholic schools from their non-Catholic counterparts. Alongside these sat history, English, sometimes a foreign language, geography, mathematics and science. History and geography

---

[43] Muir, *Stonyhurst*, p. 153.

were indeed sometimes optional with cleverer boys dropping them in favour of yet more of the classics, a pattern persisting well into the last decades of the twentieth century.

Science had traditionally been seen as an area of significant underperformance by the public schools. Arguably the First World War exposed the importance of scientific training and, in particular, a lack of trained and skilled scientific personnel. The Thompson Report in 1918 suggested that the dichotomy between the so-called "modern side" in public schools, with a balanced curriculum and significant science focus, and the "classics side", with relatively little science, was too stark. The heavy bias towards classics in school entrance examinations, in school scholarships and, ultimately, in university scholarships was, it was argued, ultimately damaging the national interest.[44] There is perhaps less evidence of this issue in the Catholic schools. The importance of science was evident in a number of ways.

First, a significant proportion of the school building programmes in these years was devoted to establishing proper facilities and laboratories for the teaching of science. A review of building programmes bears this out. At Stonyhurst, a major new physics laboratory was built in the early 1920s whilst a new science wing was built by Giles Gilbert Scott at Downside in 1932 to cater for the growth in pupils. At Douai and Cotton, new laboratories were opened in the 1930s. At Ushaw, fundraising after the Great War was used to create both memorial chapels and a new science laboratory. A further science building was created in 1931. Most of the schools in our study had similar capital building programmes to develop science education.

Secondly, one can trace a rise in the number of lay teachers on school staff lists and, especially at sixth-form level, the increasing use of specialist science lay teachers. Ampleforth, Downside and Stonyhurst all saw a growth in the numbers of lay staff in these years to cater for a changed curriculum and the pressures of external examinations. In the case of Stonyhurst the importance of lay staff was accentuated by the shift of some of the Jesuit seminarian community to teach at their new seminary at Heythrop, established in 1926. The number of Jesuits teaching in the

---

[44] Turner, *The Old Boys*, pp. 173–4.

Figure 17: Science lab and teacher, St Edmund's College *c.*1910.

college fell dramatically from 134 in 1924 to 47 some ten years later, a gap which had to be filled by qualified lay staff. At Ratcliffe, the science teaching remained in the hands of the religious throughout these years—there were no more than two or three lay teachers alongside 20 to 25 Rosminians in the entire school through the 1920s and early 1930s.[45] Science underpinned what was an increasingly broader curriculum in most public schools in these years: according to Ogilvie, "more boys turned from classics to science, history and modern languages—in which the number of university scholarships was increasing".[46]

A public-school ethos?

Galliver's insightful study of Ampleforth focused on how that school was arguably foremost amongst the Catholic boarding schools in adopting a public-school structure, ethos and style.[47] What constituted a public school was, and remains, debateable, but what is clear is that many of the Catholic schools sought to emulate some, if not all, of what they thought constituted an English public school. A simple, if not simplistic, definition of a public school was membership of the Headmasters' Conference (the HMC). It was a small club with heads of schools, rather than schools themselves, becoming members by invitation only, and members were selected on the basis of both their tangible assets (size, methods of governance, academic performance) and, perhaps more importantly, intangible assets ("tone", quality of intake, reputation). Bamford, commenting on the HMC, stressed the "significance of boarding education, a unified Anglican outlook within each school, and

---

[45] Muir, *Stonyhurst*, pp. 151–2; Ratcliffe staff data from annual issues of *The Ratcliffian*.

[46] V. Ogilvie, *The English Public School* (London: Batsford, 1957), p. 200.

[47] P. Galliver, *Ampleforth College: The Emergence of Ampleforth College as the 'Catholic Eton'* (Leominster: Gracewing, 2019).

an exclusiveness derived from a prohibitive cost and a positive restriction of the intake to the higher classes".[48]

Clearly our schools would (hopefully) all fail the Anglican test, but it is a moot point as to whether an aspiration to join such a club was in itself worthwhile. Be that as it may, by the first decades of the century our schools, or at least some members of the group, sought that cachet. Stonyhurst was the first to achieve HMC membership in 1900. Ampleforth, Douai and Downside had all been invited to join the HMC by 1914 and, in the course of the next two decades, most other schools had joined at various times, especially as a consequence of the Fleming Report (part of the Butler Education Act in 1944), which effectively defined "public schools" as those schools which were in the HMC, thereby leading to an increase in membership.

Perhaps more important than membership of the HMC was the extent to which the tangible and intangible elements of the public-school system affected how the Catholic schools were structured and run. There is a powerful case for Ampleforth, as Galliver suggests, becoming the "Catholic Eton" in these years, but it is worth remembering that the term has at various times been applied to Stonyhurst, Downside, Beaumont and Douai! And was such a soubriquet worth the effort? What is perhaps more revealing than the trajectories and relative positions in some notional league table of individual schools, is the sheer energy and effort made by almost all the Catholic schools to ape, often uncritically, the dominant public-school culture and ideology. The house system, for example, the use of boys as prefects and monitors, the cultivation of networks of influence through old boys' associations, the various forms of officer cadet forces and a cult of athleticism, especially through the adoption of rugby, were some of the elements Catholic schools sought to emulate. As Turner notes, "the public-school emphasis on character

---

[48] Quoted in Roberts, "Jesuit Collegiate Education", p. 304; see also T. Bamford, *The Rise of the Public Schools: A Study of Boys' Public Boarding Schools in England and Wales from 1837 to the Present Day* (London: Nelson, 1967), pp. 261–6.

building through the house system, governed by prefects, was increasingly picked up by Catholic boarding schools".[49]

It is perhaps revealing of the narrowness of aspirations of so many of these schools and their leaders, that there could be no greater accolade than to be considered in the same breath as Eton, Winchester or Westminster. The narrowness of their social intake, the explicit elitism that underpinned their ethos, and the political conservatism and respect for the status quo, provided a disappointingly restricted educational model for what was a growing and self-confident Catholic Church in the twentieth century.

The house system, integral to so many non-Catholic public schools, had originated in the earliest Church of England public schools as a means of providing accommodation and welfare for boys in smaller, domestic units run, at a profit, by a housemaster. In the earliest schools, a Dame would be responsible for these aspects of a boarder's life and, interestingly, it was this model that most appealed to Newman when setting up the Oratory School on explicitly public-school lines back in the 1860s. The advantage of the system was that it provided a means for a closer management of the domestic and personal needs of boarders. It was a model that some of the Catholic schools adopted. Boys would thus be taught as part of the school as a whole but would be part of a house for domestic arrangements around eating, sleeping and pastoral support. The housemaster (the Eton-model female Dames had gone by the start of the century, though female matrons remained), invariably a religious, played a key role in managing all aspects of the life of his pupils. The house would also provide a focus for organizing the gamut of sporting and cultural activities within schools that were seen as central to imbuing a Darwinian competitive spirit amongst pupils through inter-house competitions.

Most of the schools had introduced house systems of one form or another by the 1920s. At its simplest level, the house system was introduced only for sporting or cultural reasons. Up until 1928, Ratcliffe, for example, divided pupils into North and South when they joined based on where they came from. By 1928, as numbers grew, two houses

---

[49] Turner, *The Old Boys*, p. 179.

Figure 18: Talbot House, St Edmund's College, 1926.

Figure 19: College Captains at Mount St Mary's College, 1926.

were introduced which grew to three in 1938—Arundell, Lockhart and de Lisle, named after early benefactors of the college. But these houses had no particular domestic function or physical presence, and boys continued to study, eat and sleep within the college facilities. It was similar in other colleges, especially the smaller ones. Mount St Mary's, whose numbers resembled Ratcliffe, used houses solely for sporting and cultural purposes. They were never intended to be self-contained and instead had a system of college "captains" to support house activities.

At Cotton College a similar system was developed. The school was divided into two houses in 1923 and, a year later, four houses were established—Pugin, Newman, Faber and Souter—with a named housemaster over each house and with a captain and vice-captain from among the boys with a range of responsibilities including discipline. The houses competed in studies, games and sport and also produced their own magazine, plays and concerts. The house captains and vice-captains, together with the captain of the school, all acted as school prefects. But with barely 100 students in the school, the houses were very small, and, in 1929, the school finally settled on three and changed the names as well for good measure—Milner, Bowden and Challoner. Whilst the houses were not independent in terms of eating, sleeping and study arrangements, their use was seen as important for creating both an identity for boys within the school and the chief means of developing a competitive spirit. The school refectory was divided into three rows of benches for the different houses, and pupils were divided alphabetically on their arrival at Cotton. No matter which house a boy belonged to, the quality of the cuisine did not vary.

Stonyhurst sought to adopt a form of houses in this period, again, working on the assumption that what was good for the mainstream public schools would be good enough for them. As Muir notes, in the inter-war years, the position of the school was not where it might have been. Numbers were fairly stagnant, and there were concerns about the quality of the teaching, especially with the creation of the seminary at Heythrop, which led to the departure of the most senior Philosophy classes and the closure of the lay Philosophy stream at the school. The school faced significant pressures in the 1920s, just as the other two members of the "triumvirate", Ampleforth and Downside, were progressing fast. Part of the response of the school leaders was to develop a form of house system alongside the reform of academic studies. A system of "Lines"—Shireburn, Campion, Weld and St Omers—was established in 1922 to help organize games in particular and to promote a competitive spirit within the school. Again, as with a number of schools, these structures did not replicate the house system of many public schools where the domestic arrangements of sleeping, eating and socializing were carried out almost independently in smaller domestic units.[50]

The two best examples of schools seeking to fully replicate the public-school model of separate houses were undoubtedly Ampleforth and St Edmund's. At Ampleforth, the arrival of Fr Paul Nevill, who was head from 1924–54, signalled the start of a single-minded and impressive set of changes in the physical, social and academic capacities of the school. Important, sometimes difficult, meetings of the monastic chapter in the 1920s saw the development of what became something of a master plan to grow the college and establish its status as the "Catholic Eton". The creation of houses was an important part of this process. By 1926, three had been set up within the existing footprint of the school—St Bede's, St Aidan's, and St Oswald's—whilst a fourth, St Cuthbert's, was a brand-new building. Between 1933 and 1935, two more new houses were built, and a further house was established through internal reorganization.[51] The establishment of a new prep school at nearby Gilling Castle (1929) fed a constant supply of new pupils into the expanding school. Why then was the house system so central to these plans?

A first explanation is a pragmatic one. The development of new houses could be done in a planned way, reflecting the sustainability of numbers. It was, in effect, easier to build a new house for perhaps 50 boys than to try to shoehorn those new boys into an existing, sometimes cramped central infrastructure. The financial costs of these investments could thus be more easily managed. This was an important factor in mitigating the risks that some members of the Benedictine chapter at Ampleforth had baulked at, of over-extending both financial and human resources and, perhaps, compromising some aspects of the monastic contemplative life.

---

[50] Muir, *Stonyhurst*, pp. 152–3.
[51] Galliver, *Ampleforth*, pp. 98–101.

Alongside these pragmatic rationales lay important ideological ones. Fr Paul at Ampleforth was quite explicit in his wish to create a Catholic public school with all the social accoutrements such a school should supply. In this desire to create a new Catholic Establishment, it was essential, he argued, that the school should look, feel and act in ways identical to its non-Catholic rivals. The house system provided the kind of small, more intimate locale for the domestic care and management of pupils which was seen as a defining characteristic of the idealized public school. The house would provide the seedbed for developing the "character" of pupils and the "tone" of the school. The system of prefects and monitors from within the house, the use of the house for inculcating a strong sense of identity between staff and pupils, and the development of the academic, pastoral and disciplinary role of the clerical housemasters were viewed as integral to delivering the overall vision.

Other schools adopted some, rather than all, of these characteristics. Certainly the use of prefects and monitors from amongst the boys had become commonplace by the 1920s in most of our schools, though the disciplinary powers that they were able to exercise were almost always much more limited than in the traditional public schools. At Stonyhurst, Mount St Mary's and Beaumont, the Jesuit tradition of very close oversight of pupils at all times, a tradition inherited from their continental roots, was gradually replaced by the use of prefects or captains, especially during leisure time. It marked for them an important shift towards what was seen as a more "English" tradition of pupil oversight. Increasingly the prefect groups worked with the housemasters to provide what was considered an appropriate domestic environment for the boys. Corporal punishment was evident in all of our schools but almost never administered by prefects, contrasting with the public-school mores of the time. The system of "fagging" by prefects was not widespread, although at Douai new boys (known in school slang as "brats") were expected to come running whenever a prefect called, and the prefects were able to inflict limited corporal punishment on boys.

Alongside Ampleforth, St Edmund's College sought to explicitly develop a public-school ethos through the introduction of houses. In this case, however, it was the mixing of lay and church pupils that initially prompted the shift. The college had traditionally taught both groups alongside each other, apart from a brief period between 1895 and 1904, when the senior pupils destined for the Church (known as the "Philosophers") were moved to what was anticipated to become the national, central seminary at Oscott. The return of that class to St Edmund's College brought about both a set of building projects at St Edmund's and, after the war, a shift towards a house system.

Cardinal Bourne, the Archbishop of Westminster (1903–35) who had responsibility for the school, whilst recognizing the financial advantages of teaching lay and church boys in the same institution, also saw drawbacks. He recognized that "parents undoubtedly often hesitated to send their boys to Old Hall (St Edmund's) because they regarded it as too ecclesiastical, while those who were most concerned about the training of candidates for ordination were at times anxious as to the sufficiently ecclesiastical character of the school".[52]

On reading the histories of Eton and Winchester, Bourne had noted that church and lay boys were taught together but lodged in separate houses and he pushed for St Edmund's to adopt a similar system. In 1922, the decision was made to establish three houses at the college named after distinguished alumni—Challoner, Talbot and Douglass. What marked this structure off from other schools was the separation of one house—Douglass—solely for boys destined for the Church. Such boys received sets of privileges marking them off from lay pupils much to the chagrin of the latter. The system, *The Edmundian* suggested, would provide, "the advantages of the English public school, with its insistence on manliness, initiative, character and responsibility, together with its old significant advantages of Catholic training and ancient tradition".[53]

The introduction of this system required significant investment from the diocese. The building of a new central teaching block with classrooms, a music hall and an exhibition hall, together with the appointment of new teaching staff to raise the academic reputation of the college was costly. That investment had to be provided by the diocese. Schofield suggests that not only did Cardinal Bourne "syphon" much of a sizeable private bequest to the diocese to this purpose, but he also alienated some of the

---

[52] Schofield, *St Edmund's College*, p. 134.
[53] Schofield, *St Edmund's College*, pp. 135–6.

clergy who argued that more resources were needed for poorer parishes in the diocese and for the development of existing day schools, rather than being poured into an elite fee-paying public school.[54] The good Cardinal was unmoved.

A muscular Christianity?

The importance of the playing fields and the parade ground were integral to the growth and self-image of all the public schools at the start of the twentieth century. The "cult of athleticism" meant that sport played a major part in the style and ethos of the public school. Catholic schools were swift to adopt this aspect of a "traditional" public school education. Alongside sporting prowess at the level of the house and the school was the growth of a military culture (especially as a consequence of the Boer War and the Great War), reflected in the generally enthusiastic establishment of cadet corps of various kinds by almost all the Catholic schools.

Sport takes up an inordinate part of many school histories and it is not proposed to rehearse these in any detail here. It was viewed by all of our schools as being of key importance. The development of leadership, team building, a physical culture, competitiveness and mutual support were integral to the offer the schools could make to parents. It was very much a feature of the traditional public schools that the Catholic schools were keen to emulate. Whilst most of the Catholic schools had their own, often idiosyncratic sports, by the start of the twentieth century cricket and association football were dominant. It was not until the 1900s that games between the Catholic schools began to emerge. Prior to that, fixtures were usually arranged between school and local "gentleman" teams. It was often the teams you played that was more important than the results, reflecting the relative social position of the school in relation to its peers. There was a clear pecking-order and whilst matches between the Oratory, Beaumont, Stonyhurst, Ampleforth and Downside might, geography permitting, be appropriate, "lesser" schools—Ratcliffe, Cotton, Mount St

---

[54] Schofield, *St Edmund's College*, p. 136.

Mary's—could not aspire to appear on such elite fixture lists. Unabashed, the Midlands schools were content to fight each other.

At Ratcliffe, for example, the first "outside" football fixture was against a local school, Stoneygate, with subsequent fixtures against teams such as Leicester Banks, Wyggeston School and Loughborough Grammar. Cricket fixtures were also increasingly common from the turn of the century, although they first began in the 1860s. During the inter-war years, there was a significant expansion of external fixtures against outside schools. Catholic schools such as nearby Cotton College and Mount St Mary's were a regular feature of the calendar. Internal matches (against the old boys of the Ratcliffian Association for example), or inter-house competitions were integral to the school calendar. At Mount St Mary's and Cotton College, sporting activities were important to school life with football predominating until the early 1920s.

The adoption of rugby as the dominant sport alongside cricket was in many ways a clear example of a sporting shift which reflected the explicit adoption of a public-school characteristic. Rugby, an integral part of the nineteenth-century public school, offered, to quote Turner, "a sublimated violence which made it an especially powerful substitute for the knightly training of earlier centuries"![55] The adoption of rugby provides an interesting example of the diffusion of the public school ideal and of a "muscular Christianity" into the Catholic schools. Membership of the Headmasters' Conference, regarded, as we have seen, as a "badge" of a proper public school, often led to the adoption of rugby in the place of football. It suggested a better "tone", a better shaping of individual character, than the increasingly proletarian football, which found itself relegated to the casual margins of the increasingly dominant rugby pitch.

Some of our schools switched from football to rugby fairly early. Ampleforth had adopted rugby as the main winter sport in 1911, Beaumont in the same year, Downside in 1912. Both, interestingly, had joined the Headmasters' Conference at around the same time, and both saw rugby as offering a more appropriate character to their schools and giving something of a social cachet for parents, in contrast with

---

[55] Turner, *The Old Boys*, p. 99; see also J. A. Mangan, *Athleticism and the Victorian and Edwardian Public School* (London: Cass, 1981) for background.

football. Many of our other schools had fallen into line by the early 1920s. Stonyhurst adopted rugby in 1921, and by 1923 the Oratory School, Ratcliffe, Cotton, Mount St Mary's and St Edmund's had all switched to the rugby code. These switches were made, in part at least, to allow for the development of more inter-school competition. Without delving into the fine detail of teams and results, often articulated at length in individual school histories, it is hard to discern any kind of league table of sporting excellence.

Whilst schools might have adopted rugby in order to climb some notional sporting and social league table, there is little evidence that this mattered much beyond local rivalries. In the Midlands, whilst games between Mount St Mary's, Ratcliffe and Cotton may fill the pages of the school magazines, there is little evidence they played any part in parental choice. The very fact of playing rugby seemed to hold most sway. Whether they were any good was secondary. Just as well to judge by some of the early results. Ratcliffe's first game with Mount St Mary's in 1922 resulted in 97-0 loss. At Cotton, the first rugby season of 1922-3 resulted in 13 games played and 13 lost. The headmaster's promise of a holiday for the first win had to be commuted to one for the first try, which duly arrived in late November of 1922![56]

For the "big three", Ampleforth, Downside and Stonyhurst, the sports field was a key differentiating factor, and the fixture lists themselves provide at least some indication of school status. The adoption of rowing or fencing, for example, or a range of equestrian pursuits (such as hunting or beagling) also helped to reinforce the gentlemanly nature of the wider education on offer at some schools.

Few schools had the ultimate accolade of a cricket fixture at Lord's. The Oratory and Beaumont attained this elevated status with an annual fixture from 1926 until 1968 at the hallowed home of cricket! For Mangan, sports, especially cricket and rugby, were often seen as vehicles to raise the status of a school both in terms of "tone" (cricket and rugby were seen as more "character-building" than football) and especially in

---

[56] Roberts and Henshaw, *Sedgley Park and Cotton College*, p. 213.

Figure 20: The Mendip Hunt meeting in front of Downside School, *c.* late 1920s.

terms of its fixture list.⁵⁷ As Winch has argued, in the first two decades or so of the twentieth century, "a higher moral purpose emerged through games to teach sportsmanship, self-confidence, teamwork, leadership and loyalty".⁵⁸

He examines how cricket in particular became something of a vehicle for both the Oratory School and Beaumont to raise the status of their schools. In 1925, both schools were granted a fixture at Lord's alongside six Anglican public schools. When a much reduced Oratory School was temporarily lodged at Downside during the Second World War, an offer was made by Downside to act as a "caretaker" of the Lord's fixture. The head of the Oratory was unmoved pointing out that "there are only some 30 boys in the school and I'm reliably informed that only eleven of them are required for a cricket side".⁵⁹

The fixture survived until Beaumont closed in 1967. Downside did eventually get to take over the slot at Lord's, but lack of support meant it survived for only a couple of years.

The final piece in the public-school jigsaw in this period was military training which came to play an important part in the histories of many of the Catholic schools. Their adoption of a variety of cadet corps (the titles morphed over time with the OTC—Officer Training Corps—being most common by the mid-1930s) exemplified not just a desire to fit with the public-school tradition, but also to develop and project an image of a strong, nationalist, English loyalty amongst the Catholic elite. That was important at a time when Catholics were seeking to finally rid themselves of any notion that they were somehow less loyal because of their adherence to Rome in religious matters. It also coincided with political unrest in Ireland over Home Rule and, given the significant numbers of Irish boys at the Catholic schools, provided a further way of demonstrating the

---

⁵⁷ Mangan included Stonyhurst in his analysis of how sport was used to raise the status of public schools but concluded that the evidence for this, whilst strong in many non-Catholic public schools, was relatively weak in the case of Stonyhurst.

⁵⁸ J. Winch, "The role and impact of athleticism at 'two outposts of the Vatican' during the 1850s–1950s", *Sport in History* 40:2 (2020), p. 191.

⁵⁹ Winch, "The role and impact of athleticism", p. 198.

loyalty of the Catholic community. The establishment of these corps in the schools also meshed well with the notion of character-building and leadership already identified through sport. Only rarely did anti-militarist pressures lead to a questioning of this development.

Most schools established cadet corps of various kinds in the first two decades of the twentieth century. Stonyhurst was one of the pioneers, setting up a major cadet corps in 1900. Ten years later a contingent from Stonyhurst paraded at Windsor Castle. At Ampleforth and Downside, officer training corps were established in 1911 coincident with membership of the Headmasters' Conference. Mount St Mary's established a cadet corps in 1915. A circular letter to all parents secured their support, and, by the end of 1915, the corps was functioning. It was compulsory for all boys and had a military band called into service when appropriate. At Beaumont, the establishment of the cadet corps had its origins in volunteer organizations in the late nineteenth century, with the Officer Training Corps appearing just before the Great War. As one Fr Lattey noted, "on the whole the OTC has put some spirit of discipline into them, making them take orders more readily from the staff ... accustoming the bigger fellows to command and the smaller to obey".[60] The Great War was a catalyst for the establishment of military corps elsewhere. At Ratcliffe, a corps was established in 1915; at Ushaw College in 1918. At Ushaw, the 153 boys enrolled "helped to give the college the appearance of a community of Knights-Regular".[61]

The adoption of a cadet corps in one form or another was not universal, nor without controversy. At Cotton College, for example, there is no evidence that the establishment of a corps was ever even contemplated. This might reflect the fact that Cotton was run by seculars not regulars, although in the case of Ushaw, for example, that made no difference. At the most important of the schools run by a diocese, St Edmund's, a corps was established early, but it was not without some difficulties. It was set up in 1916, following on speedily from the retirement of Mgr Ward who had presided over the college for some 23 years. It was Cardinal Bourne, the Archbishop of Westminster, who was especially keen to see

---

[60] P. Levi, *Beaumont 1861–1961* (London: André Deutsch, 1961), p. 74.
[61] Milburn, *Ushaw*, p. 314.

a cadet corps at St Edmund's and the departure of Ward, a long-time opponent of a military unit at the school, gave him the opportunity. A circular letter to parents said the corps would "provide elementary military training" and "promote self-control ... confidence ... and command". By the end of 1916, it was fully functional, and by 1924, it was replaced by an Officer Training Corps with three platoons, one from each of the three new houses that had been created at the college. The dispute between Cardinal Bourne and Mgr Ward continued to rumble on. When Mgr Ward became Bishop of Brentwood, he refused to allow the seminarians from his diocese to join the corps, arguing that military service had no part in the training of a priest. In the end, Ward withdrew his diocesan students from St Edmund's; a ruling from the Congregation of Seminaries in Rome eventually decided that seminaries could not have a cadet corps and that where lay and seminary students were in the same institution (as at St Edmund's, Ushaw and Cotton), seminary students should not be part of any corps.[62] The small Dominican school at Laxton, established in 1926, was one of the very few schools taking a clear view that a cadet corps was not consonant with the ethos or values of a Catholic boarding school.

By the late 1930s then, the Catholic schools had moved a long way towards the kind of public school ideal that seemed to capture the educational and social aspirations of both the regulars and the diocesan authorities who drove the development and ethos of their schools. As well as looking after their own schools, it is evident that school leaders began to work together to try to enhance the extent, quality and reputation of Catholic secondary education more generally. A *Conference of Catholic Colleges* had been established in 1897 to act as a forum for developing Catholic education amongst the public schools, as well as a range of other day secondary schools established by the seculars and regulars. The public schools played a leading role hosting the majority of the annual conferences of the group through the century, despite being numerically very much smaller than their day-school colleagues (Table 3).

---

[62] Schofield, *St Edmund's College*, p. 130.

Table 3: Catholic Association of Teachers, Schools and Colleges Annual Conferences

Venue	Year
Stonyhurst	1891; 1905; 1917; 1924; 1932; 1941
Downside	1900; 1937; 1956
Ushaw	1901; 1907; 1916; 1923; 1934; 1949
Ampleforth	1902; 1920; 1935; 1945; 1955
Oratory	1904; 1914
Beaumont	1908; 1921; 1939; 1951
Upholland	1929; 1944
Ratcliffe	1936; 1942; 1952
Prior Park	1933; 1950
Mount St Mary's	1940

In the narrowest sense, it was perhaps only a handful of schools, indeed perhaps only one, Ampleforth, that fully met all the tangible and intangible criteria to be called a major public school, if such a classification really mattered. Certainly schools such as St Edmund's, Ampleforth, Stonyhurst, Downside, Douai and Beaumont all sought in a range of ways to emulate both the educational and social character of the mainstream public schools. Especially important was a perceived need to attract pupils of the right "tone" and class to these schools. This perhaps reached its extreme in the determination of Fr Paul, who led Ampleforth in the inter-war years, and was described colourfully as a "walking Burke's Peerage", with a single-minded determination to attract pupils from the higher social classes with a promise of achievement, Oxbridge entrance, the right form of character-building and access to a network of career opportunities.

Alongside these colleges were a significant number of schools catering explicitly for the middle classes. Their adoption of the public-school paraphernalia and ethos was perhaps more limited but striking nonetheless. A broader curriculum, a framework of character-building "opportunities" such as sport and the military, and the development of networks into business, the professions and the military were all important facets of the Catholic public-school experience across the spectrum of boarding school provision. In the two decades or so following the Second World War, the structures and experiences of that Catholic schooling were to reach their apogee as the strength and self-confidence of the Catholic community grew.

3

The Last Hurrah! c.1940–70

By the end of the 1930s, most of the Catholic public schools had consolidated their significant growth in numbers, status and influence. The Second World War brought disruptions to all of the schools, as well as loss of life for old boys. School histories recount the dubious joys of rationing, blackouts, the occasional bombing raid, and the requisitioning of buildings for various periods of time by the military authorities, as well as the loss of former school members. At Downside, tragedy struck in May 1943, when a plane crashed close to the cricket field where a match was in progress, killing the pilot and nine boys.[1] But all the schools survived a range of wartime dislocations and relocations to face the new challenges ahead. A growing Church, solid recruitment to the vocations, and a rising national presence was to characterize the first two decades or so of the post-war period. They were to be good years for both the Church and its public schools.

Post-war growth

After the difficulties and disruptions of the war, the Catholic community embarked on a period of growth in both numbers and influence, which was reflected in the ways in which its public schools developed their activities and shaped their pupils. These years saw a confidence and faith in the growing strength of the Catholic sub-culture, reflected in its liturgy and practices, the influence of its priests and bishops,

---

[1] H. van Zeller, *Downside By and Large* (London: Sheed & Ward, 1954), pp. 159–60.

its educational strategies and, of course, its increasingly visible and influential public schools. The period between the end of the war and the first pronouncements of Vatican II, in the mid-1960s, represented something of a high-water mark for the Church and the wider Catholic community. For many observers, these years before the full impact of Vatican II made itself felt in the late 1960s saw the maturing of a wide range of structures and influences in the communal and educational life of Catholics. Never were the Catholic public schools to feel as secure in their role, traditions and future as in these years.

It is evident that, through its educational activities, parish life, and organizations and events such as retreats, pilgrimages and devotional activities, the associational life of Catholics in these years could take place in an almost hermetically sealed community. Baptism, the rudiments of a nursery education, schooling by Catholics within Catholic schools of all kinds, attendance at Sunday Mass, participation in youth organizations, holiday camps run by the Church, lay groups such as the Catenians or the Society of St Vincent de Paul for men or the Union of Catholic Mothers for women, all served to knit the Catholic community together. It helped to create a kind of cocoon within which most Catholics could run their lives under the watchful eye of the parish priest and the Church Hierarchy. As Duffy eloquently argues:

> Anyone raised a Catholic before 1965 was formed in a Church which understood and presented itself as essentially timeless, its worship and its law enshrined in the immemorial splendours of the Latin language, its authority structures dominated by its clergy, its principal teachings infallible and therefore irreformable.[2]

Now whether this cocoon constituted a "Catholic fortress" or a "Catholic ghetto" is a matter of some debate amongst historians.[3] But three important

---

[2] E. Duffy, *Faith of Our Fathers* (London: Continuum, 2004), p. vii.
[3] For an excellent summary of the issues see A. Harris, *Faith in the Family: A Lived Religious History of English Catholicism 1945–82* (Manchester: Manchester University Press, 2013), pp. 36–41; S. Bruce, "Secularisation,

factors did contribute to the sense of identity and self-regulation for Catholics in these years: separate and distinctive Catholic schools, the continuing power of the pulpit and the Hierarchy to shape and control social mores and religious attitudes, and the enforcement of strict laws governing mixed marriages to ensure Catholics were dissuaded from marrying "outside the community". Taken together these three factors were central to what seemed to be the continuing internal cohesion and external strength of the Church. Ordinations were up, conversions up, and Catholic marriages and baptisms were up. This helped consolidate a confidence which had begun in the 1920s and 1930s. Overall the Catholic population grew from around 2.4 million in 1945 to 2.8 million in 1952 and 3.6 million in 1962, reaching almost 4 million by the end of the 1960s. The numbers of Catholic priests also grew from around 5,600 on the eve of the war to 6,200 in 1945 and 7,800 in 1965.

Table 4: Roman Catholic demographics 1939–65

Year	Catholic population	Catholic priests	Catholic marriages as per cent total
1939	2.4 m	5,642	7.9 per cent
1950	2.4 m	6,257	9.2 per cent
1952	2.8 m	6,684	10.2 per cent
1962	3.6 m	7,887*	13.0 per cent

*Figure for 1965. Source: Faith Survey (University of Roehampton, 2018).

As in earlier decades, immigration was an important component of that growth. Refugee populations settling in England following post-war disruptions brought, for example, significant numbers of Polish immigrants, many of them strongly Catholic. Migration from Ireland was also important. The "pull" factor of employment in England, especially in the building industry for men, and the new National Health Service

---

Church and Popular Religion", *Journal of Ecclesiastical History* 62:3 (2011), pp. 543–61.

for women, combined with the "push" of an economically stagnant and socially immobile Republic of Ireland, brought many Catholic individuals and families from across the Irish Sea. Irish priests were also very important in serving the new, growing parishes in urban and suburban England. Interestingly, the key concern of the Irish Church Hierarchy was less population loss, and more the supposed moral laxity of life in England.

The Catholic Truth Society of Ireland, for example, published a pocket-sized handbook in the 1950s for those migrating to England. Men and women foolhardy enough to make that journey were warned of the evils of dancing, drinking, gambling and sex to be found everywhere in England. As one priest put it: "you are leaving a country where the Christian way of life shines clearly and are entering the darkness and confusions of twentieth-century materialism". Dangers were best resisted, it was argued, by immersion in the cleansing waters of a good parish life—Sunday Mass, daily prayer, regular Confession and Communion, the recital of the rosary when things got tough.[4] Sending children to a Catholic school was an essential. In the large urban Catholic communities in cities such as Liverpool, Manchester and Birmingham, those networks of structures (Church, church hall, primary school) and associations (prayer groups, rosary circles, the Union of Catholic Mothers, the Catenians) could serve to create what became almost a "tribal identity" for the growing Catholic population.

Alongside the arrival of Catholic immigrants, the 1950s saw an upsurge in new religious orders arriving in England. The White Fathers, for example, grew from only four small centres in 1946 to eight just four years later, staffed by 40 priests making a considerable impact on English life both locally and nationally. Orders of nuns were also expanding and making a significant impression in both the Catholic mainstream schools

---

[4] C. Wills, *Lovers and Strangers: An Immigrant History of Post-War Britain* (London: Penguin, 2017), pp. 123–5; see also C. Wills, *The Best Are Leaving: Emigration and Post-War Irish Culture* (Cambridge: Cambridge University Press, 2015), pp. 23–60.

and in the expansion of convent education for girls.[5] The traditions of Catholicism were ingrained into the daily lives of the faithful, whether in the parish, the day school or the boarding school: "Benediction and rosary, the nine first Fridays, plenary indulgences ... minor seminaries ... filled with hundreds of small boys from working-class homes trained in their teens in Latin and celibacy ... The Catholic Church remained indeed a law unto itself."[6]

The Catholic school, whether public or otherwise, continued to play a very important part in the knitting together of that community, especially with the growth of government interest in the expansion of secondary education. The Butler 1944 Education Act heralded significant state intervention in secondary education. It enshrined free access to secondary schooling for all children up to the age of 15, and numbers in secondary schools rose from 1.1 million in 1944 to 2 million just over a decade later. State spending on education rose by 80 per cent over the same period. The Act put significant pressure on the Catholic community and Hierarchy to provide adequate Catholic schools in the secondary sector.

Much political effort was devoted to maximizing government capital and recurrent funding for Catholic schools, amid fears that an inability to fund new and existing secondary schools might lead to the absorption of financially stretched Catholic schools into the mainstream. Intense lobbying by the bishops led to some improvements to overall funding conditions for Catholic schools, but the community still needed to raise its own monies for such schools.[7] By the early 1950s, many Catholic

---

[5] A. Hastings, *A History of English Christianity 1920–2000* (London: SPCK, 2001), pp. 474–6.

[6] Hastings, *History of English Christianity*, p. 490.

[7] On the Butler Act, see S. J. Curtis and M. Boultwood, *An Introductory History of English Education since 1800* (London: University Tutorial Press, 1964), pp. 197–206; G. Davie, *Religion in Britain since 1945* (Oxford: Blackwell, 1996), pp. 131–2; F. Greene and D. Kynaston, *Engines of Privilege: Britain's Private School Problem* (London: Bloomsbury, 2019), pp. 32–7; J. Davies, "'L'Art du Possible': The Board of Education, the Catholic Church and negotiations over the White Paper and the Education Bill, 1943–4", *Recusant*

secondaries, especially those created by religious orders in the first three decades of the century, had become grammar schools, but creating new, secondary modern schools was a continuing challenge for dioceses. In Birmingham, for example, between 1952 and 1966, some 42 new Catholic secondary schools were built with around 20,000 new secondary places being catered for. At about the same time, the diocese experienced the biggest growth of churches in its history with over 60 new churches built and paid for from parish funds.[8] In the Clifton diocese, similar pressures were evident, with an inadequate building stock to deal with the expanded numbers, and curriculum changes especially in physical education and science.[9] The financial and resource challenges faced by all the Catholic dioceses dwarfed those of their public schools.

The growing size, affluence and confidence of the Catholic community, especially amongst the sizeable middle classes, was to leave a clear mark on the public schools. But there were also a number of other important changes in the external environment which all the public schools, Catholic or otherwise, had to navigate. As part of the 1944 Butler Act, the Fleming Commission had been set up to look at the public-school sector as a whole. The Labour Party, which came to power in 1945, had a hostile attitude to public schools on grounds of access and social equity, and because of the enormous and disproportionate influence exerted by ex-public-school pupils in the corridors of power. The latter was, of course, a central, often explicit, part of the public-school marketing pitch. As one educationalist noted: "We can hardly continue to contemplate an England where the mass of the people coming on by one educational path are to be governed for the most part by a minority advancing along a quite separate and more favoured path."[10] The notion that the public

---

History 22:2 (1994), pp. 231–50; A. B. Morris, *Fifty Years On: The Case for Catholic Schools* (Chelmsford: Matthew James, 2008), pp. 23–4.

[8] J. J. Scarisbrick (ed.), *History of the Diocese of Birmingham, 1850–2000* (Strasbourg: Editions du Signe, 2008), pp. 48–51.

[9] J. A. Harding, "Catholic Education and the Diocese of Clifton: A Brief History", in J. A. Harding, *The Diocese of Clifton 1850–2000* (Clifton: Clifton Catholic Diocesan Trustees, 1999), pp. 251–2.

[10] Greene and Kynaston, *Engines of Privilege*, p. 30.

schools, Catholic or otherwise, might eventually need to be wholly absorbed within a new national education system, was a chronic political concern in the immediate post-war period.

For a while then, the very survival of Catholic public schools was threatened because of changes in the political environment. School heads and the Hierarchy regularly bemoaned the threat that seemed to be posed by the new Labour government in a range of areas such as welfare and education, and the Catholic public schools joined the rest of the sector in seeking to dilute any proposed changes. But the Fleming Commission ultimately changed very little, other than creating a mildly hostile environment but not scaring the horses too much. It proposed setting up a national scheme to open up a quarter of all places in the public schools to non-fee payers in return for government support, but that proposal quietly lapsed. Many schools were recruiting well and thus saw no need to free up 25 per cent of their places in return for government money (which was very welcome) and potential government interference (certainly not welcome), and, whilst noises about the public schools remained, there were no further concrete threats to their survival. The Conservative governments of the 1950s and early 1960s posed no threat to the political support for a continuing public-school sector.

There were other, more forceful sets of changes which fed through into the Catholic public schools. First was the impact of a wider interest in the academic performance of schools. That pressure came from a number of areas. The introduction of the GCE A level examination in 1951 gave parents a good indication of where "their" schools stood since, by the end of the 1950s, almost all the public schools had adopted the examination. Many of the public schools were initially hostile to the exam (and often had poor results in the early years) and continued to focus solely on gaining Oxbridge entry which until the late 1960s depended largely on performance in specific entrance examinations and an interview, rather than A level grades. It was a system which naturally favoured the public schools which could both facilitate extra tuition and accommodate pupils for the additional "seventh term" required to take the entrance exams, in return, of course, for the extra fee income.

It may well be that the more middle-class Catholic public schools were more fleet of foot in realizing that good A level performance was the key to high numbers of university entrants. Certainly by the late 1950s, all of the schools were extolling their academic performance in A levels, as well as Oxbridge entry, in their magazines, prospectuses, speech days and parental communications. Of course the university environment itself was also changing. The number of places grew through the 1950s and 1960s, as existing universities expanded their places and, following the Robbins Report, new universities emerged. Whilst there were more places there was also more competition from expanding, free grammar school places to contend with. Many of the major Catholic day schools in cities such as Birmingham (St Philip's, St Chad's) or Manchester (St Francis Xavier, St Bede's) provided stiff competition for the boarding schools. A key effect then was to increase parental pressure on schools to secure university entrance. Oxbridge entrance remained the gold standard, but securing places outside Oxbridge was becoming increasingly important. And, perhaps for the first time, parents were able to judge and compare school performance through the metric of national exam results. The die was cast, though it was not until the early 1970s that the forerunner of today's league tables first appeared.[11]

A second feature of the wider environment came with the introduction of inspection regimes. Inspections of public schools by government had begun in the early post-war period, but they could hardly be described as rigorous. None of our schools failed. A tighter regime began to develop in the late 1950s, with a focus on the curriculum and facilities, especially in the sciences. In the mid-1950s, the *Industrial Fund for the Advancement of Science in Schools* was set up; it brought significant capital funding into all the public schools for improving the teaching of science and helped to sharpen changes in the curriculum, favouring a slow shift away from the traditional focus on the classics. The funding was essential in helping schools to modernize their teaching facilities and start the process of improving the pedagogic and subject knowledge of their staff, both religious and lay.

---

[11] D. Turner, *The Old Boys: The Decline and Rise of the Public School* (London: Yale University Press, 2016), p. 185.

Life at the top?

The Benedictine schools of Ampleforth and Downside, together with the Jesuit school at Stonyhurst and the diocesan college of St Edmund's, were arguably the most influential of our schools in these decades in terms of their numbers, their ability to secure university and especially Oxbridge entrance and scholarships, and the influence of their alumni. Almost all the schools progressed in numbers and influence in this period, but these four were perhaps most significant in the public arena. Downside (10th) and Ampleforth (17th) were, for example, the only Catholic public schools placed in a table of the 20 top public schools in terms of Oxbridge scholarships and exhibitions between 1957 and 1961.[12] The influence that they were able to exert on the creation of a Catholic Establishment was significant. Building on the growing confidence of these schools and their alumni, positions of influence in the Church itself (a large number of bishops were drawn from these schools), in academia, business, journalism, politics and the media were taken up by a new Catholic elite. For Sewell, "the master narrative of Britain's Catholic community during the twentieth century became one of relentless social progress".[13] The confidence of the Catholic public schools generally was reflected in the values, academic and sporting aspirations, and the intimate interlocking of daily academic, cultural, sporting and spiritual life within the schools.

We can get some idea of that growing influence by examining data from the *Who's Who in Catholic Life* published in 1997. The entries reflected a group of people who were educated between about 1935 and 1965, and who came to national prominence some three or four decades later. Their educational background is interesting. Looking just at lay persons in that group of around 1,000 individuals, over one-third (34 per cent) of what we might term a Catholic elite were educated in that group of a dozen or so schools that have been the subject of our study. As Table 5 shows, Ampleforth, Stonyhurst and Downside dominated by some considerable margin. How had this been achieved?

---

[12] T. Bamford, *The Rise of the Public Schools* (London: Nelson, 1967), p. 309.
[13] D. Sewell, *Catholics: Britain's Largest Minority* (London: Viking, 2001), p. 4.

Table 5: Educational background of lay, male entrants in Catholic *Who's Who* (1997)

School	Number	Percentage of total entrants in the Catholic *Who's Who*
Ampleforth	121	12 per cent
Stonyhurst	91	9 per cent
Downside	49	5 per cent
Prior Park	19	2 per cent
Ratcliffe	11	1 per cent
Mount St Mary's	11	1 per cent
Douai	9	
Oratory School	9	
Others	25	

Source: *Who's Who in Catholic Life 1997* (Manchester: Gabriel Communications Ltd., 1997).

As we saw in the last chapter, Ampleforth had embarked on a strategy of growth in numbers and an overhaul of its structures from the 1930s under the leadership of Fr Paul Nevill. As Galliver argues, by the late 1950s, Ampleforth "was counted as a leading public school because of the social composition of its intake and its record in sending its boys on to Oxford, Cambridge and Sandhurst".[14]

The development of the house system and the success of its preparatory school meant a school population of well over 500 in the post-war decades. That remarkable figure, a doubling of its numbers from the late 1920s, created a sound financial footing for the expansion of buildings, with a new Abbey church opened in 1961. Critically, Ampleforth was also able to draw the Catholic aristocratic and gentry elite into its orbit, groups for whom the tone and social standing of a public school were as important as academic performance and facilities. A steady stream of

---

[14] P. Galliver, *Ampleforth College: The Emergence of Ampleforth College as the 'Catholic Eton'* (Leominster: Gracewing, 2019), p. 5.

influential Catholics paid regular visits to Ampleforth in the 1950s and 1960s—Catholic politicians, writers, distinguished academics. Building the "right" social composition and tone of the school was as important as building the right facilities, and Fr Paul was pre-eminent in doing precisely that.

One of the ways in which the quality and external performance of the education provided by the public schools was improved was by the increased appointment of academically well-qualified lay staff to work alongside the large monastic community. Their role was not only to prepare pupils for external examinations and, especially, Oxbridge entrance, but also to improve the network of connections into Oxbridge colleges and the Establishment through which the school would continue to enhance its reputation. Access to that Establishment depended on the networks and contacts that heads and their staff could draw on. The house system was also integral to the success of Ampleforth. Houses were largely self-contained: a pupil's life was determined within and by the house. Senior pupils acted as monitors who exercised discipline, including corporal punishment, and academic performance was closely monitored. Every individual was ranked in a form order which determined where boys appeared on the school list, seating arrangements in the refectory, and even their position in church. This degree of control and competition set the school apart from most of its Catholic contemporaries.

Religious observance and ritual remained strong, even though the school was often explicitly seeking to mirror the elite, non-Catholic public schools where the emphasis on religious formation was much weaker. All the housemasters in these years came from the religious community, and at Ampleforth some 70 per cent of the staff in the 1940s and 1950s were monks. Well into the 1960s, all of the academic heads of department were clerics, emphasizing the extent to which the levers of control in the school were concentrated in the monastic community.[15] Mass for the whole school was celebrated at around 7.30 a.m. with prayers for the house at 9 a.m. House prayers closed the day at 9 p.m. The houses had their own early Mass on Sundays, followed by a High Mass for the

---

[15] A. Marrett-Crosby, *A School of the Lord's Service: A History of Ampleforth* (London: James & James, 2002), p. 118.

whole school with Benediction in the early evening. The whole school stopped for the Angelus prayer at midday and 6 p.m. That was a religious regime that was not uncommon in most of the Catholic public schools through to the 1960s. Retreats and school pilgrimages were also a regular occurrence.

School life was dominated by rituals, packed timetables and a mix of academic, cultural and sporting activities. The house provided the domestic environment for the boys, with the nature of the religious housemaster governing much of the character of daily life. Sport loomed large. Within the school, inter-house competitions were meant to serve the purpose of cementing cohesion within the house, whilst external fixtures against schools regarded as their social and academic equals were important reputationally. Cricket, rowing and fencing gave a social cachet to the school, as did beagling and the regular visits of the local hunt to the school. It was a training in upper-class mores for a school population which was predominantly upper class. For the middle-class parents able to afford the fees, it was seen as an aspirational sacrifice worth making. Overlaying everything was the constant presence of the monastic community which intermingled with the daily life of the school.

Stonyhurst, historically perhaps the pre-eminent Catholic public school in England, had been somewhat eclipsed by the growth of Ampleforth and, to a lesser extent, Downside in the 1930s and 1940s, as both those establishments sought to attract a higher class of pupil and parent, who were increasingly measuring the Catholic public schools against the competition in the non-Catholic sector. A series of reforms at Stonyhurst in the late 1930s had laid greater emphasis on the pastoral role of housemasters as well as on academic performance, which were to reap benefits after the war. The college also established a separate Junior House (St Mary's Hall) in 1946 which proved a swift success, and the original complement of some 60 boys at St Mary's in 1947 had reached almost 140 by the early 1960s. The Common Entrance exam (in existence since 1911) was finally adopted by Stonyhurst in 1948, in order to begin measuring the performance of the school intake against wider benchmarks. There were some 417 boys enrolled in the prep and main school in 1947, and numbers remained at that level well into the 1960s.

The growth of the junior school in particular drove a number of building projects in this period. The creation of a gym at the junior school and a new chemistry block in 1958 improved facilities, with the latter project, as with so many schools, benefiting from the national Industrial Fund for Science. A further expansion of science facilities was built in 1963. A new Rhetoric Wing (the term used for the most senior classes at the school) was opened two years later; it was a building largely designed by the Rector, Fr Vavasour, and was opened with much ceremony by the Earl of Derby in 1965.[16] The life of the pupils continued to be bounded by tradition and conformity in these years. Academic performance remained very important, with entrance to Oxbridge a key measure of success placing it, as we noted earlier, alongside Downside and Ampleforth, at the top of our schools. Sport remained very important, perhaps as a test of "character", more likely as a reputational measure.

As with all of our schools, participation in national public-school competitions was eagerly sought. Drama, the arts, and the tradition of "Great Academies" (academic entertainment, prize giving and gymnastic displays) remained part of daily life. Spirituality remained integral to school life in these years. All the boys were required to remain at school throughout Holy Week, and the liturgy was enhanced by a nationally distinguished choir. Daily Mass was compulsory, and there were three-day spiritual retreats for all boys at the start of the academic year. The somewhat spartan living conditions, corporal punishment with the *ferula* and rigid discipline and timetabling controlled every aspect of daily life. It was a challenging regime.

By the end of the 1960s, some changes began to be felt, with the advent of a degree of liberalization. Muir suggests that by the mid-1960s parents were beginning to question some of the traditional aspects of school life: "They demanded higher academic and cultural standards and, perhaps as a consequence of this, they were less willing to sacrifice material prospects in the cause of religious education."[17] Changes crept in slowly, perhaps too slowly for some generations of boys. New buildings

---

[16] T. E. Muir, *Stonyhurst College 1593–1993* (Cirencester: St Omers Press, revised edition, 2006), pp. 161–4.

[17] Muir, *Stonyhurst*, p. 164.

Figure 21: Cross-country running, Stonyhurst, 1950s.

accompanied some liberalization of the regime in the late 1960s as, one by one, old traditions were adapted or removed. Compulsory daily Mass, the three-day religious retreats which had traditionally begun the academic year, and compulsory membership of the Cadet Corps slowly but surely shifted, altering the daily life of the school through to the early 1970s.[18] Alongside Stonyhurst, Beaumont remained a distinguished southern Jesuit partner, continuing to develop with a range of building projects completed in the early 1960s. Numbers remained on the small side, but the school continued to attract a well-connected and well-networked international intake.

For Downside, these years saw a consolidation of numbers and prestige. The school had grown to around 550 by the late 1960s and, at that date, was perhaps at the height of its educational and intellectual reputation. Both school and monastery continued to expand physically with very significant capital investment from the monastic community. The science wing was significantly expanded in the 1950s and, following a major fire in 1955, a new theatre and gym, together with additional accommodation, were opened in 1961.[19] At the same time, plans were drawn up by the monastic community for a new monastic library with guest accommodation, which was completed in 1970 with a radical modernist design.[20] These developments reflected the confidence of the monastic community, or at least of their leaders, in a secure and sustainable future for both school and community. The school continued to perform outstandingly well in getting students into Oxbridge. Through the 1950s and early 1960s, the school regularly sent 15 or 20 students to Oxford and Cambridge and secured significant scholarship awards. By the late 1950s, there were regularly over 30 Downside boys in residence at Oxford and close to 60 at Cambridge.[21] It was something of a golden era for the school, with academic and sporting achievements placing it

---

[18] Muir, *Stonyhurst*, pp. 166–7.
[19] *The Raven: Downside School Magazine* 53, 229 (1963).
[20] D. A. Bellenger (ed.), *Downside Abbey: An Architectural History* (London: Merrell, 2011), pp. 201–16.
[21] Data from *The Raven* 1963–9.

comfortably alongside most of the major non-Catholic public schools in public esteem and reputation.

The monastic community at Downside was integral to the academic, social and pastoral character of the school. In the 1950s and 1960s, all of the housemasters, a key role as we have seen, were monks or brothers, and within the school, around one-third of all the teachers were part of the monastic community. The practice of the faith was central to school activity. Compulsory attendance at daily Mass was part of what the headmaster in 1964 called, "the central importance of Godliness and good learning" in the work that the school carried out.[22] The practice of retreats and pilgrimages (ranging from nearby Glastonbury Tor to Lourdes and Rome) was celebrated at Downside. Groups such as the League of Christ the King, and prayer groups dedicated to the Virgin Mary, were strong. In 1964, the school celebrated Easter Week as a community with a range of celebrations. The climax was the Easter Vigil, "which has a character all of its own and the hundreds of candles in the darkened Abbey church, the sudden illumination at the *Gloria* and the Easter communion at the hour of the Resurrection, are likely to linger in the memory as a corporate and compelling experience".[23]

At the same time, there were veiled warnings about the issue of vocations to the Benedictine community, which were not keeping pace with the growing demands on the community by school and parish commitments. Increasingly, the pace of new vocations from within the school were tailing off by the early 1960s. It was a pattern beginning to be replicated in other schools.

The fabric of daily life for the pupils was similar to most other schools. Academic performance remained fundamental to the reputation of the school with a rising number of well-qualified lay teachers coming on to the staff. The academic results of the school were consistently high in these decades. Sport was important too, with rugby and cricket providing the opportunity to test both sporting prowess and, especially, to measure the school against its peers. Public School Rugby Sevens, as with both Ampleforth and Stonyhurst, were a key national competition

---

[22] *The Raven* 55, 231 (1964).

[23] *The Raven* 55, 231 (1964).

from the early 1950s. The school, emulating a long-standing practice at Ampleforth, also introduced its own pack of beagles in 1947. For one historian, a Downside monk, the introduction of the beagles, "marked the peak of Downside's glory . . . it is the one post-war development which stands in a class of its own".[24] One suspects the remark was not ironic. They were not to survive much more than a decade.

St Edmund's College continued to grow and, significantly, was the first of all of our schools to appoint a lay head for the period 1940–9. The school maintained a somewhat different character from Ampleforth, Downside and Stonyhurst. It was controlled by the diocese, it was also involved in training seminarians for the priesthood, and it was financially helped through recruiting a number of day pupils, first introduced in the mid-1950s. As with so many other schools, the early 1950s saw considerable rebuilding and renovation to deal with increased numbers. New playing fields were laid out, a new infirmary developed, and boarding facilities were improved. But the financial position was, as Schofield notes, a very challenging one, with significant deficits in the early 1950s, deficits which fell to the diocese to try and resolve.[25] Unlike the Benedictine and Jesuit schools (who nevertheless often struggled), the diocesan schools (St Edmund's and Cotton) did not have recourse to any wider funding from the orders.

By the mid-1950s, thanks to the recruitment of day boys and raising fees, the financial position was improved. The admission of day boys, a feature well in advance of all the other schools, did raise objections. Commenting on the fact that three boarding pupils had been withdrawn as a result of the change, the President, writing to Cardinal Griffin, noted that "I cannot think that we are doing anything other than what is our duty to the Catholics of the neighbourhood. It would be a terrible thing if we were to stand aside and see these [day] boys go to non-Catholic grammar schools."[26] It was an argument that would be rehearsed at all of our schools by the late 1970s.

---

[24] van Zeller, *Downside*, p. 167.
[25] N. Schofield, *The History of St Edmund's College* (Ware: The Edmundian Association, 2013), pp. 153–4.
[26] Schofield, *St Edmund's College*, p. 158.

The college buildings were renewed and renovated in the 1950s to improve living conditions for the boys, whose numbers rose to between 200 and 250 by the mid-1960s with day boys being about one quarter of that figure, much higher than any of the other Catholic public schools. The usual range of sporting and cultural activities governed daily life. When needed, school sports teams might be supplemented by one or two "ringers" from the senior seminarians training at the college to ensure a good result. The cadet force celebrated its fiftieth anniversary in 1960 and remained important through these years. Scouts, annual camps, theatrical performances, traditional sporting matches against the old boys of the Edmundian Association, marked the annual calendar. The college was quietly successful although perhaps less "well connected" than the "big three". The key change, the announcement that the seminary would move from St Edmund's to a new home in London, Allen Hall, was made in 1968 but not achieved until 1975.[27] As with so many of our schools, it was a change that reflected the upheavals of the late 1960s.

Across the sector

Douai, always a smaller school than its bigger brothers, Downside and Ampleforth, had nevertheless grown in the post-war period, with 160 pupils in the late 1940s, 220 by 1959 and 260 by the end of the 1960s. In part, this was a reflection of the establishment of a prep school in 1948 at Ditcham Park near Petersfield. It was, the school noted, an ambitious undertaking at a time of economic challenge but it recruited well. The pressure to increase numbers at the main school, together with buoyant demand for junior places, meant the venture paid off, and before long a virtually guaranteed 15–20 boys progressed to the main school each year.

As in many other schools, the bulk of the teaching continued to be carried out by the monks. In 1948, there were just four lay teachers alongside 35 religious staff. That proportion changed very slowly; by the mid-1960s there were still only eight lay teachers alongside the 34 monks. Whilst the school remained relatively small, it is still quite striking that

---

[27] Schofield, *St Edmund's College*, pp. 167–9.

the Benedictines were able to take on such a high proportion of the teaching, as well as providing the senior staff and housemasters.[28] This came at a time when the proportion of lay to religious staff was changing quite fast in some other schools. At the same time, the Benedictine community at Douai was also serving a significant number of parishes across the country. In 1964, there were 83 members of the monastic community at Douai, of whom 12 were not yet ordained, and 35 were working away from Douai on missionary work in the parishes.[29] These figures help to explain some of the conflicting pressures beginning to face the Benedictine schools in particular. As in the period of expansion at Downside and Ampleforth in the 1920s and 1930s, not all members of the monastic community were entirely comfortable with having to continually balance the interests of school and parish responsibility with the inherent need to maintain the contemplative life which had perhaps drawn them to the order in the first place. It was a pressure that was ultimately to lead to the closure of the school by the end of the century.

The steady growth of the school, as elsewhere, was reflected in building programmes. As well as the significant investments in the prep school, the main school itself saw new building work. From the outset, at Douai there had been a significant mixing of the school and monastic spaces, something which had concerned various abbots over the decades because of the tensions between the quiet, meditative aspects of the monastic life and the much busier, bustling life of the school. It was not until the late 1940s that clearer spatial differentiation came as a consequence of building work. By the early 1960s, plans were begun for a major new monastic space and Abbey church which was eventually opened in 1964. The layout of the church reflected the changes introduced by Vatican II, with a forward-facing altar and a design facilitating concelebration of Mass by several priests.[30] The buildings were to be a testament to these years of confidence in the Catholic faith and a Catholic public-school education.

---

[28] Scott (ed.), *The English Benedictine Community of St Edmund*, pp. 33–6.

[29] *Douai School Magazine*, Spring 1964.

[30] *Douai School Magazine*, Autumn 1965.

The experience of the pupils in these years was a familiar one of tight regulation and discipline within a well-articulated structure of orthodox religious observance. The school, one visiting bishop noted in 1949, was "carrying on the great tradition of Benedictine education; and by education I do not mean academic studies alone, but the daily life and recreation of the boys which is based upon the rule of St Benedict and sound Benedictine tradition".[31]

As always, one doubts how much the boys appreciated such insights. In the early 1960s, boys entering, after taking the Common Entrance at 13, faced an open dormitory of some 60 beds in long rows. They had no private space or cubicle, just a chair and a coat hook, no names, just a school number. These were features common to most Catholic boarding schools at the time.

Meals were served in a single large refectory. Uniform was three-piece grey suits, and a blazer in summer. Corporal punishment was a part of daily life and administered by either the housemaster or the head, but never by fellow pupils. Compulsory sport and regular attendance in church and at house prayers were an integral part of the regime. High days and holydays provided some relief from the tedium. At the annual Corpus Christi procession, the school marched through the Benedictine parish in nearby Reading, attracting a large following in a town which apparently had no idea it had so many Catholics in its midst![32] Sport remained important as in all our schools. Interestingly, the school adopted fencing as a major sport which provided school teams with access to fixtures with a public-school elite—Lancing, Charterhouse, Winchester, Bradfield, Wellington—which was seen as integral to the social standing and tone of Douai.

It is interesting to note the extent to which the external environment impinged on the life of the school. As with every other school, lectures and debates on particular social or political issues, ranging from capital punishment to the role of the trades unions, were part and parcel of school life. On a number of occasions visitors from some of the organizations working under the broad heading of "Catholic Action" visited schools.

---

[31] *Douai School Magazine,* Autumn 1949.
[32] *Douai Society Magazine,* Autumn 1948.

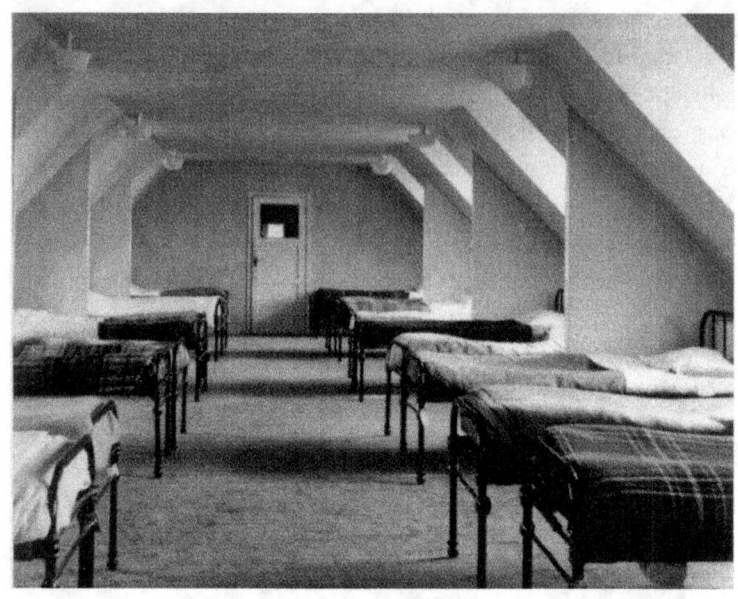

Figure 22: School dormitory, the Oratory School, late 1950s.

Figure 23: School washrooms at the Oratory School, late 1950s.

Movements such as Distributism (a movement advocating a kind of middle way between the "extremes" of unfettered capitalism and communism) were widely discussed at school meetings, and the role of organizations such as the Society of St Vincent de Paul and the Catholic Evidence Guild in guiding the practical actions of boys at the school was highlighted in talks and presentations.

One of the more interesting ones was the Catenians, who were influential at a number of the smaller Catholic public schools from the 1930s onwards. Founded in 1908, they constituted a kind of "Catholic Rotary" organization, which sought to provide a network and support for young professional Catholics seeking to make their way into business and the professions. They expanded significantly in the 1950s, and generally received support from the Hierarchy and from a number of our schools, especially those catering for a more middle-class clientele.[33] The Catenians could provide help to pupils leaving the school, noted one editorial, emphasizing that the pupil "will find Brothers ready to help him in his business or profession".[34]

By the late 1930s, Mount St Mary's was in some financial difficulties because of poor recruitment and, whilst having the strength of the Jesuit community behind it, a strategy to secure sustainable numbers was needed. As in a number of other schools in the 1930s, that solution was a prep or junior school. The Mount had opened Barlborough Hall School, some two miles from the Mount, in April 1939. After a brief period of wartime requisition, numbers grew to around 60 or 70 pupils a year, many of whom subsequently progressed to the Mount helping to secure numbers. In 1942, the Mount had celebrated its centenary. The traditional patterns of a Solemn Mass presided over by the Bishop of Nottingham, and including the ordination to the priesthood of two old boys, was followed by a Past v Present cricket match and a formal dinner

---

[33] J. Hagerty, *The Catenian Association: A Centenary History* (Coventry: Catenian Association, 2008), pp. 95–106.

[34] *Douai School Magazine*, Autumn 1959.

in the evening. Solemn Mass the following day, a march past of the cadet corps, prizegiving and solemn Benediction ended the celebrations.[35]

What then was life like in the Mount at this time? Joining at the age of 12, some 60 of the youngest boys slept in an open dormitory presided over by a Jesuit housemaster. A daily life of worship, study and sport (compulsory rugby of course) was not dissimilar to schools elsewhere. Discipline was enforced, as in all Jesuit schools, with the *ferula*, a kind of pivoted cane and paddle, usually when all other measures (lines, compulsory cross-country runs and so on) had failed. Boys never administered corporal punishment. The teaching staff of those years was varied. It included young men in training for the priesthood, ex-Army personnel, trainee lay teachers and, especially, members of the Jesuit community which numbered between 20 and 30 in this period. The Combined Cadet Force was "reborn" in the early 1950s. Rugby was the most important sport, and classes continued well into the evening. As Beattie noted, there was also an increasing awareness amongst senior members of the staff of the need to prepare for a gradual handover of the running of the school to non-Jesuits.[36] Lay teachers had of course long been a small but important component of the public schools, but management had almost always remained vested in the religious community. The first hints of a need to reconsider this model had begun to appear by the late 1950s.

Ratcliffe celebrated its centenary in June 1947. Numbers had stabilized at around 200, and the celebratory weekend was presided over by the Bishops of Nottingham and Northampton with the usual mixture of religious ceremonies, sports, and a celebratory dinner, with a blessing from Cardinal Griffin, the Archbishop of Westminster. At High Mass, the Cardinal spoke of the important role schools such as Ratcliffe played in bringing "sound Catholic teaching, doctrinal and social, into English life

---

[35] M. Beattie, *Portrait of our College: Mount St Mary and Barlborough Hall, 1842–2017* (London: Society of Jesus, 2017), pp. 100–1.

[36] Beattie, *Mount St Mary*, pp. 115–18.

and culture by men of proven knowledge and virtue (bringing) untold benefit to the Church and to the country".[37]

The celebrations coincided with the appointment of Fr Leetham to the role of President. He was to remain in post until 1963, and oversaw a continued growth in the numbers, facilities and status of the school. The expansion of Grace Dieu, the preparatory school for Ratcliffe, from the late 1940s, meant a secure supply of new entrants through the 1950s, and by the end of the decade there were over 300 students, the largest in the history of the school.[38] Recruitment remained strongest in the middle classes, and was geographically focused on the Midlands and the south-east. Patterns of activity were familiar ones. An emphasis on sport sat alongside strong performances in the academic arena. Through most of the 1950s and 1960s, the college sent between seven and twelve students each year to Oxbridge, many on open scholarships or exhibitions, and in 1953 the college reported, somewhat surprisingly, that it had the second highest number of former pupils at Cambridge of any of the Catholic public schools.[39] For a school of its size, this was a significant achievement. Along with strong performances in external examinations, especially the new A level exams, this focus chimed well with the changing parental aspirations of the time at all of the schools.

As with many other public schools, Ratcliffe took advantage of external monies to improve facilities for the teaching of science, with new chemistry and physics facilities, and took pride in the fact that religious staff were responsible for all the science teaching at a time when other schools were recruiting more and more lay teachers in those areas. Other developments included the re-founding of the Combined Cadet Force in 1954, and the expansion of the footprint of the college through the purchase of a neighbouring aerodrome in 1950, with the help of funds from the Ratcliffian Association.[40] The place of religion in the ethos and daily life of the school remained strong. Plans for a new

---

[37] C. R. Leetham, *Ratcliffe College 1847–1947* (Leicester: Ratcliffian Association, 1950), p. 104.

[38] *The Ratcliffian*, Autumn 1959.

[39] *The Ratcliffian*, 1953.

[40] *The Ratcliffian*, February 1950.

chapel were announced in the late 1950s, and the chapel was opened by 1960. A Pontifical Mass was celebrated by the Bishop of Nottingham at the opening. Later building projects in the 1960s included a large sixth form centre (1966) and new language labs (1969).

As with many of our schools, engagement with the wider Catholic community was important. The school took part in the Rosary Crusade of Fr Peyton in the early 1950s and sent a large group of boys to the rosary events in Leicester in 1952. The link with the Catenian Association (something of a hallmark of middle-class identity) remained strong. The annual "Catenian Sunday" at Ratcliffe regularly had attendances in excess of 200 for a range of religious and sporting events, which served to emphasize the importance of a strong Catholic presence in the professions and business. That focus contrasted with the more explicitly elitist tone of the connections sought by schools such as Ampleforth and Downside. By the mid-1960s, the school was in a strong position. Pupil numbers were consistently above 300, the prep school was buoyant, and A levels and university entries, especially to Oxbridge, remained strong.

There were, however, as in other schools, some harbingers of future change. Pressures on the Rosminian community were regularly highlighted in parental communications. The Rosminians, unlike the Jesuits or Benedictines, were not a large order, yet their activities had continued to grow in the two decades after the war. A new school and seminary in New Zealand, significant parochial responsibilities in south Wales, the staffing of a school in east Africa educating the children of white expatriates, and establishing a grammar school in Huddersfield, placed growing demands on human resources. By the mid-1960s, the pressures were becoming apparent. In his 1967 Address, the President wondered prophetically, "how far the Institute of Charity may in the future be able to find the men needed to carry on Ratcliffe in its present form".[41] In 1952, there were 18 religious and 5 lay members of staff; in 1958, the figures were 26 and 8 respectively. By 1962, however, the number of religious was static at 26 whilst lay teachers had increased to 14. By 1967, lay teachers outnumbered religious teachers for the first time.[42] It was a

---

[41] *The Ratcliffian*, 1967.
[42] Data from annual issues of *The Ratcliffian*.

sign of the pressures on the religious community and an inevitable shift towards a lay majority within the teaching staff of the school, a pattern replicated at many other schools. That not only placed pressures on the existing religious community—and unsurprisingly prompted a number of appeals by the President to parents and boys alike to reflect on the need for new vocations—but it also shifted the business model of the school. Little wonder that concerns about financial viability and the need to raise school fees dominated school business towards the end of the 1960s.

This picture of expansion in numbers and facilities, coupled with pressures on the traditional financial model, was replicated elsewhere. Cotton College was in many ways at its most successful and influential in these years. From around 150 students in the immediate post-war period, numbers grew to a peak of 225 in 1962, made up of both "church" boys funded by the dioceses intended for the priesthood, and fee-paying boys from Catholic families, especially from the Midlands.

A new Faber wing with study bedrooms, new facilities for an expanding sixth form and new classrooms were built to accommodate higher pupil numbers in what seemed to be a period of real optimism for Catholics. One priest working at the college noted: "There was no time quite like it; no quarter expected or given. Mass, Office, Class, Rugger/Cricket/Hockey, pick and shovel. Study, food, bed, start all over again."[43]

If that was the routine of the priests, that of the boys can be imagined! The headmaster from 1948–67 was Mgr Doran who quickly brought in a new group of priests to maintain high standards at the college. Rugby and cricket dominated the calendar, all within an atmosphere of strong discipline and self-sacrifice. The tone was set by the head, described thus by John Cornwell: "The smoothness of his pale hair, the correctness of his manner of speaking, the precision of his Roman collar, the starch of his white shirt cuffs were the epitome of Catholic clericalism."[44]

At the Cotton bicentenary in 1963, the successes of the school were celebrated. During that period, Cotton, and its predecessor Sedgley Park, had educated some 9,000 boys from whom there were over 1,000

---

[43] F. Roberts (with N. Henshaw), *A History of Sedgley Park and Cotton College* (Privately published, 1985), p. 237.

[44] J. Cornwell, *Seminary Boy* (London: Harper, 2007), p. 160.

Figure 24: Archbishop Griffin, an old Cottonian, with pupils at Cotton College, 1946.

Figure 25: Cotton College Bicentenary celebrations, 1963.

priests, 15 Bishops, four Archbishops and one Cardinal Archbishop. It was an impressive tally of vocations, reflecting the significant presence of diocesan-funded "church boys" at the school, most of whom went on for their priestly training to Oscott in Birmingham.[45]

School life continued to be dominated by religious ritual and observance. Daily Mass remained compulsory, unlike many Catholic public schools which had begun to relax this requirement in the late 1950s and early 1960s. The centrality of religion, and the way in which the religious community teaching at Cotton influenced so many aspects of a boy's life, has been evocatively (and critically) articulated in John Cornwell's *Seminary Boy*. As a pupil funded by his diocese with the expectation of progressing to the priesthood, he provides a picture of life at Cotton in the 1950s. Describing a highly disciplined, ascetic education in a bleak, cold corner of north Staffordshire, he captures the claustrophobic environment, the authoritarian structures and the rigid hierarchies which existed at the school. A strong academic focus, obsessional religious observance, corporal punishment, the mixing of "church" and "lay" boys, and the sometimes dangerous intimacies of a boarding school life in which the religious community has absolute power and control are perfectly captured: "The single most important focus of our routine was the sanctuary where we created a daily pageant of music, precise rituals and rapid rhythmic prayers. The tabernacle on the high altar where resided the real presence of Jesus Christ was the centre of our lives."[46]

Of course it is a portrait of one school at one point in time, but it nevertheless conveys some of the general features shared by all of our schools in this period of what has been described as "Catholic triumphalism". For many, it seemed as if nothing could or would change.

Belmont Abbey School, a Benedictine school established in 1924, whose numbers had rarely exceeded 50 in the years before the Second World War, expanded too in these years of confidence. Pupil numbers grew

---

[45] Roberts and Henshaw, *Sedgley Park and Cotton College*, p. 239.

[46] Cornwell, *Seminary Boy*, p. 76; See the material of Cotton in John Cornwell, *The Dark Box: A Secret History of Confession* (London: Profile Books, 2014) pp. 169–78.

during the war because of the geographical security of its Herefordshire base, and by the mid-1950s numbers were close to 200. New buildings were put up for both science teaching and accommodation, and novices were taught alongside lay boys, although the numbers of the former were always small. Fees were kept low to attract predominantly middle-class parents (mirroring Ratcliffe and Mount St Mary's in this respect), and by the early 1960s, numbers were capped by the monastic community who ran the school at around 250. A prep school near Matlock, which was somewhat speculatively opened in 1949 (the community decided to buy an existing prep school lock, stock and barrel, including the boys in it!), proved successful in ensuring steady recruitment to Belmont.[47]

The Benedictine community at Worth Abbey, initially founded as a dependent monastery of Downside, and the location of the Downside prep school from the early 1930s, became an independent Abbey in 1957 and two years later founded a new boarding school. It thrived and in 1965 a new junior school was set up alongside the senior one with a strong sense of optimism for the future.

Prior Park was also redeveloping in these years. After it suffered significant bomb damage during a raid on Bath in 1942, the Christian Brothers who ran the schools embarked on a rebuilding programme, together with a determined effort to grow numbers and reputation within a firm Catholic ethos. In a pattern familiar from elsewhere, the school established a prep school at Cricklade in 1946 to feed into the main school, leading to a secure school roll of around 250 by the mid-1950s. The school also began to take on more day pupils taking advantage of the immediate proximity of Bath, whose population could gaze up at the magnificent Palladian mansion at the heart of Prior Park looming above them. It grew in both numbers and reputation in the two decades after the war with its old boys' association supporting the development and social connections of the school.

Faith, discipline and academic results were central to Prior Park. By the late 1950s, concern about a relative lack of success in A level

---

[47] B. Whelan, *The History of Belmont Abbey* (np. 1956); The Belmont Association: <https://www.cyberarc.co.uk/belmontabbey/index.php>, accessed 17 August 2023.

performance was being articulated by school leaders. The President, Brother Curran, noted in 1956 that, alongside religion and piety, parents also wanted study and sound scholarship and were unwilling to buy into the former without getting something of the latter. By the late 1950s, there were murmurings of a need for change in terms of thinking about co-education and a reduced reliance on boarding. The school continued its core traditions. The Christian Brothers took on all of the pastoral, and a great many of the teaching roles. Lay staff were called "visiting staff" and were restricted to a nine-to-five role. Rather late in the day compared to other schools, a cadet force was established in 1949. A major new science block, the expansion of music and drama, and the continued centrality of Catholic spirituality placed the college firmly within the public-school tradition.[48]

Not all schools made this kind of steady and stately progress in numbers, activity and reputation. The Oratory School, having transferred from its Birmingham home to Caversham in 1922 to allow for an expansion of its footprint, continued to have a difficult transition to sustainability. Numbers remained critically small—on the eve of the war there were barely 50 pupils at the school. The Birmingham Oratory, founders and trustees of the school from its foundation in 1859, had been unhappy with the running of the school and with its financial viability, and were unwilling to continue to bankroll operations in 1941. Lloyds Bank effectively foreclosed on a significant overdraft the school had run up, and the school home at Caversham was put up for sale. The school migrated temporarily to Downside, whilst the Oratorian Fathers (who wanted out of the operation) and a group of school governors (who wanted the school to continue) argued over whether the school should have a share of the considerable monies raised by the sale of Caversham to the BBC. After lengthy legal actions, the school was eventually able to use some of the sale monies to move the Oratory school to a new site at

---

[48] P. Cornwell, *Prior Park College: The Phoenix* (Tiverton: Halsgrove Press, 2005, revised with additional material by D. Clarke, 2018), pp. 89–93.

Figure 26: Prior Park Alumni, 1947.

Woodcote in Oxfordshire. There the school sought to rebuild numbers and financial stability.[49]

Securing the future of the school meant the effective abandonment of the old Newman ethos of keeping the school small. Small may have been beautiful, but it was not sustainable. By the early 1950s, there were financial problems again. The new head, Dom Adrian Morey, arriving in 1953, discovered the bank account was empty and paid a final demand from the gas board on his sister's cheque book! Policy changed fast, and numbers and facilities were expanded from the mid-1950s. After one inspection noted that the science facilities were "the second worst they had seen in their whole tour", significant investment in teaching facilities was sanctioned.[50] Numbers grew to 100 in 1954 and over 230 by 1962. Membership of the Headmasters' Conference was gained, and the future of the school secured, with a strong preparatory school near Bournemouth opened in 1946. Facilities, academic results and sporting prowess grew through the period on firm financial grounds.

In the early 1950s, as part of rebuilding all aspects of the school, a new school uniform was introduced alongside a revamp of the rugby team which, interestingly, the leadership saw as fundamental to the school's reputation. A new boarding house was built in 1957 and, for the first time, the governors of the school explicitly sought lay housemasters, ideally married ones, as the key to providing the right kind of pastoral and emotional support for pupils. It was a contrast to the traditional dominance of religious staff in that role across the sector and a harbinger of the changes to come. A new refectory, swimming pool, squash courts and tennis courts followed as the school celebrated its centenary in 1959. The Provost of the Birmingham Oratory (the founding fathers of the school) and the Archbishop of Birmingham presided. A new gymnasium/theatre and a cricket pavilion funded by the Old Oratorians in 1963 celebrated the "rebirth" of the school. As at Prior Park, the alumni associations were important in rebuilding the confidence and reputation of their schools.

---

[49] T. Tinkell, *Cardinal Newman's School: 150 Years of the Oratory School* (London: Third Millenium Publishing, 2009), pp. 87–95.

[50] Tinkell, *Newman's School*, p. 121, 124.

By the mid-1960s then, the future trajectory of so many of our schools seemed secure. Recruitment from a growing and increasingly affluent Catholic community had become more solid than ever. The schools of both the regulars and the seculars had strong reputations, and catered, often explicitly, for different sectors of the community. Academic performance was on a par with the public and grammar schools generally, and the religiosity of our schools, whilst far from identical in every school, was the foundation for the distinctive education that a Catholic public school might offer to those who wanted it. But there were undoubtedly some signs of change. There was a heavy dependence on new vocations to the religious life feeding through to the communities involved in running schools. Conflicting demands on the monastic communities that ran a number of the schools was also evident. There was pressure to increase lay teachers in some subject areas, as educational demands, inspections and competition increased. The reforms of Vatican II were beginning to be felt within both the Church Hierarchy and the community. Social attitudes towards religion and authority were under pressure from wider social, cultural and political change. Whether and how the traditions, structures and patterns of authority in the Catholic public school could adapt to the coming changes is the subject of the next chapter.

4

Reinventing the model? *c*.1975–2010

In May 1961, Queen Elizabeth II visited Beaumont College, near Windsor, on the occasion of its centenary celebrations. The school was buoyant, recruiting well and basking in the sunlit uplands of a confident English Catholic community. The Queen formally opened a new classroom block, funded by voluntary subscriptions from parents and a powerful alumni body, and planted a commemorative tree before taking tea on the lawn. It was the first visit by a reigning monarch in England to a Catholic school since the Reformation.

The school, Jesuit-run and somewhat socially exclusive, was in the orbit of Windsor and Eton and, since its foundation in 1861, had consciously sought to educate an English Catholic elite. Yet just four years later, the decision to close the school of 250 boys was announced. Amidst a climate of falling vocations, the Jesuit order had determined that amongst all the growing demands on their dwindling numbers of priests—running parishes and a range of schools, missionary activity and charitable work—maintaining a boarding school for privileged English boys was not a high priority. In the summer of 1965, just as the boarders were to head home for the summer, the decision to close was announced. It was a bombshell for the school and for the wider community of Catholic public schools. It created uproar and bad publicity for the next two years as its well-connected pupils, parents and old boys fought to get the decision changed. To no avail, and in the summer of 1967 it closed.[1]

The speed and public impact of the closure exemplified the breadth of challenges that were to face Catholic public schools in the last quarter of the twentieth century. These were years when the confidence, authority

---

[1] <http://www.beaumont-vision.co.uk/school.html>, accessed June 2022

Figure 27: Queen Elizabeth II visiting Beaumont College, 1961.

and financial sustainability of those schools was challenged by a range of external and internal pressures. These challenges were swift and often unanticipated. The early 1960s had actually been marked by the development of a range of new church and monastery buildings at many of the public schools. At Douai, an ambitious project to remodel the complex of monastic buildings was announced in 1963. Ampleforth (a new chapel in 1961), Downside (new monastic library and monastic accommodation), Cotton (major church renovations begun in 1962) and Ratcliffe (new chapel in 1961) also embarked on significant religious and school buildings in the early 1960s. Yet within just a few years the environment had shifted dramatically from that notional high-water mark of the "Church triumphant". What had changed?

New challenges

For the first time in their history, the demographics of expansion that had underpinned the growth of our schools for so many decades had altered. After many years of continued growth, the Catholic population stagnated and remained at around the 4 million mark between the late 1960s and into the new millennium. If one looks beneath that total figure of around 4 million, the underlying trends were clear. Annual baptisms and marriages fell by almost one half, from around 136,000 and 45,000 respectively in 1965 to 71,000 and 27,000 respectively some 20 years later. By 2005, whilst the overall estimate for the Catholic population remained at around 4 million, the numbers of baptisms (60,000) and marriages (11,500) had continued to fall.[2] That stagnation in religious populations affected the Church of England and non-conformist faiths as well as Roman Catholics. Once the "baby boom" generation had passed through the population, many schools began to face real challenges in recruitment. During this period as well, boarding seemed increasingly

---

[2] Faith Survey (University of Roehampton, 2018).

to fall out of fashion for all the public schools, Catholic or otherwise, creating yet more issues for school budgets.[3]

The resources available to both the regular and secular authorities in the Church were stretched by the continued, remarkable commitment of the Catholic authorities to ensuring a Catholic primary and secondary schooling was available to as many Catholic children as possible. The growth of Catholic secondaries and grammar schools continued to dominate the planning of the Church Hierarchy. This may well have meant a weakening of commitment, and certainly of financing, for the much smaller Catholic public-school sector, coming just at the time when individual school resources were most stretched. The swift closure of Beaumont, something of a showpiece for Jesuit education in the south, showed that the impact of changed circumstances hit schools run by the regular and secular authorities alike. For the important Benedictine schools, financial and resource commitments by the individual monastic communities that controlled the schools continued to grow, creating significant pressures.

These years also saw continuing, significant interventions by the state in the educational sector. As we saw in the last chapter, the public schools had succeeded in seeing off the perceived threat to their survival from government action and, by the mid-1970s, the key threat to survival was economic and social rather than political.[4] State intervention through a range of inspection regimes also made itself felt in these years. Public schools were regularly inspected from 1957 onwards by both government and the Headmasters' Conference (HMC). The Independent Schools Inspectorate (ISI) also acted in this role from the 1990s onwards. Their reports had the effect of establishing greater transparency over academic performance which, combined with the emergence of published league tables from the 1980s, highlighted both the competition between the Catholic public schools and other sectors, and the relative standings of the Catholic schools themselves which were not always where their

---

[3] D. Turner, *The Old Boys: The Decline and Rise of the Public School* (London: Yale University Press, 2016), pp. 207–8.

[4] J. Rae, *The Public School Revolution: Britain's Independent Schools 1964–1979* (London: Faber and Faber, 1981), pp. 163–76.

leaders thought they should be. The scrutiny of the market was to become ever more intensive and unforgiving.[5]

As a result of a Public Schools Commission in 1970, a large body of so-called direct grant schools, which fell somewhere between the independent and state sector, were required to choose to become either comprehensive state schools or private, independent ones. Around 100 such schools opted to become fully independent, swelling the ranks of the HMC, whilst almost all of the Catholic grammar schools opted instead for the comprehensive route. By the early 1980s, and the advent of a more benign, Conservative government, the security and standing of the public-school sector was assured.

The effects of these changes on the Catholic public schools were mixed. On the one hand, the decision by the Catholic authorities to support the shift of some of the old (and academically very successful) Catholic grammars into the more inclusive comprehensive sector might have had the effect of lessening competition with the public schools, given the strong academic focus and performance of many of these grammar schools. They certainly could have provided a significant challenge to the Catholic public schools, especially when coupled with the declining appetite of many parents for a full boarding education. Any such challenge was weakened by the decision to take the comprehensive route.

A shift away from boarding, beginning in the early 1970s, was reflected across all the public schools, Catholic or otherwise, and had major effects on school business models, especially when combined with the recession of those years. Rising costs (the 1974 Houghton Committee, for example, brought about a 30 per cent rise in salaries for teachers), and the growing numbers of lay teachers in the Catholic public schools, created a challenging economic environment. As Rae noted, fees at the major boarding schools in the wider sector grew by over 400 per cent between 1966 and 1980 as costs rose. In the single year 1974–5, the

---

[5] On the Independent Schools Inspectorate see F. Greene and D. Kynaston, *Engines of Privilege: Britain's Private School Problem* (London: Bloomsbury, 2019), p. 51; M. Peel, *The New Meritocracy: A History of UK Independent Schools, 1979–2015* (London: Elliot & Thompson, 2015), pp. 7–34.

average rise in HMC boarding school fees was almost 33 per cent.[6] As public school numbers began to fall right across the sector from around 510,000 in 1955 to just 403,000 in 1978 (a fall from 6.7 per cent to 4.5 per cent of the school population), the context within which Catholic public schools were operating was radically new.[7] Quite when this new era began to make itself felt is a moot point. Certainly by the mid-1970s our schools were regularly reporting economic challenges, with pressures on fees especially difficult at a time when recruitment was no longer as secure as it had been 15 or 20 years earlier. For one historian these changes impacted right across the wider Catholic school sector: "the year 1974 was in some respects a high-water mark for the Catholic education project in England and Wales ... after 1974, [there was] a decline in pupil numbers and a depressed economic environment".[8] These shifts impacted private and public education and relentlessly squeezed the finances of both the dioceses and the religious orders.

The trends set in place by the mid-1970s continued to impact on Catholic education generally, and the public schools in particular. The number of pupils in Catholic secondary schools, whether public or private, had fallen to around 525,000 in 1980 and 392,000 in 1996. Over the same period, there was a 39 per cent fall in the number of Catholic independent schools of all types, and a fall in the number of pupils in such schools from 79,000 to just over 50,000.[9] Quite clearly, there had been a sea-change in the demographic and economic environment as Catholic populations stagnated and the fashion for boarding fell. These challenges in the external environment within which the public schools operated were further compounded by very significant internal changes within Catholicism in the last quarter or so of the twentieth century.

---

[6] Rae, *Public School Revolution*, p. 163.
[7] Turner, *The Old Boys*, p. 207.
[8] B. O'Keeffe, "Reordering perspectives in Catholic schools", in M. Hornsby-Smith (ed.), *Catholics in England 1950–2000: Historical and Sociological Perspectives* (London: Cassell, 1999), pp. 242–65.
[9] O'Keeffe, "Reordering perspectives in Catholic schools", pp. 246–7.

Changes within Catholicism

When Pope John XXIII called the Second Vatican Council in early 1959, he sought to establish a forum for discussion and debate about the Church, which, he hoped, would be pastoral rather than dogmatic, an opening-out of the Church to both its religious and lay communities. The Church's bishops and priests, and the heads of the main religious orders—male, of course—female heads were not directly involved—helped to set out an agenda which was intended to guide the work of some 2,500 bishops assembled in Rome in 1962. A series of commissions debated particular issues—moral, social, liturgical, theological—which then fed back into the formal assemblies of the Council.[10]

Different factions were at play—a rigid, traditionalist Roman curia, conservative groups of bishops alarmed by the new liberalism of the 1960s, and more radical groups that sought an accommodation of the Church to the rapid pace of social and economic change. Change ended up being radical and far-reaching, transforming many aspects of the outward form of worship, such as the use of the vernacular in place of Latin, an increased role for the laity in Church affairs (albeit within reason ...), the nature of priestly training in the seminaries, and the reinvigoration of the missionary role of the Church.[11] What then was its impact on English Catholicism and, in particular, on its public schools?

Perhaps the most obvious, and controversial, changes were in the outward forms of worship which were transformed in all of our schools (and, of course, in the wider Catholic community) in a relatively short space of time. The use of English in the Mass became universal, and to all intents and purposes compulsory by the late 1960s in both parish and school. This led to the abandonment of the range of Latin plain chant and sung liturgy which had been ubiquitous for some 150 years and had been such an important part of public-school spirituality. Liturgical practice and language were also fundamentally changed. The "folk Mass", with

---

[10] A. Hastings, *A History of English Christianity 1920–2000* (London: SPCK, 2001), pp. 563–9.

[11] Hastings, *History of English Christianity*, pp. 519–31.

guitars and other instruments, and new "popular" English hymns became part of the school services.

Alongside the use of English, other, very visible changes transformed how the Mass was experienced. The priest now officiated facing the congregation, and the physical layout of churches had to be altered to accommodate the change. The practice of Communion, the climax of the Mass, was changed and communicants now received the host, the "body of Christ", in their hands rather than delivered by the priest onto the tongue. Consecrated wine, the "blood of Christ", also became part of Communion practice. Other innovations such as the greater involvement of the congregation in reading lessons, or the "kiss of peace" (often replaced by a rather cursory and embarrassed handshake), made their way into the Mass. The very heart of school spirituality, the communal sacrament of Mass, which was so central to the daily life of the Catholic public school, was significantly changed in the space of just five years or so.

Accompanying these visible changes in the form and function of worship was a reconsideration of the importance of the worship of Mary (especially through the practice of the rosary, which had been of such importance in the 1950s), and a steady relaxation of the rules surrounding practices such as fasting before Communion and abstaining from meat on Fridays.[12] These shifts in the nature of Church worship may seem small and trivial, but to schoolboys regularly attending Mass in the school chapel, or serving on the altar, and to their parents, brought up in an environment dominated by Latin, by the physical and psychic distance between the priest and his flock, by centuries-old prayers, rituals and patterns of activity, they represented some considerable shift. Remember too that tradition, ritual and patterns of authority had long been absolutely central to life in the Catholic public schools. The reasons for these alterations in patterns of worship and Catholic life were not always well articulated by the Hierarchy. For Duffy, for example, "the abandonment of fasting and abstinence was symptomatic of a more

---

[12] For a summary of key liturgical changes, see A. Hastings (ed.), *Modern Catholicism: Vatican II and after* (London: SPCK, 1991), pp. 68–73, 151–62, 240–5.

widespread drift... the disappearance of much that was distinctive in the symbolic lives of Catholics, the network of observances and prayers which shaped and sustained our lives".[13] The impact of change within the closed, almost claustrophobic, environment of the boarding school was perhaps even more marked than in the parish community.

These changes were also taking place at a time of major social, political and cultural transformations in English society as a whole. A liberalization of social attitudes, social legislation on, for example, homosexuality and abortion, wider political movements around colonialism (the Vietnam War, for example), and huge shifts around popular culture, especially for young people, placed significant stresses on what had traditionally been the "natural" authority of the Church and its leaders which, within the public schools, were a fundamental feature. The collision between a popular youth culture in the boarding schools, articulated through access to radio, TV, a new music press and the Virgin Record deliveries, and a sometimes autocratic teaching authority long accustomed to deference and automatic respect played out in all our schools. The continued growth of an educated middle class may also have placed pressures on their relationship with a seminary-trained, sometimes rather inward-looking priestly community, accustomed to a high degree of deference and automatic authority. That professional middle class was, of course, a key constituency served by many Catholic public schools. Not only were the attitudes of the young being altered, but their parents were also experiencing significant social and religious changes.

It is clearly an oversimplification to lump the impact of Vatican II alongside these wider changes and see it simply as a pattern of secularization. It would also be misleading to suggest that the "swinging sixties" sounded the death-knell of the traditional pieties, practices and priestly authority in the parish or the public school. It may well be that the traditional "lived religious history", to use Alana Harris' evocative phrase, lasted longer in the working-class community than elsewhere. But there is certainly much to suggest that, amongst the educated, and increasingly affluent, upper middle classes that were the bedrock for so many of the Catholic public schools, there was an increased questioning

---

[13] E. Duffy, *Faith of Our Fathers* (London: Continuum, 2004), p. 184.

of assumptions about the innate and immutable authority of the Church to govern all aspects of their lives, or of the lives of their children, destined (or not) to attend public school. As Brown suggests, "the lampooning of organised Christianity signalled less a growth of organised anti-religious secularism as a rejection of Church and parental controls".[14]

This distancing from authority was undoubtedly accelerated by the overwhelmingly hostile reaction to the papal encyclical *Humanae vitae* in 1968, which forbade "artificial" means of birth control and which seemed to wilfully ignore the realities of so many people's lives. Perhaps for the first time, many Catholics (and many of their priests as well) felt justified in ignoring a key ruling of the Church.[15]

A disappearing workforce?

We have argued that the maintenance of the character and ethos of the Catholic public school depended, first and foremost, on the support of the regular and secular authorities who had founded the schools and on a steady supply of their novices, lay brothers, priests and monks, as well as money, to support them. It was that large majority of religious staff that had traditionally provided the academic, pastoral and spiritual infrastructure of the schools. There was a critical need for a constant flow of new recruits to the priesthood or the religious orders, moving into teaching within the public schools, sometimes for just a few years as part of their wider training for Holy Orders, sometimes as long-term members

---

[14] Alana Harris' *Faith in the Family* provides a remarkable and evocative account of the stability and longevity of Catholic practice in English working-class communities during this period of dramatic religious change. It is suggested here that the impact of changes in this period may have been more rapid in the middle-class Catholic communities that were the market for many of the schools. See also C. Brown, "What was the Religious Crisis of the 1960s?", *Journal of Religious History* 34:4 (2010), p. 473.

[15] J. Marshall, "Catholic Family Life", in M. Hornsby-Smith (ed.), *Catholics in England 1950–2000: Historical and Sociological Perspectives* (London: Cassell, 1999), pp. 67–77.

of the teaching and management staff of the schools. Many of these staff were ex-pupils, and they were essentially unpaid, although clearly schools and their diocesan or monastic authorities were responsible for board and lodging, other expenses and provision for old age. For the major orders, such as the Benedictines, this "free" labour played a key part in the sustainability of the business model. For the diocesan schools, the pressures were perhaps even sharper, because of the pressures on diocesan authorities from all the other demands on their resources. Of course lay teachers had always played a role in staffing schools, but clerical teaching and pastoral support had been the norm throughout their history. It was precisely what made the Catholic public school distinctive and unique. That began to change from the mid-1960s onwards.

What drove the changes in the nature of Catholic public-school education was, first and foremost, a serious fall in vocations to the priesthood and the monastic life. The number of secular priests in England and Wales peaked at 7,887 in 1965; by 1982 numbers had fallen to 6,995, and by 2000 they had fallen again to 6,194. In 2010, there were some 5,453 secular priests working, a fall of some 30 per cent in around 40 years. The average age of those priests continued to rise inexorably as the number of ordinations fell. In 1962, there were 213 ordinations to the priesthood in England; by 2000 that figure was just 29.[16] It was a similar picture for the regulars. The number of English Benedictines, for example, the bedrock of so many public schools, fell from a peak of 727 in 1965 to 479 in 1996, and there were similar pressures in other orders such as the Jesuits.[17] Seminaries that were once full in the early 1960s were half-empty, mothballed or closed within a decade.

This collapse in vocations was felt just as strongly in the religious orders for women, with membership of religious orders diminishing and ageing. In 1989, the total number of new women entrants into the religious life was just 31, and this fall in recruits had significant effects

---

[16] Faith Survey (2018); Hastings, *Modern Catholicism*, pp. 630–48.

[17] D. A. Bellenger, "Religious Life for Men", in V. A. McClelland and M. Hodgetts (eds), *From Without the Flaminian Gate: 150 Years of Roman Catholicism in England and Wales, 1850–2000* (London: Darton, Longman & Todd, 1999), p. 150.

on independent education for girls. Many Catholic convent schools closed in the 1970s and 1980s as their female religious staff dwindled: "by the end of the 1980s the traditional convent school was an institution of the past".[18] Ironically the shift of the public schools to co-education was facilitated, in part at least, by the movement of girls from their rapidly disappearing convent schools into the once all-male bastions. The Catholic public schools were ruthless in plundering the best female pupils from the convent schools from the early 1980s.

Alongside this fall in new entrants to the religious community, the years immediately following Vatican II also saw the departure of a cohort of priests and monks, many of whom were increasingly at odds with the Church as it stumbled to deal with the conflicting pressures of tradition and liberalism. It was, noted Hastings, "a tragically high proportion of the intellectually ablest members of the younger generation" who departed.[19] In the writings of Anthony Kenny, John Cornwell or Peter Levi, all products of the Catholic public schools, and distinguished scholars and priests, we have vivid accounts of their individual journeys away from the Catholic Church.[20] At St Edmund's College, where internationally renowned theologian Fr Charles Davis taught, his departure in 1966 "was compared at the time to the secession of Newman from the Church of England in 1845".[21] Alongside these losses, the number of converts to Catholicism also fell, from an annual figure of around 10,000 in 1965 to 5,000 in 1970 and 3,000 in 1995, further accentuating what to the

---

[18] S. O'Brien, "Religious Life for Women", in V. A. McClelland and M. Hodgetts (eds), *From Without the Flaminian Gate: 150 Years of Roman Catholicism in England and Wales, 1850–2000* (London: Darton, Longman & Todd, 1999), p. 130.

[19] Hastings, *Modern Catholicism*, pp. 631–2.

[20] See for example J. Cornwell, *Seminary Boy* (London: Harper, 2007); A. Kenny, *A Path from Rome* (Oxford: Oxford University Press, 1986), pp. 23–42, 191–204; P. Levi, *The Flutes of Autumn* (London: Arena, 1985), pp. 35–40 (on Prior Park School); pp. 57–60 (on Beaumont).

[21] N. Schofield, *The History of St Edmund's College* (Ware: The Edmundian Association, 2013), p. 165.

optimist might appear a temporary halt in the inevitable growth of the Church, but to the pessimist suggested an almost terminal decline.[22]

The fall-off in vocations undoubtedly compromised the ability of both the regulars and seculars to staff their schools with religious who could both teach and provide the backbone for school spiritual and pastoral life. But changes in the economic environment noted earlier (inflation; pension and salary changes for teachers), coupled with social changes in the Catholic population meant that the status quo was not an option. By the mid-1970s, almost all the schools in our study had begun to contemplate very significant changes which would fundamentally alter their character and composition. The ability to develop long-term survival strategies was critical; not all schools had the leadership and governance skills to be able to do this. The model had to be reinvented if it was to survive.

Towards a new school model?

For all of our schools, the last two decades or so of the century were marked by unprecedented pressures for change. These changes fundamentally altered the nature of education in the Catholic public school and brought to an end many of the characteristic features and traditions that they had built up over many decades. Put bluntly, the successful schools became almost indistinguishable from mainstream public schools; they had to in order to survive. The Catholic public school was replaced by the public school providing a Catholic ethos for a rapidly changing set of parents and pupils. The *chapel*, for so long the very heart of the school and the locale for a collective spirituality and religious observance, was increasingly replaced by a *chaplaincy* service, run by a very limited number of clerics, offering some pastoral and religious advice and support to a much larger and more diverse pupil community. That process of change might be sudden or more gradual but, ultimately, the pattern of a school where priests, monks and lay brothers were at the core of the community, were numerically and spiritually dominant, and

---

[22] Data from the annual *Catholic Directory*, 1965-95.

occupied the key management roles of heads and housemasters, gave way to a lay teaching and management community, often, though not always, Catholic, and largely divorced from the religious orders and diocesan structures that had been so formative in the creation of their schools. For better or worse, it was a fundamentally new model.

The laicization of the teaching community was fundamental to this transformation which impacted on so many aspects of school experiences. If we look at individual schools, we can trace the steady replacement of religious by lay teachers within the school community. Of course lay teachers had always been a part of school teaching staff, but historically their numbers were relatively small in relation to the religious community. And, before the 1980s, very few occupied the key academic, pastoral or management roles in the schools. The priest or monk dominated. At Douai School, for example, the 1963 staff lists included just eight lay teachers alongside 42 teachers who were in orders. By 1973, the proportions had altered and there were now 12 lay teachers alongside 30 religious. By the late 1970s, the proportion of lay teachers had grown again to almost 50 per cent.[23] Taking another example, at Ratcliffe College the proportion of lay staff had historically been a little higher than many of the other schools because the Rosminians were a fairly small order. By the late 1960s, lay staff outnumbered religious staff for the first time (in 1968: 17 lay and 14 religious) and that trend was accentuated over the following two decades. What is perhaps most striking was the almost precipitate decline in the size of the religious teaching community at the school from twelve in 1974 to seven in 1982 and just four in 1990 and 1995. In what was for much of that time a fairly small school (it didn't reach 400 until the end of the 1980s), the increasing absence of a sizeable Rosminian community in lessons, sports, pastoral activity and religious celebrations would have been readily apparent to external observers and the pupils themselves.[24]

At Ampleforth, a large and thriving Benedictine community had always been at the heart of the school, but it was far from immune to this fundamental change in personnel. In 1971, lay staff outnumbered

---

[23] *Douai Magazine*, Autumn 1963; Autumn 1978.
[24] *The Ratcliffian*, annual issues: 1968, 1974, 1982, 1990, 1995.

religious staff for the first time (49 lay and 42 religious). By 1980, the figures were 51 lay and 32 religious and, through 1990 (62 lay and 24 religious) and 2005 (61 lay and 8 religious) the proportions of religious involved in the school significantly declined.[25] The Benedictine community at Downside, which had made up about one-third of the teaching community in the early 1970s, had fallen proportionately to around 12 per cent in 2002. Ten years later, there were just five religious involved in any teaching or administration at the school at what had been a flagship school for the Benedictines. In 2022, there were none, as the monastic community left Downside Abbey, relocating temporarily to Buckfast Abbey in Devon to consider their future.[26]

The pattern was similar elsewhere. The religious communities in the widest sense, embracing teachers and support staff—priests and monks, lay brothers who may have taught as well as performing a range of services from maintenance and caring for the grounds, to sacristan roles looking after the church—were disappearing at a sometimes precipitate rate. They were obviously much less visible in the fabric of everyday school life and, as they became less visible and inevitably played a less active part in the work of the school, so the character of the school altered. The absence of younger novitiates in particular, who would traditionally work in the boarding schools during their period of training, meant that there were fewer young religious staff engaged in the range of sporting and other activities within the school than was the case prior to the late 1960s. The cycle of new teachers who came to the schools for a few years before moving on to further training had meant a constant rejuvenation within the religious staff. That "virtuous circle" of ex-pupils leaving school for the seminary, returning to the school during training and, once ordained, returning again as teachers to inspire new vocations, had gone.

The gap between a shrinking and ageing religious community in many schools and a young, increasingly self-confident, articulate and diverse pupil population was to become increasingly stark. Abbot Madden of

---

[25] *Ampleforth Journal* LXXXI (1971); LXXXV (1980); CXV (1990).
[26] *The Raven* 285 (2002–3). On the monastic community leaving Downside see: <https://www.thetablet.co.uk/news/14915/fears-over-future-of-abbey-church-at-downside>, accessed 22 August 2023.

Ampleforth articulated the issue of this declining religious community in the school concisely, when he wrote in 2005 that "it is difficult to see how we can be a Benedictine school if monks are not visible within the life of the school on a day-to-day basis".[27]

For all of our schools this was a central dilemma from the late 1970s. How were schools to maintain the daily presence of the Catholic religion in all aspects of a holistic Catholic education, which had been so central to the establishment of these schools, at a time when the religious presence within the schools was ageing and disappearing? Strategically it was an enormous issue for both the schools and the religious communities, secular or regular, that were their bedrock. There was a real danger that what marked schools out from their peers, namely the constant, lived Catholic spirituality from the religious community in the school, might disappear. At Downside too, the issues facing the religious community servicing the school were stark. For the Abbot, commenting in 2002, when there were some 11 or 12 members of the community working at the school, "one of the great distinguishing marks of a Benedictine school is the stability of the monastic community". A few years later, he was to note that "the greatest threat to Downside's future is the serious shortage of vocations to the monastery".[28]

The declining numbers of religious within all of our schools posed immediate financial issues of paying for well-qualified teaching staff at a time when boarding education was falling out of favour, and inflation and economic downturns threatened having to raise fees to uncompetitive levels. These pressures coincided with a period of rapidly growing competition, both within the Catholic independent sector and, more especially, between them and the wider public-school sector. If the Catholic public schools no longer had the significant and visible religious presence that had characterized them for so many decades, why would parents send their children there rather than to other public schools in the wider sector, who might have a much stronger academic performance, and who sat much higher in the increasingly ubiquitous school league tables?

---

[27] *Ampleforth Journal* 110 (2005).

[28] *The Raven* 283 (2002); 288 (2005).

A number of options to deal with this looming crisis presented themselves at different times in different schools. The first was to begin to accept larger numbers of day pupils. These had always been a part of some school intakes, albeit in fairly small numbers. Certainly St Edmund's was amongst the earliest schools to strategically plan for substantial numbers of day pupils, and began to take sizeable numbers of day boys as early as the mid-1950s. By the mid-1960s, almost 25 per cent of boys at St Edmund's were day pupils and one report noted complaints that "the College is becoming more of a grammar school than a smaller public school, and yet public-school fees are being charged".[29]

At many of our schools, it was the economic difficulties of the 1970s that prompted this change. The President of Ratcliffe announced a plan to accept just three day boys for entry in 1975, although that number was gradually increased through the decade, and weekly boarding was available from the early 1980s.[30] For most of our schools, the decision to increase the numbers of day pupils was financially driven. Proximity to significant urban centres was clearly important in facilitating the growth in numbers of day pupils. For schools such as Ratcliffe (Leicester/ Nottingham), the Oratory (Reading) and St Edmund's (Hertfordshire) there were geographical advantages; for others in more isolated rural environments such as Ampleforth, Stonyhurst and Cotton, the option of shifting to significant increases in day pupils was rather more challenging.

Did an increase in day boys change the character of the schools? It is interesting that the nature and strengths of many schools, at least as articulated by their leaders over many years, had traditionally resided in the fact that they were boarding schools. The academic and spiritual development of the boys benefited, it was argued, from the constant rhythms of boarding school life for some two-thirds of the year. The provision of study time, a full curriculum, a wide range of sporting and cultural opportunities and, most especially, the constant exposure to the spiritual aspects of the Catholic life, were viewed as being integral to the boarding-school experience. Even as the wider religious environment began to alter from the early 1970s, and the amount of compulsory

---

[29] Schofield, *St Edmund's College*, p. 165.
[30] *The Ratcliffian* 1975.

religious attendance began to tail off, that boarding environment was celebrated by the school heads. The building of cohesion and community through the house, the school and the chapel was arguably much easier when all the boys were boarders and, for those having gone through the prep school system, had been boarding from the age of eight or nine.

It is striking, however, how quickly the supposed advantages of boarding-only were conveniently forgotten as economic realities began to bite. By the early 1980s, the numbers of day boys began to grow in almost all of our schools—the Oratory, Mount St Mary's, Ratcliffe, Belmont Abbey—but especially in those that catered for middle-class, professional families, keen on the academic side of school cultures, but perhaps less willing or able to embark on the cost of a boarding-school option. A number of other schools, Ampleforth, Downside and Stonyhurst for example, expanded day-boy numbers much more slowly, arguably because their reputations in the Catholic community kept applicant lists fairly buoyant. Life at the top, for the moment, meant boarding!

Something of a bigger sea change was the decision of schools to become co-educational. Again this was driven in large part by financial expediency, and in lesser part, and usually in retrospect, by a wish to impart a different ethos to the suddenly discovered disadvantages of the all-male school. The financial incentives were considerable, in part because, as we noted earlier, the 1970s had seen something of a collapse in Catholic convent boarding education for girls because of the precipitate decline in female religious congregations, and their shift into wider missionary work. And, of course, girls automatically enhanced academic and therefore league table performance!

The speed with which schools chose to become co-educational varied. For some schools, Ampleforth, Downside and Stonyhurst for example, applicant lists remained strong until the late 1990s and the financial imperative was perhaps less than elsewhere. St Edmund's (girls accepted in 1974), Ratcliffe (1978), Mount St Mary's (1979) and the relatively newly established Princethorpe College in Warwickshire (1978) were amongst the innovators but, even so, were probably a decade behind the wider public-school sector in making the change. At Mount St Mary's, the first girls arrived as day pupils throughout the different years and, we are told, "exercised a decidedly civilizing influence on the boys".[31] Even amongst the innovators, the process of becoming co-educational throughout the school took both time and very significant capital investment. New or repurposed accommodation was required, together with significant increases in female staff. Married lay staff became an increasingly attractive option as part of the school community, bringing with them changes in school culture. The establishment of boarding facilities for newly arrived girls was a challenge in the early years, but the move to a fully co-educational sector, whilst coming later than the mainstream public schools, was successful. It made finances more sustainable, broadened the social spectrum of schools and, most importantly, as league tables developed, undoubtedly improved the overall academic performance of schools. The innovators were joined by others—Cotton in 1983, Douai in 1997, Ampleforth (sixth form in 1999; across the school in 2004), and Stonyhurst (sixth form in 1989; across the school in 1997).

At Downside, the decision to become co-educational came quite late. The numbers of pupils had fallen by the end of the century to around 350 from previous highs of 500 to 550 in the late 1960s. As Fr Antony Sutch noted in 2003, "we thought Catholic parents would just go on sending their children here as they always had. But they leaked away, our reputation slumped and we were disappearing downhill."[32] Whilst there had always been small numbers of day girls at the school (usually the daughters of lay masters), the decision to go fully co-educational was finally made in 2005. It provided enhanced recruitment and raised academic standards. It was seen by the authorities as enhancing the position of the school: "Catholic families that have transferred to Marlborough and Radley, Charterhouse or Sherborne are again looking seriously at Downside." Predictably, some traditionalists expressed concern—a fall in the standard of school rugby seemed a particularly common gripe and the provision of rugby bursaries for girls was discussed—but the arrival of girls, caused "hardly a ripple

---

[31] M. Beattie, *Portrait of our College: Mount St Mary and Barlborough Hall, 1842–2017* (London: Society of Jesus, 2017), pp. 123–4.

[32] Quoted in M. Peel, *The New Meritocracy: A History of UK Independent Schools, 1979–2015* (London: Elliot & Thompson, 2015), p. 40.

to the smooth flow of our social and academic life" according to one report.[33]

Alongside the growth of day pupils and co-education, a third set of changes took place relating to governance and leadership. Historically, the Catholic public school was governed by the secular or regular authorities, led by a religious head, managed by religious staff, and taught to a significant degree by the religious themselves. That created the kind of cohesive, almost self-contained, perhaps self-satisfied, Catholic cocoon within which particular moral and religious values were imbibed alongside academic, sporting and cultural activities. As the numbers of priests and monks declined, and the number of lay staff grew, that model came under increasing strain. In the last two decades or so of the century, the importance of clear, transparent governance and leadership within schools of all kinds became apparent.

For state schools, the use of public money brought with it a range of responsibilities and requirements, together with an increasingly powerful set of inspection regimes. In the independent sector, the requirements were less onerous, although issues over admissions, financial sustainability and authority were no less significant. Within the Catholic public schools, lines of authority and control were sometimes dangerously opaque, with the role of the diocese and bishop (in the case of the secular schools) and the headmaster, abbot or provincial (in the case of the regulars) being central but not always transparent.

Taking the Benedictine schools as an example, the abbot of individual and independent monasteries such as Belmont, Downside, Ampleforth or Worth had responsibilities towards both their school and monastery, the wellbeing of staff and monastic members and the wellbeing of the pupils. Lines of responsibility between the abbot (as head of the monastery), the school head (always until recently a monk appointed by the abbot) and the teaching staff were much less clear than would be the case in a state school. If a member of the monastic teaching staff transgresses against a pupil, the abbot must act both in the interests of the transgressed (the pupil) and the transgressor (the staff member), who might be a member

---

[33] *The Raven* 285 (2003–4); 286 (2005).

of the monastic community for whom the abbot takes responsibility. That potential conflict of interests could, and did, create significant difficulties.

Alongside increased state interest in school governance from the 1980s, the role of the Headmasters' Conference (HMC) which, in 1993, decided to develop an inspection regime of its own, also put pressure on schools to have clearer lines of authority and decision-making, as did the growth of regulations governing the management of charities.[34] The increasing requirements for clear and robust arrangements for the safeguarding of children was also very important and, as we will see in the next chapter, was to almost fatally undermine the position and standing of some schools. Laicization, a necessity because of the decline in priests and monks, became an important engine for change as the Catholic public schools entered ever-more challenging and competitive times.

Within the space of some 20 years then, almost all of our schools, whether by strategic design or adventitiously, had appointed lay members to key roles such as housemaster or headmaster, and developed more transparent systems of governance with their boards or councils, which had a mix of lay and religious representation, and which provided less opaque lines of authority for the management of school affairs. In some ways, the appointment of a lay head seemed the most symbolic of acts, but the consequent changes were far more deep-seated than that. At St Edmund's, often something of an innovator, lay teachers had been important for many years, and lay housemasters were important from the late 1960s. In 1984, a married layman was appointed as head. Bishop Butler, a former headmaster of Downside, told parents at the time that "it was soon very clear to the governors that it would not be possible to replace Fr Garvey [the previous head of St Edmund's] by another priest: no suitably qualified priest was available; indeed, such is the shortage of priests in the Westminster diocese, that it seems likely that it will not be possible in the foreseeable future to spare a priest for this post".[35]

At Stonyhurst, another innovator, the development of a strategic charitable fund in the early 1970s, which was managed with significant lay involvement, was something of a trojan horse: "it fitted in with the

---

[34] Greene and Kynaston, *Engines of Privilege*, p. 112.
[35] Schofield, *St Edmund's College*, p. 190.

increasing trend towards lay management in the College generally".[36] By the mid-1980s, all the housemasters were lay, as were most of the academic heads of department. The pressure to appoint a lay head came in part from the growing shortage of priests to fill that role but was also in line with the view from Vatican II that the laity should be allowed to play a greater role in religious affairs. The first lay head, Giles Mercer, a married man and a parent, was appointed in 1985. At Mount St Mary's, the process of greater lay governance followed a similar pattern. A board of governors, established in the mid-1970s with significant lay involvement and expertise, had paved the way for greater lay involvement in management roles. As Beattie noted, the mid-1980s saw a rapidly diminishing Jesuit community at the Mount: "from a relatively stable community of twenty-six the numbers were down to three or four" and greater lay management was a necessity. In 1991, the first lay headmaster was appointed.[37]

At Ratcliffe, issues of declining recruitment to the Rosminian order had been raised by school presidents on a number of occasions in the 1960s and early 1970s. The governing body of the school, the majority of whose members were religious, was able to manage recruitment issues through increasing numbers of day pupils and co-education, but by the early 1980s was continuing to warn about the consequences of falling vocations. In 1984, the Father Provincial of the Rosminian order wrote to parents to say that insufficient vocations meant the school management and governance would increasingly be under lay control. He reassured parents that "what has been built will not be abandoned" and that the Rosminians would remain the trustees and legal owners of the school.[38] The process of appointing lay staff to key management roles took some time though, and it was not until 1996 that the first lay head was appointed.

Similar processes, albeit at different speeds, took place elsewhere. At Ampleforth, it was not until 1988 that the first lay housemaster (there

---

[36] T. E. Muir, *Stonyhurst College 1593–1993* (Cirencester: St Omers Press, revised edition, 2006), p. 169.

[37] Beattie, *Mount St Mary*, pp. 128–9.

[38] *The Ratcliffian* 1984.

were ten houses at the time) was appointed. By 2014, all the housemasters and mistresses were lay, and a first lay head was in place.[39] At Cotton, it was not until the new Archbishop of Birmingham, Couve de Merville, decided in 1982 that the diocese could no longer maintain a large religious presence at the school, that diocesan ownership was ended, and a majority lay board of trustees set up to run the school. In September 1982, a new lay head joined the school with just a single priest in place as a chaplain.[40] At Downside, as with co-education, the process seemed less than fleet of foot. Lay housemasters remained in a minority until the late 1990s, and it was not until a new governance deed was drawn up in 2013 that the first lay head of the school was appointed.

For many schools, change was sometimes a slow process, often piecemeal rather than strategic, and underpinned by tensions between tradition (boarding, all-male, religious governance and management) and modernity (day pupils, co-education, transparent governance). In some instances, schools did not have the luxury of a gradual transition to a new order but had to make very rapid decisions. Prior Park, run by the Christian Brothers from 1924, faced a crisis when, in March 1980, they announced they would be leaving the college. Despite a search for a new order to take over their role, none could be found, and the college faced closure. An Action Committee was established with influential alumni playing a major role. Deciding that here was an opportunity to build a new structure and ethos for the college whilst retaining "the spirit of the place", a lay headmaster was appointed who set in train rapid changes. Married lay staff were appointed to key house roles, numbers of lay staff were significantly increased, non-Catholic numbers grew and, in 1983, the college went co-educational. Sets of changes that had often taken a couple of decades to permeate many of our schools were adopted within the space of just a couple of years at Prior Park. The college was able to celebrate 150 years since its founding by Bishop Peter Baines,

---

[39] P. Galliver, *Ampleforth College: The Emergence of Ampleforth College as the 'Catholic Eton'* (Leominster: Gracewing, 2019), p. xiv.

[40] F. Roberts (with N. Henshaw), *A History of Sedgley Park and Cotton College* (Privately published, 1985), pp. 256–61.

as pupil numbers recovered, and the blending of new changes and the old Catholic ethos began. Change was swift and ultimately successful.[41]

Closures

The magnitude of change in the closing decades of the century is clear. Declining vocations, an ageing population of existing priests and monks, economic pressures, competition from the rest of the independent sector, let alone the shifts in lay Catholic attitudes following Vatican II, all presaged the need for a new model. Not all schools were able to deal with these changes and, perhaps, closures were inevitable. We have already noted how the female convent schools were especially hard hit in these years. It was a fortunate coincidence that their collapse came just as traditional boys' boarding schools shifted into co-education and sought to grow numbers and poach as many girls as possible from the crisis-struck convent school sector.

For some schools change was swift, unanticipated and terminal. Beaumont, as we have seen, closed in 1967, ironically at a time when numbers were fairly buoyant, and the Jesuit community at the school strong. The decision was certainly informed by concerns over falling numbers of vocations, though the major falls in Jesuit numbers did not come until the late 1970s. It is more than likely that the closure was a consequence of a wider repositioning of the work of the Jesuits consequent on some of the outcomes of Vatican II. The Council, notes McClelland, "forced many orders and congregations to reconsider employing large numbers of their subjects in teaching the children of wealthy and privileged parents".[42] Given the existence of the other two Jesuit public schools, Stonyhurst and Mount St Mary's, the order may well have felt able to close Beaumont without fatally undermining parts of the Jesuit educational mission.

---

[41] P. Cornwell, *Prior Park College: The Phoenix* (Tiverton: Halsgrove Press, 2005, revised with additional material by D. Clarke, 2018), pp. 119–22.

[42] V. A. McClelland, "Great Britain and Ireland", in A. Hastings (ed.), *Modern Catholicism: Vatican II and after* (London: SPCK, 1991), p. 370.

It was not just the Jesuits who had to grapple with closures. That also was the case for Franciscan interest in Catholic boarding education. The Friars Minor, always a small order in England, had founded a seminary and school at Buckingham which had developed into a medium-sized boarding school, St Bernardine's College. A preparatory school at nearby Stony Stratford, almost entirely staffed by Franciscan priests and brothers, was established as late as the early 1960s, primarily to feed boys into the senior college. Yet within just a few years the project collapsed, as the Franciscans refocused their work on wider missionary activity rather than private education. St Bernardine's closed in 1969, and the prep school closed a few years later, having survived for only ten years.[43] Some of the Franciscans who staffed the schools moved to a range of parochial and missionary roles elsewhere. Others simply left the order. The old college buildings were sold off, becoming the nucleus for the new, independent, University of Buckingham.

These closures were replicated elsewhere. Cotton College, left pretty much to its own devices by the decision of the Birmingham diocese to remove support in 1982, lasted just five more years. Under pressure from the decline in "church boys" that had long been the mainstay of the school a new, largely lay, board instituted a flurry of changes. Remodelled buildings to improve boarding accommodation, the admission of girls in 1983, and efforts to attract day pupils (always a challenge in this remote part of north Staffordshire) were not enough, and Cotton closed in 1987. The decision was swift and unexpected. The Archbishop of Birmingham, Couve de Merville (an old boy of Downside School), celebrated Association Day (for alumni) at the college and just one month later announced the closure. The *Catholic Herald* underlined the parallels with the Beaumont closure that opened our chapter, noting that "the parents are naturally up in arms, as were those with boys at Beaumont, who felt unfairly treated when that other distinguished, if much newer school, was disposed of so precipitately only just after a major appeal".[44]

Cotton, together with colleges at Ushaw (Co. Durham) and Upholland (Lancashire), were for parts of their history both school and seminary.

---

[43] Hastings, *History of English Christianity*, pp. 633–4.
[44] *Catholic Herald*, 17 April 1987.

They therefore accommodated both "church" students, intending to follow a vocation, and lay students. The fall in vocations and the withdrawal of "church" students was undoubtedly a factor in the closure of Cotton. The seminary schools of Upholland and Ushaw also struggled, as applicants for the priesthood fell steeply. At Upholland, a short-lived upsurge in vocations in the early 1960s was replaced by significant challenges at the end of the decade. Reforms to seminary training as part of Vatican II called into question the very closed and sometimes introverted pattern of training traditionally practised in often remote, rural seminaries such as Upholland. It was argued by some that such an environment was no longer appropriate for the training of priests destined to work in much more fluid and engaged urban and suburban settings. Upholland had both a junior and senior seminary, and it was the high cost of educating junior students that lead to closure. In 1974, for example, none of the 33 junior seminarians who had been through the college at significant expense to the diocese had become priests. The last senior students left in 1975, and the land and buildings were sold by the diocese.[45] The seminary functions were transferred to Ushaw, which itself ultimately closed in 2011 despite proposals in 2002 to merge with the major remaining seminary at Oscott. Oscott continues to function as an important seminary.

There were two further closures of schools in the 1990s—the Benedictine schools at Belmont Abbey in 1994 and Douai in 1999. Belmont Abbey had grown to a medium-sized school with around 270 boarders and 50 day pupils in the mid-1970s, when it held its fiftieth anniversary. It had invested heavily in new boarding facilities from the mid-1960s, but despite going co-educational in the mid-1970s and taking day pupils from the early 1970s, it was unable to arrest a decline in numbers from its peak of around 320 in the late 1970s to just 200 in 1990. When it closed in 1994, boarding numbers had fallen to just 82

---

[45] D. Atherton and M. Peyton, *St Joseph's College, Upholland: One of the glories of Catholicism in England. Its rise and fall.* Unpublished (2013), <https://www.academia.edu/48825759/St_Joseph_s_College_Upholland_One_of_the_glories_of_Catholicism_in_England_Its_rise_and_fall_Revised_and_Updated>, accessed on 17 January 2023.

with significant losses being incurred by the school and monastery. In part, this was due to changes in the appetite for boarding we saw for so many schools at this time and, given its rural location, the difficulties of attracting large numbers of day pupils. At the same time, the role of the school in encouraging new vocations had rapidly diminished. Even at its peak, vocations had dried up—by the mid-1970s, pupil numbers had quadrupled in some 20 years, but vocations had more than halved.[46] For the Abbot of Ampleforth, asked to comment on the closure, the remedy was obvious: "if all Catholic parents used Catholic schools, there would be no problem!"[47] Would that it were that simple.

The closure of Douai school, founded in 1903, and with a distinguished history, followed a similar path. It had always been a relatively small school, closely connected to the Benedictine Abbey which had been rebuilt in 1963. Numbers in the early 1970s were about 260, and both day boys and girls were admitted during the 1990s to try to secure more sustainable growth. A rural location made major growth in day numbers difficult, and by the mid-1990s, the school was incurring significant annual losses. A lay head was appointed in 1996 to work with the board to grow numbers. The problem of achieving sustainable growth could not be resolved and the monastic community took matters into its own hands. A review suggested the school needed at least £1.5m to rebuild its finances, a sum which the monastic community decided it could not, or would not, provide. That decision in itself was an interesting one which reflected, in part at least, the long-standing issue of balancing the tensions between the contemplative, missionary and educational roles within monastic communities, previously highlighted. The community decided to legally separate the Abbey and school and to close the latter, deciding, in effect, to cease their educational role in favour of other, perhaps more contemplative, forms of activity. Pressure from parents and alumni led to the establishment of a new, lay, board, and a rescue plan was announced with much fanfare. Within a matter of months, however, the plan had

---

[46] Belmont Association. See <https://www.cyberarc.co.uk/belmontabbey/>, accessed 22 August 2023, for archived information on the school.

[47] *Daily Telegraph*, 2 March 1994.

collapsed, and the school closed in 1999.[48] What the closure served to emphasize was just how important the nexus between Abbey and school was in generating reputation and resources, especially financial ones, from monastery to school. Breaking that link was fraught with risk.

Events at both Belmont and Douai in the 1990s underline some of the issues facing Benedictine schools in particular. Alongside the wider pressures that all schools faced, the issue of the nature of the Benedictine vocation continued to be felt. As in previous decades, the Benedictine communities, all of whom were independent and largely self-governing, were not always of one view as to their role. The contemplative monastic life in the Abbey did not always fit with a bustling, busy, business-focused life running a school. Decisions over allocating resources were also more sharply felt in these decades. As the economic climate shifted and the financial sustainability of their schools increasingly required resources to be shifted from monastery to school, a number of communities began to question the rationale of staffing and financing school structures. For the communities at Belmont and Douai the time had come to separate monastery and school and to leave the latter to its own devices.

Expand to survive?

From the late 1980s, Turner, reviewing the public-school sector as a whole, pointed to what he termed a "facilities arms race" as public schools faced ever greater demands from parents for high performance and facilities to match the high fees that they were charging.[49] The description is an apt one. Those Catholic public schools that were able to adapt sufficiently to the financial, social and religious pressures of the 1970s and 1980s in reasonable shape, found themselves part of a wide and very competitive network of schools keen to recruit from the growing professional middle classes. Facilities were now a central part of a very challenging market which extended well beyond the traditional, loyal Catholic sector that our schools had relied on.

---

[48] *Douai School Magazine,* 1998.
[49] Turner, *The Old Boys*, p. 222.

At the millennium, the Catholic public school had changed irrevocably from its heyday in the late 1950s. The priest, monk or lay brother had virtually disappeared from the school. Authority, governance and management was lay, not religious. A chaplaincy service and a Catholic ethos remained part of schools, and prospectuses and websites certainly continued to articulate their Catholic origins and history. But the constant presence of priest and monk, the frequent religious ritual and observance, the regular communal celebration of the liturgy was no longer there. That is not to say that the schools are less Catholic than they were. It is impossible to know that and, happily, that can't be measured. But the schools are now much bigger, and more religiously diverse. They are co-educational, they are multi-national, and they have, in almost all cases, a higher proportion of day than boarding pupils. The context is different, the experience is different and the place of the schools within the wider public-school sector is different.

The natural competitor now is not the other Catholic public schools, rather it is the public-school sector, day or boarding, as a whole. That competition has shaped the schools into the new millennium. This is not the place to explore in any detail the physical growth, character and financial sustainability of what are rapidly changing enterprises. It is difficult in any case for the historian to have sufficient perspective and distance when dealing with what are near-contemporary institutions. But it is possible to pick up a number of generic features across the sector. What do they look like now?

First and foremost, almost all of the schools have grown very fast since the turn of the century. To take a few examples: Mount St Mary's had over 600 on the main and prep school roll in 2017; Ratcliffe has grown from around 550 in 2000 to 838 in 2018; Stonyhurst had over 800 on the roll in 2018, up from 450 in 2005; St Edmund's College has grown from around 500 in the mid-1990s to 850 in 2019. Princethorpe, which abandoned boarding altogether in 2004, has now grown to a school of almost 900 pupils. The growth in school numbers has been driven primarily by growth in day pupils and international boarders. For most schools, the percentage of boarders has rarely been above 25 per cent and many of those boarders are international students. The international student market accounts for some 15 to 20 per cent of the pupil intake in many of our schools, with southeast Asia and China of increasing importance. There has been growth in weekly boarding, but for most schools it is the day pupil market that has been most significant.[50]

There are exceptions. Two of the traditionally "elite" schools—Ampleforth and Downside—have taken a somewhat different route. Both have remained relatively small in comparison with both their fellow Catholic schools, and the wider public-school sector. At around 500 in the mid-1990s, Ampleforth has grown only marginally to 560 in 2018. Boarding remains central to the school with around 80 per cent being boarders; the monastic community remains but now plays a much-reduced role in school affairs and governance. Downside remains the smallest of the schools with some 350 pupils in 2018 of which over 80 per cent were boarding. There is now no monastic community and no direct Benedictine involvement in the school. The trajectories of these two schools perhaps reflect a conscious separation from the rest of the sector, preferring to sit themselves alongside some of the traditional, expensive elite public schools where boarding remains significant, rather than competing as successful mixed day/boarding schools as the remainder of the sector has. Such a model may well succeed but carries obvious financial risks.

All of the schools have been physically transformed over the last two decades in the search for a competitive advantage. School websites and marketing literature, always to be treated with care, nonetheless serve to illustrate just how massive the capital investment in building stock has been. Academic buildings such as new science blocks, IT suites and language lab facilities have appeared across the piece. The prospectuses and websites of the schools spell out the sporting and cultural offer—all-weather pitches, floodlit tennis and netball courts, synthetic running tracks, indoor pools and fitness suites, new theatre and performing arts facilities, large and lavish sixth-form centres, ensuite boarding accommodation. Some schools have also built new prep schools on site.

Academic facilities and high-quality teaching staff all require major investment, especially as all of the schools are now ranked in national

---

[50] Data on recent pupil numbers from the annual reports of the Independent Schools Inspectorate.

league tables, reflecting performance at GCSE and A level and a range of "value-added" metrics. The strength, or otherwise, of a Catholic ethos, the presence, or otherwise, of a significant religious community on site, the frequency, or otherwise, of communal worship or individual meditation may be relevant and flagged up but is difficult to evaluate.

These schools are now ranked alongside all others in the tables and stand or fall accordingly. Without putting too much faith (perhaps not the most judicious word to use . . .) in the variety of league table measures available to the prospective parent (and all schools are in any case adept at picking the "right" table to focus on), it would be fair to say that amongst its public school peers the Catholic public school performs perfectly adequately, but only very rarely do any of the schools feature consistently in the top quartile of the most important and widely-read tables.

The life of pupils in our schools around the millennium was certainly different from the experiences of 30 years previously. In some ways, the academic pressures are greater now than was the case. With greater transparency comes greater scrutiny, and both pupils and teachers face the pressure of achieving the best results. Access to higher education is a necessity, not a luxury, for all our schools, and this is reflected in the busy timetables, expectations about homework, and the place of extra-curricular activities for both day and boarding pupils. The days of schools being able to celebrate Oxbridge success as the sole pinnacle of their achievement have long gone. And Oxbridge success itself is much more difficult. Competition from a strong state sector and pressures for a more diverse intake to Oxbridge in particular have altered the rules of the game. The abandonment of seventh-term examinations to Oxbridge in the mid-1980s, a system which favoured public schools who could provide the extra tuition needed to take entrance examinations after A Levels, has meant the days of say Ampleforth, Downside or Stonyhurst each sending 20 or so pupils a year to Oxbridge have long gone.

School spirituality is different and is no longer all-pervasive. The visible signs of that spirituality have weakened in most schools, with the communal celebration of Catholic liturgy and spirituality being much more challenging as numbers grow and the clerical presence falls. Interestingly, the "facilities race" has not included any expansion plans for church or chapel. It is much more difficult to comment on the less visible aspects of personal faith. Daily compulsory Mass has long gone; weekly services, perhaps for the house rather than the whole school, may form part of the calendar. High Mass on Sundays, once the focal point of school worship, features much more rarely, in part because of the substantial growth in day pupils. Where boarders remain a clear majority—Ampleforth and Downside for example—a communal High Mass on Sundays is more common. The visit of the local bishop to administer the sacrament of Confirmation is a very much rarer occasion. This spirituality has changed, especially as the religious composition of the pupils is now so much more varied, with significant numbers of non-Catholic pupils within the mix.

Other aspects of what might be regarded as traditionally Catholic practice have sometimes fared rather better. The charitable work of school pupils has remained strong, with a range of fundraising initiatives supporting charitable work, echoing the long-established tradition in many schools of working in deprived parts of the country with boys' clubs and summer camps. All the schools have their own, often long-established charitable links, both national and international, which provide a focus for pupil activity. For many schools, the pilgrimage was an important part of school life. Visits to Rome and an audience with the pope featured, for example, at St Edmund's (1993) and Stonyhurst (2006), and annual pilgrimages to Lourdes remain an almost universal part of school life as do a range of charitable activities in deprived parts of the country.

Mirroring to some extent the "cult of athleticism", which was so important to the public schools in the early decades of the twentieth century, it is in the area of sporting facilities that the greatest changes have been evident. School facilities today bear no relation to those of perhaps 20 or 30 years ago. At Mount St Mary's, the school historian notes that the arrival of girls into the school not only led to proper ballroom dancing lessons, but also to the establishment of an all-weather hockey pitch for the newly arrived girls. Uniquely, the Mount also took the rather unusual step of allowing all its playing fields to be dug up in 1994–5 to extract a quantity of valuable open cast coal. The money helped to provide new, flood-free pitches for a wider range of sports and a new Health and

Sports Club. Clearly, location on a coalfield, not necessarily something the marketing literature might celebrate, brought particular benefits.[51]

As schools expanded their numbers, the pressure for more attractive sporting facilities grew. At almost all of our schools, new floodlit all-weather pitches, tennis courts, all-weather athletics tracks and revamped swimming facilities have emerged in the new millennium and dominate the marketing offer. The financial stability that larger pupil numbers have brought has meant constantly enhanced facilities for a range of sports from fencing and tennis to rowing and equestrianism. It is hardly surprising to see the dominance of public-school-educated sports men and women in national teams, given the quality of facilities and coaching on offer. Sporting success of various kinds—rugby sevens trophies, international caps, international cricket and rugby—sit alongside academic league tables in the glossy websites reflecting the continued search for new pupils. The Catholic public school has joined the mainstream independent-school sector.

After the high point of the late 1950s and early 1960s, the Catholic public schools have faced enormous change. The fall in vocations, the weakening of clerical authority, the changes introduced by Vatican II, economic challenges and social change have all had their impact on the schools. There have been closures with some—Beaumont in 1967, Cotton in 1987, Douai in 1999—having a particular resonance in the wider Catholic community. Most of the schools have survived by changing, arguably out of all recognition. The staffing and management of the schools is now entirely in the hands of lay authorities. Whilst the long Catholic heritage of many of the schools is celebrated, at least in the "History" section of many websites, the contemporary school is very, very different. Perhaps better, perhaps worse but undeniably different. It is bigger, there are virtually no cassocks in sight, the chaplaincy rather than the chapel provides the religious overlay to the work of the school, and the pupils are much more socially and ethnically diverse—girls as well as boys, domestic and international, day as well as boarders. That has made them, perhaps, better, more rounded, more reflective, yet still undoubtedly elitist places. But one further, damaging, set of challenges faced some of these schools in the last decade or so, with the emerging scandals around child abuse.

---

[51] Beattie, *Mount St Mary*, pp. 131–2.

5

A crisis of authority:
The schools and child sexual abuse

By the early 2000s, the model of strong clerical input into the public schools had largely gone. In nearly all the schools, the teaching, management and governance was very much in lay hands, with a Catholic presence delivered primarily through a chaplaincy service and religious education in and out of the classroom, rather than a sizeable and permanent religious community. As Chapter 4 noted, the challenges that schools faced, and the ways in which they had begun to adapt to the new environment, significantly altered many of the features that had characterized traditional Catholic public schools in the past. Those changes, however, were to be overshadowed by the Catholic child sexual abuse scandals which began to emerge into public light towards the end of the twentieth century. Those scandals were rooted in shameful behaviour and activities by priests, lay teachers and members of religious orders in a range of settings. The Catholic public schools featured significantly in a number of those cases, alongside abuse committed in a range of parish and day school settings. Adding to the impacts of the abuse itself, it became increasingly evident that both Church authorities and religious orders had sought to cover up abuse, to protect some of the abusers, and above all to seek to preserve the reputation of the Church itself at all costs. For the Church, the crisis seemed to be dealt with more as a public relations exercise than a fundamental moral and religious issue. Not until the millennium did some of these attitudes begin to change. The impact on the structures and reputations of a number of Catholic public schools was to be highly significant and damaging.

The chronology of abuse cases in the Catholic Church has been well established. The most recent authoritative source for much of the evidence relating to abuse within the Catholic Church generally, and in some of its public schools in particular, was the Independent Inquiry into Child Sexual Abuse, which was commissioned by government in 2015 and chaired by Professor Alexis Jay.

Independent Inquiry into Child Sexual Abuse

The Independent Inquiry into Child Sexual Abuse was a major inquiry into abuse in a range of different settings and over a significant period of time. Table 6 indicates the reports of particular significance to this study.

Table 6: Independent Inquiry into Child Sexual Abuse

2015	Inquiry commissioned by the UK Government
August 2018	Ampleforth and Downside (English Benedictine Congregation Case Study) Investigation Report
June 2019	The Roman Catholic Church Case Study
October 2019	Roman Catholic Church (English Benedictine Congregation) Case Study: Ealing Abbey and St Benedict's School Investigation Report
November 2020	The Roman Catholic Church Case Study: Archdiocese of Birmingham Investigation Report
October 2022	The Report of the Independent Inquiry into Child Sexual Abuse

Two reports in particular contained significant material relating to the public schools: the *Ampleforth and Downside Investigation Report* (2018) and *The Roman Catholic Church Investigation Report* (2020) with the final summary report of the Inquiry appearing in 2022.[1] The reports are available in full and are online and in the public domain. They provide a key source for this chapter. They are significant, well-researched and very detailed judicial reports. We refer to the two reports most relevant to the public schools as the *Ampleforth and Downside Report* and the *Roman Catholic Church Report*.

Both reports highlighted data from the Bullivant Report of 2018, which was commissioned by the Catholic Church, to consider the chronology of child sexual abuse cases. Between 1970 and 2015, there were some 3,000 complaints of sexual abuse against 900 individuals connected to the Catholic Church in England and Wales.[2] These complaints were both historic and contemporary, and related not just to Catholic boarding schools but to the whole range of parish and other settings in which abuse took place. The cases of reported abuse were concentrated in the period between the late 1950s and early 1980s, whilst the complaints themselves were primarily made from the late 1990s onwards.[3] However, as the reports noted, allegations have not stopped, with around 100 allegations of sexual abuse against individuals connected to the Church being made annually since 2016, again in a variety of settings.[4] The report of the Inquiry, which had full legal powers, has provided for the first time a forensic, detailed, and carefully evidenced account of the nature and extent of child sexual abuse by named individuals, often acting within particular religious environments in the parish or in schools, together

---

[1] The Independent Inquiry into Child Sexual Abuse Reports are referenced in the notes as *Roman Catholic Church Report* (2020) and *Ampleforth and Downside Report* (2018). The author is grateful to the Home Office for permission to quote at length from the Inquiry. The reports are available in full on the website, together with witness statements and commentary, at <https://www.iicsa.org.uk/reports-recommendations>, accessed 4 December 2023.

[2] The chronology of child sex abuse cases is covered in *Roman Catholic Church Report*, pp. 15–17. See also valuable background material in R. Hattersley, *The Catholics* (London: Vintage, 2018), pp. 539–53.

[3] *Roman Catholic Church Report*, p. 18.

[4] *Roman Catholic Church Report*, p. 18.

with the actions taken by Church authorities within either dioceses (for the secular clergy), or within religious orders (for the regulars), in response to both allegations and convictions. In addition, the Inquiry has also provided a very detailed examination of the nature and management of child sexual abuse within two of the most important schools whose history has featured significantly in this book, Ampleforth and Downside. As well as using material evidenced in the reports, this chapter will also cover incidents at a number of other schools. The reports themselves, and press coverage of other incidents, do not make for easy reading but are an important part of the history of Catholic public schools and cannot be ignored.

Child safeguarding: The state and the Church

A sizeable number of both allegations and prosecutions for child sexual abuse have taken place within educational environments run by Catholic, Anglican and non-conformist groups. It is not possible to estimate what percentage of those cases have taken place within Catholic public schools, but it is evident both from examining reported prosecutions, and from using the details provided in the IICSA reports, that some of the features of the schools that we have described in previous chapters did, unwittingly, provide enhanced opportunities for abusers to carry out their activities. As the last chapter emphasized, at their zenith between the 1940s and 1970s, the schools had high percentages of clerical staff, whether diocesan or religious, in key teaching, pastoral and leadership roles.

The schools at that time were still largely single sex and boarding. Housemasters, who played such an important part in caring for the boys, were almost all clerical as was overall school management and governance. The boys and their masters shared physical space; they inter-related in every aspect of school life—academic, disciplinary, sporting, recreational, spiritual—and shared close proximity for perhaps two-thirds of the year. This was particularly the case in the preparatory schools that were integral to the system. In those schools, boys from perhaps the age of seven or eight shared those kinds of spaces. Boys could feel isolated, unhappy, and uncomfortable at being away from home, perhaps subject to a harsh disciplinary regime, certainly emotionally and physically vulnerable. These kinds of environments, it should be stressed, do not of themselves automatically produce abusers, but if individuals were pre-disposed to becoming abusers, the conditions may well have made carrying out their activities easier.

The identification of vulnerability, the use of physical and emotional power, the loneliness and isolation of abused individuals, the lack of recourse to authority, were all themes that emerge from the accounts of how abuse developed and continued within a number of schools in our study. In the Benedictine schools, for example, "many monks were teachers, housemasters with a very close link to the boys ... and girls now. There is a very close, family relationship ... some matters were very difficult to explore because of the nature of that friendship."[5]

Interestingly, the fact that abuse allegations were not confined to a particular historical period, but have continued into recent decades, suggests systemic issues around safeguarding within the Catholic public schools which have taken a significant amount of time to begin to be resolved. It is also worth noting here that such conditions of emotional and physical isolation and potential abuse were certainly not the sole preserve of the Catholic public schools but were evident elsewhere within the public-school sector. As one author noted, "the failure to tackle this culture of intimidation and fear must rank as the most shameful legacy of the old public school system".[6]

The role of government in opening up the issue of child sexual abuse within society as a whole was an important factor in helping to uncover issues within the Catholic boarding schools. It may perhaps be somewhat surprising that the development of a government-led child safeguarding strategy, outside of simple recourse to the law, did not emerge until the late 1980s, with the amended Children Act (1989), which laid responsibilities on Local Education Authorities to provide proper education, training and administrative procedures to ensure the safety of children. Together

---

[5] *Ampleforth and Downside Report, Part B: Ampleforth*, p. 67, point 180.

[6] M. Peel, *The New Meritocracy: A History of UK Independent Schools, 1979–2015* (London: Elliot & Thompson, 2015), p. 39.

with the *Working Together for the Protection of Children* legislation of 1988, it created for the first time a set of mechanisms to ensure children were properly protected within school environments. Inspection regimes delivered through OFSTED (the Office for Standards in Education), for example, identified and reported on safeguarding issues within all state schools. The Education Act of 2002 emphasized the key role of governing bodies in ensuring the education and training of staff in dealing with safeguarding issues and required all schools to have named safeguarding leads.

That basic framework, obligatory in state schools, was applied with more flexibility in the independent sector. For some Catholic public schools, the issue was properly recognized and resourced but, inevitably, not all schools were at the same level of awareness or indeed, commitment. The oversight responsibilities of school governing bodies, critical in ensuring standard procedures were followed, were also sometimes opaque. Improved inspection regimes from the Independent Schools Inspectorate required governing bodies to ensure safeguarding issues were discussed at board level. As we have noted before, religious staff in key management positions might face divided loyalties in reporting issues concerning their brethren, since they also had responsibilities for their welfare to their diocese or religious community. Issues such as these were sometimes to seriously undermine the exercise of child safeguarding within the schools. Again the evidence from IICSA supports this view.

Alongside the role of government, the Catholic Church itself had commissioned a series of reports as the issue of child sexual abuse was becoming more prominent in the 1990s. A 1994 report, *Healing the Wound of Child Sexual Abuse*, emphasized that the misuse of power and control were at the heart of sexual abuse issues within the Church.[7] The *Nolan Report* in 2000 was very important in recognizing the extent of the problem and the enormous damage it caused to victims of abuse. It set up an infrastructure to tackle abuse, creating the *Catholic Office for the Protection of Children and Vulnerable Adults* (COPCA), to advise religious authorities on the correct way to deal with and report abuse

---

[7] *Healing the Wounds of Child Sexual Abuse* (Catholic Bishops' Conference of England and Wales, 1994).

and abusers.[8] This marked an important stage in Catholic safeguarding, but came up against two particular difficulties.

First, whilst the role and authority of the diocese (and ultimately the Archbishop of Westminster) was clear, the position of the religious orders such as, for example, the members of the English Benedictine Congregation (EBC) who played such an important role in many of our schools, was opaque. The bishop and diocese, for example, had no clear, unequivocal right of intervention into the affairs of religious orders under canon law. And the religious orders themselves had historically resisted any centralization. The idea of creating a single, unified line of authority was a significant challenge. Thus for an order such as the Benedictines, individual Abbeys and their abbots had much more power than the central English Benedictine Congregation in managing their affairs. They had become fully independent, self-managing communities in the 1890s and were reluctant to give up any of that independence to either the EBC or to the Church Hierarchy as a whole.

A second, seemingly minor, but in reality very significant, issue was the reporting and disciplining of priestly abusers. From the perspective of the Church, they were answerable, first and foremost, in canon law, rather than civil law, for disciplinary matters. A simple issue of disciplining or removing a priest who had offended was rendered complex and legalistic. But the *Nolan Report* was an important starting point. It is interesting that the Chair, Lord Nolan, was an ex-pupil of Ampleforth, but the report did not contain any significant discussion of the potential issue of abuse in the Catholic boarding-school sector. The focus was almost exclusively on the parish and the family, which were viewed as the key locales for abuse.

In 2007, the Church commissioned Baroness Cumberledge to chair a group to consider the progress made since Nolan. It was optimistic in tone, suggesting that 79 out of the 83 recommendations in Nolan had been accepted and implemented by the authorities. But it flagged up again the persistent issue of lines of authority and responsibility, especially in the case of the religious orders. Nolan had anticipated the

---

[8] *The Nolan Report: A Programme for Action* (2001); see also Hattersley, *Catholics*, pp. 546–8.

creation of a single, uniform framework for dealing with safeguarding, driven by the dioceses but applicable equally to the religious orders. Such a structure would replicate the kind of framework operating within the state sector. That had not happened, and the orders had been very slow in even discussing how integrated lines of authority, and single sets of procedures envisaged by the proposed "One Church" approach, might be established.[9] Again, as with Nolan, there was little discussion of issues within the public schools.

The establishment of the child abuse inquiry by government in 2015, and the subsequent publication of its report on the Roman Catholic Church in 2019, served to underline just how much work remained to be done in establishing procedures and lines of authority in the identification, reporting and management of child sexual abuse. The report prompted a wholesale reform of processes. A new agency, the *Catholic Safeguarding Standards Agency* (CSSA), was set up in 2020. A commitment to the "One Church" process was paramount and a dedicated part of the agency was established to ensure that the regulars (called the Religious Life Groups) were brought swiftly into a single, unified process.[10] That work remains ongoing and critical to the restoration of confidence.

The new legal environment—police investigations and convictions

The significant number of accusations of child sexual abuse against the Catholic Church from the early 1990s inevitably had an impact on many of the public schools whose history we have traced. A range of local police enquiries and trials prefigured the inquiry that was to come. At Stonyhurst in 1996, there was a wide-ranging police investigation, Operation Whiting, into long-standing sexual abuse accusations, some

---

[9] *The Cumberledge Commission* (2007); see also Hattersley, *Catholics*, pp. 550–1.

[10] *Roman Catholic Church Report*, pp. 40–1; *Catholic Safeguarding Standards Agency: Policy documents* at <http.catholicsafeguarding.org.uk>, accessed 22 August 2023.

of which dated back some 20 years or more. Five teachers, one of them a priest, who had taught at the school, and at St Mary's Hall, the prep school for Stonyhurst, faced investigation and a series of high-profile trials over such allegations, which caused significant damage to the reputation of the school.[11] Ultimately the one conviction was reduced from a five- to a three-year sentence on appeal. A further high-profile case was quashed on appeal. In at least one case, the decision was taken to "stay" prosecution, because at the time the abuse was uncovered, the parents of the abused pupil had signed an agreement not to involve the police in exchange for a settlement. Charges against a former Jesuit head of the college were also stayed. The collapse of that case led to the county court judge making serious criticisms of the police for failing to pass on key information to the judge. Judge Openshaw was especially critical of the circumstance in which, back in 1971, the school had failed to inform the police or social services about a key incident. He argued that "the Jesuits gave undue weight to the need to prevent scandal and damage to the reputation of the Society and the College".[12] A later letter about the abuse that had taken place in 1971 noted that it was the school solicitors, as part of a non-disclosure deal with the parents of the abused child, who took on the responsibility of ensuring that the abusive priest concerned left the school.[13]

Similar issues were also coming to light in both of the northern seminary colleges, Ushaw and Upholland. At St Joseph's Upholland, which closed in 1987, a priest was convicted in 2019 of a series of sexual offences against teenage boys at St Joseph's in the 1970s and 1980s. He was initially found guilty in 2017, a conviction quashed by the Court of Appeal. A retrial was ordered, and he received an eighteen-year sentence. The judge at the case noted that "what you did ... effectively destroyed

---

[11] BBC News, 21 April 1999; *The Guardian*, 18 January 2000; *Lancashire Telegraph*, 22 March 2000; T. E. Muir, *Stonyhurst College 1593–1993* (Cirencester: St Omers Press, revised edition, 2006), pp. 177–8.

[12] *Lancashire Telegraph*, 28 March 2000.

[13] Letter quoted in <https://www.catholicculture.org/commentary/british-jesuits-chapter-contemporary-history/>, accessed 22 August 2023. See also *The Times*, 22 October 2003.

the remainder of his childhood and did a good job of destroying any faith he ever had". The judge also noted how difficult it was for the victims to report these crimes: "the way you acted left them with a sense of shame and of guilt as well as the sense that no-one would believe them".[14]

A second priest, who was facing five charges of indecent assault whilst teaching at the college, committed suicide prior to his trial. At Ushaw College, which closed in 2011, a priest pleaded guilty in 2021 to abusing pupils in the college during outdoor activities in the 1960s and received a twenty-eight-month sentence. John Cornwell, writing about his experiences as a pupil at Cotton College in the 1950s, noted how the relationship between pupil and priest as exercised through the confessional could create what were sometimes unhealthy and potentially abusive relations towards pupils.[15] Elsewhere, Catholic public schools experienced similar police investigations into historical abuse claims, as the wider environment became more conducive to disclosure, and victims of abuse felt more confident about making formal complaints.

At Douai School, which closed in 1999, one priest received a nine-month sentence in 1992 for molesting a boy. A prolific offender, he committed further offences as a scoutmaster in Liverpool and, in 2017, he received a five-year prison sentence for further offences committed whilst at Douai. Sentencing, the judge emphasized how the particular circumstances of a boarding environment put this individual in a position of enormous authority and trust which he had betrayed.[16] At the Oratory School, a former lay teacher had abused boys of between 10 and 16 years of age in the 1980s and was jailed in May 2014 for 13 years, which was upheld after appeal. The judge noted that the teacher had exploited lonely pupils with alcohol and pornographic material. He had been forced to leave the Oratory School after a victim complained in the late 1980s. The school, however, did not report the matter, and it only came to light in 2013 after a victim spoke to police. Whilst it could be argued that procedures for reporting abuse were less clear in the 1980s, a pattern of

---

[14] *Liverpool Echo*, 11 August 2019; BBC News, 30 July 2020.
[15] *Northern Echo*, 22 December 2021; Cornwell, *The Dark Box*, pp. 169–96.
[16] *The Independent*, 6 August 1992; *Liverpool Echo*, 3 May 2016.

seeking to minimize any bad publicity, and move any offenders elsewhere was, unhappily, to become a chronic and systemic issue.[17]

At Ratcliffe, a Rosminian brother was jailed for 12 months in 2014 for the abuse of a pupil in the 1980s. The victim had received no support from the school at the time and was even forced to write a letter of apology to his abuser. The judge later commented that "the Order which you served seems to have swept it under the carpet and moved you elsewhere".[18] The school also faced major investigations into the way it ran its own preparatory school, Grace Dieu Manor, between the 1950s and 1980s, as well as a boarding school, St Michael's, for expatriates that the Rosminians had run in Tanzania between 1952 and 1973. Serious physical and sexual abuse of young pupils was exposed as a result of a class action by a group of 22 former students at the two schools. Grace Dieu, it was said, was for some pupils a place of beatings, of sexual abuse, even of being shot at with an air rifle. One priest who worked at Grace Dieu used to sexually whip young boys. When a parent complained, the priest was not disciplined, but instead was moved to St Michael's School in Tanzania, which was described by one former pupil as a "loveless, violent and sad hellhole". Another pupil abused at Grace Dieu spoke of "being beaten regularly as part of a sadistic and sexually violent ritual".[19]

A BBC TV documentary about abuse at Grace Dieu and St Michael's, *Abused: Breaking the Silence*, was broadcast in 2011, exposing not just the cases of abuse that were the subject of the class action, but also the catalogue of denials and evasions about the issues from the Rosminian order.[20] Whilst the head of Grace Dieu argued that such events had no relevance to the Grace Dieu of today, the difficulties the complainants experienced in seeking redress reflected poorly on the order and the school. One priest, a leading, well-connected Rosminian, was exposed as culpable for some of the abuse, and his involvement elicited significant press coverage. Writing in *The Guardian*, the journalist Peter Stanford,

---

[17] *Berkshire Live: Reading and Berkshire News*, 16 January 2015.
[18] *Leicester Mercury*, 11 September 2014.
[19] *Leicester Mercury*, 9 March 2013.
[20] BBC TV documentary, *Abused: Breaking the Silence*, broadcast on 21 June 2011.

a friend and admirer of the priest (he had written his obituary when the priest died in 2010), came to realize the crimes that had been committed and hidden. For Stanford, "the Rosminians appear ... to be placing defending the institution above a heartfelt acceptance of the catalogue of depression, broken marriages and suicide attempts recounted by victims in the [BBC] documentary".[21]

The cases did not go to court. The Rosminian order chose instead to make an out-of-court settlement with the plaintiffs to cover compensation and legal costs. The amounts paid were not disclosed. Fr Myers, provincial of the order, wrote: "I apologize without reservation on behalf of the Rosminian brethren in the UK to all those who have suffered. Such abuse was a grievous breach of trust to them and their families."[22] Despite significant capital investment at the site, Grace Dieu prep school closed abruptly in 2019 and was transferred to a new building on the main college site at Ratcliffe.

It is clear that there is a significant and unhappy catalogue of recorded offences and convictions relating to abuse cases within the Catholic public schools, which are both historic and contemporary in nature. A school environment characterized by isolation, rigid structures of authority and automatic deference may have been conducive to the perpetration of abuse. That it should be inflicted by priests or monks, often on very vulnerable young people, is especially reprehensible. It ought also to be the case that the infrastructure of processes, policies and training around safeguarding issues in the last three decades should have made a recurrence of what sometimes seems a torrent of child abuse cases very unlikely. Catholic public schools today are undoubtedly subject to more rigorous inspection regimes than was the case 15 or 20 years ago, with the Independent Schools Inspectorate seeking to be stricter than ever in ensuring public schools comply with existing legislation. But, as the *IICSA Report* has shown, in two of the best-known Catholic public schools in England, Ampleforth and Downside, both of them Benedictine foundations, an inability or unwillingness to address safeguarding issues characterized both schools over a number of years.

---

[21] *The Guardian*, 18 June 2011.
[22] *Leicester Mercury*, 21 June 2011; *Catholic Herald*, 22 June 2011.

Ampleforth, Downside and the English Benedictine Order

Ampleforth and Downside, both Benedictine schools, had, as we have seen, been at the pinnacle of the Catholic public-school sector—long-established, traditional in ethos, successful in attracting a well-connected set of pupils, and competing with some of the top non-Catholic public schools. They reflected the ideal model of a Benedictine monastery integrated physically and academically with a school on the same site, a model which had underpinned a number of other Benedictine boarding schools such as Douai (closed in 1999), Belmont Abbey (closed in 1994) and Worth. Both schools went into the millennium years, with all the changes and new developments that resulted from the falling numbers of monks and priests, with a sense of optimism. Neither school, however, had dealt properly with child safeguarding issues, and the leadership of both schools, and their adjacent monasteries, had seemed, despite Nolan, reluctant to embrace the notion of external safeguarding protections being imposed on what they saw as independent, self-regulating, school and monastic communities.

This focus on independence, and on the desire of the schools to "manage their own affairs", was to prove hugely damaging in terms of the ability of both schools to deal properly with historic and contemporary child abuse issues. Boundaries between the school and the monastic community had always been porous and, for the monks who governed the school and monasteries, either as heads (until lay heads were appointed), or as abbots at the head of the monastic community, any kind of external scrutiny of school safeguarding, commonplace in the state sector, was regarded with suspicion. Dom Charles Lombard-Fitzgerald, Abbot of Downside from 1990–8, later reflected:

> Looking back over the 20th century, I would say that local agencies such as the police and district or even county councils seemed generally content to leave the abbey and school to manage their own affairs. This deferential attitude was complemented by the abbey and school's rather conservative, paternalistic "we know best" approach to deal with matters which would now be

reported ... Downside was run on convention, precedent and tradition.[23]

At Ampleforth, the ethos was similar with an inherent notion that self-regulation was right and appropriate in dealing with the increasingly strong regulatory environment around safeguarding. For Fr Leo Chamberlain, headmaster between 1992 and 2003, the growing regulatory burden was not just onerous, but seen as positively damaging. Writing in 2000, he argued:

> There is too much prescription, too much emphasis on rights and all too little on ancient duties of the pupil like obedience, courtesy and diligence ... all these measures can be barriers to a child's development and hostile to our work.[24]

The Inquiry into Child Sexual Abuse, as part of its overall investigations, looked in forensic detail at three Catholic Benedictine schools where there had been significant instances of abuse—Ampleforth, Downside and St Benedict's day school at Ealing. Our focus is on the first two whose story has been such an integral part of Catholic boarding school history. The findings for St Benedict's were very serious and concerning but are not examined here. The Inquiry report itself ran to over 200 pages with at times sickening detail of the nature and extent of sexual abuse and sexual sadism, linked to a culture of corporal punishment at Ampleforth and Downside stretching back many decades. Two themes dominate the report. A first underlying theme is the nature of the abuse perpetrated by both religious and lay teachers within a boarding-school environment, where authority and power relations were so closely inter-connected with the lived, day-to-day experience of the pupils. A second theme concerns the failure of leaders to deal properly and appropriately with cases of abuse as the law required, and, in particular, failures to report offenders and to ensure that such offenders could never have any contact with children again.

---

[23] *Ampleforth and Downside Report*, p. 167, point 264.
[24] *Ampleforth Journal* 105 (2000).

The summary of the *IICSA Report* into Ampleforth and Downside is stark. It is difficult, it notes, "to describe the appalling sexual abuse inflicted over decades on children aged as young as seven" at the schools. It continues: "ten individuals, mostly monks, connected to these two institutions have been convicted or cautioned in relation to offences involving sexual activity with a large number of children, or offences concerning pornography. The true scale of the abuse, however, is likely to be considerably higher."[25]

The report noted a wide range of abuse such as physical chastisement for sexual gratification, mutual masturbation, fondling of genitalia and oral, anal and vaginal penetration. "Many perpetrators", the report noted, "did not seek to hide their sexual interests from the children."[26] It indicated that at Ampleforth, three priests and two lay teachers were convicted or cautioned between 1995 and 2016, whilst at Downside one priest and one lay teacher were convicted or cautioned between 2003 and 2012.

The report revealed a catalogue of abuse in a detail which would not be appropriate to reproduce here. It is, however, important to note how the environment of abuse was certainly facilitated by the close daily lives of teachers, monks, priests and pupils within a traditional boarding school context. Both Ampleforth and Downside remained overwhelmingly boarding colleges at a time when, as we saw in the last chapter, other Catholic public schools were shifting to a much more mixed pattern of schooling with a mix of day pupils, co-education, and a range of weekly boarders and international students. That is not to say that a boarding system alone accounts for patterns of abuse; a separate report catalogues the serious sexual abuse committed within the day school of St Benedict's in Ealing over the same period.[27] But the exercise of power over preparatory and main school pupils aged from 8 to 18 who studied, lived, prayed and played within the school for some two-thirds of the year, meant that abuse could perhaps be more easily

---

[25] *Ampleforth and Downside Report*, Executive Summary, p. iii.

[26] *Ampleforth and Downside Report*, Executive Summary, p. iii.

[27] *The Roman Catholic Church (EBC) Case Study: Ealing Abbey and St Benedict's School Investigation Report* (October 2019).

perpetrated within that closed, sometimes claustrophobic environment. An environment where clerical abuse seemed to be tolerated created in its turn a climate of bullying, of fear, of intimidation and of uncertainty about moral boundaries. Such a climate impacted on pupils of all ages.

At Ampleforth, the main school was complemented by a prep school at Gilling Castle, which became St Martin's Ampleforth in 2001. Separate embryonic safeguarding arrangements for the school and monastic community were developed from the late 1990s alongside an increased physical and legal separation between school and monastery. In terms of management, governance and leadership, however, the connection between monastery and school remained central to the nature and ethos of Ampleforth, and was, indeed, a key part of its own powerful self-image. A number of allegations about child sexual abuse had been made since the 1960s, but the majority came to light only as a result of a police operation, Operation Ellipse, in 2005.[28] The IICSA report described the environment between 1960 and 1980 as one of physical and emotional abuse of children as young as seven or eight boarding at Gilling Castle. Physical violence, sometimes entirely random, was sadistic and veered into sexual sadism. Abuse was committed by both religious and lay members of the school. Extra-curricular activities (walking, climbing, camping expeditions), a central part of boarding school life, took place in an environment in which one master indulged in child sexual abuse in both individual and group settings. One priest, the report noted, "would give and receive oral sex in front of other pupils in the workshop. The pupils would then independently go off in groups for oral sex with each other in the woods."[29]

Another abuser taught at the Junior House at Ampleforth in the 1970s and 1980s. He was the warden of Redcar Farm near the school, which was used for outdoor education activities. That environment, away from the school, but where the priest had full control and authority, proved conducive to his abusive activities.[30] A third abuser taught in the

---

[28] *Ampleforth and Downside Report, Part B: Ampleforth*, p. 33, point 19.

[29] *Ampleforth and Downside Report,* Conclusions, p. 38, point 45.

[30] *Ampleforth and Downside Report, Part B: Ampleforth*, p. 45, points 76–7.

Junior House at the school which had what was described as a "culture of violence" with physical abuse for the purposes of sexual gratification.[31]

Girls were admitted into Ampleforth across the age range from 2001. One lay teacher, employed between 2003 and 2016, used his position to groom a female pupil from the age of 13. The pupil was lonely and felt isolated and vulnerable, and the attention she received from him made her feel special. The grooming continued over a number of years and included serious sexual abuse. The victim disclosed the abuse after leaving the school and it was noted that the issue became "less about what was best for the child, and more about what the school should do if a false accusation or ... allegation was made against a member of staff. It was more an atmosphere of fear, rather than an atmosphere of caring and commonsense."[32]

The teacher was convicted and sentenced in 2017. The descriptions of child sexual abuse within the report point to an environment and culture where power and authority were taken for granted by some staff, and where it was very difficult to report abuse and seek help, because to do so would be to expose oneself as somehow "different" and "difficult". Silent acceptance was often the only response for pupils.

How then did the authorities at Ampleforth seek to address these issues as they came to light? In some ways, the *Nolan Report* had provided a watershed. Prior to the *Nolan Report*, the school sought to deal with individual cases in a piecemeal fashion. Offenders were transferred out of the school and sometimes given treatment, where recommended by psychiatrists. A short guide on dealing with allegations of abuse was produced by the school in 1993. A further policy statement in 1994 involved the solicitors of the school in the process and left the solicitors, rather than the school or monastery leaders, to report abuse cases to the statutory authorities.[33] It was not until the publication of the *Nolan Report* that there was a framework outlining what any Catholic public school should do in relation to safeguarding.

---

[31] *Ampleforth and Downside Report, Part B: Ampleforth*, p. 47, points 86–7.

[32] *Ampleforth and Downside Report, Part B: Ampleforth*, p. 64, points 161–8.

[33] *Ampleforth and Downside Report, Part B: Ampleforth*, p. 65, point 174.

The initial response of the school to pressures for the establishment of a more robust safeguarding framework was characterized by a "strong reluctance ... to engage with the Nolan recommendations" with Abbot Timothy Wright (who was abbot from 1997 to 2006) especially reluctant to act with any decisiveness. He was heavily criticized in the report as having "prioritised the interests of his monks ahead of the needs and welfare of children in his care".[34] Amongst external groups, the safeguarding situation at Ampleforth also began to be of some concern. The general manager of North Yorkshire County Council Children's Social Services in 2003 commented:

> I do not believe currently that the organization as a whole understands or accepts their responsibilities for child protection issues ... We appear to be dealing with obfuscation, denial or downright obstruction.[35]

The issue of when an offender should be reported to the police and social services was to prove very difficult, with the Abbot suggesting that offenders should make only an "admission" that something might have happened, rather than a "disclosure" giving details of a particular abuse. The former, he argued, need not be reported to the authorities, whereas the latter should. Such a distinction was totally contrary to the Nolan recommendations. The IICSA report highlights a whole series of internal documents and commentaries at the school which contradicted the spirit and recommendations around good safeguarding practice set in place by Nolan.[36]

The appointment of Abbot Madden at Ampleforth in 2005 seemed to mark a period of greater openness and transparency between the school and the statutory authorities, and the emergence of a clearer safeguarding strategy for both the school and the monastic community. Certainly a series of external inspections on the main school and preparatory school

---

[34] *Ampleforth and Downside Report, Part B: Ampleforth*, pp. 66–7, points 177–8.
[35] *Ampleforth and Downside Report, Part B: Ampleforth*, p. 67, point 179.
[36] *Ampleforth and Downside Report, Part B: Ampleforth*, pp. 69–73, points 189–203.

by both the Independent Schools Inspectorate (ISI) and OFSTED between 2005 and 2017 found that the main school and junior school "met the appropriate standards" both for boarding conditions and for safeguarding, suggesting that the issues around the lack of a safeguarding culture were being properly addressed.

In November 2016, however, the Charity Commission, alarmed at reports about safeguarding at Ampleforth, decided to open a statutory inquiry into the handling of such issues by the school trustees. The Ampleforth trustees also decided at the same time to commission their own independent, external review (chaired by Professor Proctor) into safeguarding and child protection at the same time. The Proctor Review was broadly positive about safeguarding issues, identifying some areas for improvement and making 90 recommendations which were accepted by the school.[37] Over the last decade or so, the school noted, the ISI had consistently reported positively on safeguarding and child protection, but an ISI Inspection in March 2018 found the college no longer met all the required standards with difficulties reported around record-keeping, referrals, staff recruitment and lines of responsibility.[38] The Charity Commission inquiry reported in April 2018 that the current safeguarding framework at the school was not working properly. It noted that "we are not satisfied that the trustees of these charities have made enough progress in improving the safeguarding environment for pupils in schools connected to the charities".[39] The trustees were provisionally stripped of their control over the charity that ran the school, and an interim manager was appointed. The school faced a very real and very public crisis with future pupil admissions being suspended for a period because of the findings.

At Downside, whilst the numbers of monks involved in school teaching and management had begun to fall by the late 1990s, the co-location of school and monastery meant that physical boundaries between the two were largely absent. Again, like Ampleforth, lay headmasters appeared quite late (2014) compared to other schools. Boarding dominated, and

---

[37] *Ampleforth and Downside Report, Part B: Ampleforth*, pp. 93–4, points 302–4.

[38] *Ampleforth and Downside Report, Part B: Ampleforth*, pp. 94–5, point 305.

[39] *Ampleforth and Downside Report, Part B: Ampleforth*, pp. 95–6, point 306.

that continues to be the case through to the present. The monastic community was, however, small and declining and for the last two decades or so has only been able to deliver a chaplaincy service to the school. Unlike the situation at Ampleforth, the school did not have a clear and separate legal identity, forming part of a General Trust which was responsible for school and monastery alike. That situation did not alter until 2017 when a number of assets were sold by the monastery in order to facilitate the financial support of the school, as monastery and school formally separated.

There had been a significant number of child sexual abuse cases within the school dating back to the 1960s. An assistant housemaster in 1969 had admitted engaging in mutual masturbation with a sixteen-year-old pupil and had been sent away from the school. The head reported the incident to the Department of Education and Science, but no police report was made because the parents did not wish to pursue the matter.[40] The priest was banned from teaching for three years by the Department. The ban was then lifted, and the priest moved into adult education. In 2011, police investigated the case, and the priest was placed on the Sex Offenders Register.[41]

A second serious case was that of a priest who worked at Downside in the mid-1980s, left the school in the 1990s, but returned at the end of the decade.

One of his victims, an eleven-year-old who had experienced a recent family trauma and was especially vulnerable, was taken by the priest into the private monastery gardens, and he later masturbated with the pupil in the monastery library. The abuse continued for some time, and the victim reported the issue to his father who was told the school "would sort things out". However, on entering the senior school in 1988, the victim was rightly horrified to find that his new housemaster was the very person who had abused him and was now responsible for almost every aspect of his daily life. The abuse continued and at no time did the victim feel able to report it to anyone in authority. When he realized the priest had abused and raped another boy, he reported it to his father who again

---

[40] *Ampleforth and Downside Report, Part C: Downside*, p. 107, points 21, 28–31.
[41] *Ampleforth and Downside Report, Part C: Downside*, p. 110, point 51.

took the matter up with the school. The parents of both boys obtained an injunction to try to avoid press coverage of the issue, but an article was published in the *News of the World*, and at that point the priest was removed from the school and monastery.[42] The matter was not taken up by the Bath police. It was not until 2011 that he was finally arrested and prosecuted. Following the conviction, two former pupils made further allegations against him. The first victim, commenting on his experiences in Downside in the 1980s, noted that "if you have an organisation that neatly partitions good and evil, then, you know, you go in as a young child and you believe that stuff; these guys are the representatives of God. But of course, to put it melodramatically, unexpressed sexual tension stalked the corridors of Downside."[43]

The abbot at Downside sought a range of external parish placements for the abusive priest, and he was eventually moved to Fort Augustus Abbey School in Scotland, remaining there until it closed in 1998, a school which has itself been the subject of recent investigation over child sexual abuse by the Scottish authorities.[44] He returned to the Downside monastic community in 1999. Concerns about the adequacy of monitoring the priest when he was in close proximity to the school remained, and a group of ex-Downside boys even sought independent legal advice as to whether the school and monastery were justified in accepting his return to the school.[45] There were recurring issues over the next decade or so surrounding his presence at the school and monastery, especially given the lack of a clear physical border between the two. After an audit by the Clifton diocese and the police, the original complaints against the priest were uncovered, and he was finally prosecuted and given a five-year sentence.[46]

---

[42] *Ampleforth and Downside Report, Part C: Downside*, pp. 111–14, points 52–70.

[43] *Ampleforth and Downside Report, Part C: Downside*, pp. 112–13, point 61.

[44] *Scottish Child Abuse Inquiry: Case study No 5: Benedictines* (2021) at <https://www.childabuseinquiry.scot/evidence/case-study-findings-benedictines>, accessed 22 August 2023.

[45] *Ampleforth and Downside Report, Part C: Downside*, p. 117, point 84.

[46] *Ampleforth and Downside Report, Part C: Downside*, p. 119, point 95.

Other episodes reported from the school included issues of drinking and inappropriate sexual contact, where the issues of how and when to remove offenders from the school, coupled with uncertainties and irregularities in maintaining a degree of scrutiny over the offender, seemed to pose chronic, systemic issues for the school authorities.[47] The case of a monk and teacher at Downside in the 1990s, who accessed pornographic images of children on school equipment, was first uncovered by the head of IT at the school. He was consistently critical of the very slow pace with which the school reacted to the downloading of the material and the attitude of school leaders seemingly mostly concerned with managing the impact on school life and reputation. The report is clear that the school did "not adequately respond to this as a safeguarding issue" and that the monk, required to stay in the monastery and away from the school, was not adequately monitored. "Out of sight, out of mind" seemed to be the standard response. He was even moved to a role as novice master in the monastery, responsible for the training and pastoral care of young men contemplating entering the order.[48] It was not until 2004 that he was reported to the police who found incriminating pictures, 98 per cent of which related to young children, on his computer. He was convicted in 2004 and sentenced to 18 months' imprisonment.[49]

Following the recommendations of Nolan, a number of historic cases of abuse allegations were re-examined. In one case, a 1992 Somerset County Council report had identified that corporal punishment was being used in one of the boarding houses when only the head had the authority to administer it. A number of other notes showed that one particular teacher was using caning very regularly and on bare flesh. As one witness to the IICSA noted:

> I would not be surprised if this satiated a sexual sadistic desire of his, for it certainly was not a "normal" sort of caning. I have felt deeply humiliated and traumatized by such an experience.

---

[47] *Ampleforth and Downside Report, Part C: Downside*, pp. 120–8 provides a narrative of various systemic failures in safeguarding.

[48] *Ampleforth and Downside Report, Part C: Downside*, p. 135, point 164.

[49] *Ampleforth and Downside Report, Part C: Downside*, p. 141, point 174.

> Surely the school authorities knew about his infamous caning. It is bewildering to know they turned a blind eye to this illegal and condemned act.[50]

The cases noted above represent just some of the issues relating to child sexual abuse that took place at Downside from the early 1970s, and highlight in particular the lack of oversight from the school and monastery leaders. In the pre-Nolan period, the characteristic response was one of confusion over whether key responsibility for safeguarding lay with the head of the school or the abbot of the monastery. It was a confusion that dogged the institution through to the recent past. It was a confusion that also meant there was no clear guidance or proper training around safeguarding for staff, despite the 1990 legislation for state schools. The publication of Nolan not only provided a clearer framework for Catholic safeguarding but also highlighted that the issue of lines of authority which were clear for secular priests and institutions (i.e. the bishops and the diocese) were much less clear for orders such as the Benedictines. In addition, the requirement to investigate both historic and contemporary allegations of abuse raised some concerns and trepidation. From 2002, Downside sought to align its processes and procedures with the Clifton diocese in which it sat, and the relationship with the safeguarding coordinator was generally good. In addition, inspections were positive. The County Council inspection of 2002 noted only the quality and quantity of food as being an issue at the school, and the inspections by the Commission for Social Care in 2005, ISI in 2006 and OFSTED in 2007 were positive about the child protection policies in place.

Two allegations made in 2010 about sexual abuse of a female pupil at the school prompted a multi-agency meeting and a police investigation. Accounts of that investigation in the IICSA report suggest chronic difficulties between the school leadership and other agencies, and also allude to the powerful external political connections of the school and monastery, some of which were especially hostile to the scrutiny the

---

[50] *Ampleforth and Downside Report, Part C: Downside*, p. 141, point 190.

school was under.⁵¹ An ISI interim report from the 2010 inspection found overall governance inadequate and that child protection policies were incomplete. A series of meetings of agency representatives alluded to a lack of leadership and transparency amongst trustees of the school.⁵² A Charity Commission regulatory compliance case was opened in late 2010, and an OFSTED inspection in December 2010 rated child protection inadequate. There was, noted one observer, "a clear cultural divide between the more elderly monks who did not understand safeguarding and saw no role for it, and the younger group who did understand and were frustrated by the resistance of the older group".⁵³ By 2011, the school faced a real issue of being de-registered by the Department of Education. By late 2012, the school had begun to address safeguarding issues in a way that satisfied the Charity Commissioners, the ISI and OFSTED. There had at least been the beginnings of a cultural shift.

Issues at the Abbey itself have also shifted. The separation of the school and monastery has now been physically and legally completed. The close personal and physical proximity of the monastery and school, something that was so central to the Benedictine educational ethos of the last 150 years, has gone. That the culture has been slow to shift is exemplified by the fact that in 2012, Dom Leo, the Prior Administrator, felt able and entitled to take several trips with a wheelbarrow full of personal files into a distant part of the monastery gardens to burn. No-one knows what the files contained.⁵⁴ The monastic community, rapidly shrinking over the last 20 years, yet based in a large monastery with an Abbey which is one of the finest Catholic churches in the country, has now left Downside altogether and is based at Buckfast Abbey in Devon where it is deliberating on the future. Dom Leo's comment in 2013 that "a Benedictine school needs a permanent Benedictine community as its nucleus" seems especially resonant at Downside today with an empty monastery sealed off from the adjacent school by signs, fences and gates.⁵⁵

---

51 *Ampleforth and Downside Report, Part C: Downside*, p. 164, point 316.
52 *Ampleforth and Downside Report, Part C: Downside*, p. 186, points 357–9.
53 *Ampleforth and Downside Report, Part C: Downside*, p. 165, point 311.
54 *Ampleforth and Downside Report, Part C: Downside*, p. 171, points 345–6.
55 *The Raven* 64 (2013).

The impact of these inquiries on both schools and on the wider Catholic community has been immense. The press coverage was noteworthy: a "culture of acceptance of sexual abuse at two Catholic schools" (*Guardian*), "two top Catholic schools hid claims of appalling sex abuse over four decades ... scale of sadistic attacks was worse than feared" (*Daily Mail*), "culture of sex abuse flourished at Ampleforth and Downside" (*The Times*) and "Damning catalogue of sex abuse at top Catholic schools" (*The Tablet*).[56] These damaging headlines, and the ongoing fallout from the report of the Inquiry, have continued to impact directly on both schools, and indirectly on the sector as a whole. A recent *Telegraph* article by a Downside old boy underlined the extent to which child sexual abuse helped to corrode relationships between pupils and contributed to an atmosphere of bullying and intimidation in the school.[57]

At Ampleforth, a continued issue over the adequacy of safeguarding procedures and processes led to the Charity Commission in November 2020 suspending any new recruitment of pupils to the school, a suspension overturned in April 2021. For Edward Stourton, an Ampleforth pupil and head boy in the late 1960s, writing in 2023, the school today is "a place of locked doors and electronic keypads". The school, he writes, is utterly changed: "The presence of the monks was once considered Ampleforth's greatest asset, something that set it apart; today it is the school's greatest handicap ... The damage has been done by the monks themselves."[58]

It is also interesting to reflect on issues of child abuse in Benedictine boarding schools elsewhere. We do, for example, have a detailed account of issues at Fort Augustus School, near Inverness, Scotland, for the period 1948–91 which was one of the case studies for the Scottish Child Abuse Inquiry. Whilst outside the geographical confines of this book, it identifies a range of similar issues. Bullying and intimidation,

---

[56] See *Guardian*, 9 August 2018; *The Tablet*, 9 August 2018; *The Times*, 10 August 2017; *Daily Mail*, 5 September 2018; *The Tablet*, 18 February 2023.

[57] Alex Diggins, "The abbey abandoned following decades of sexual abuse", *The Telegraph Magazine*, 29 July 2023, pp. 20–7.

[58] E. Stourton, *Confessions: Life Re-Examined* (London: Doubleday, 2023), p. 247.

grooming, sexual, physical and emotional abuse coupled with an inability or unwillingness to properly instigate child safeguarding, deal with offenders and report matters to the appropriate authorities. The English Benedictine Congregation which exercised oversight of the school (as it did at Ampleforth and Downside) admitted that lasting damage was inflicted on children at the school and that the monks were a dysfunctional group incapable of providing appropriate care and education. Whilst the detailed findings relate only to this school, the systemic failings of management and leadership have a strong resonance with the situation at Ampleforth and Downside and with other Catholic public schools facing these issues.[59]

The history of child sexual abuse in the Catholic public school is not edifying. What the recent history of the roles of safeguarding and child protection in the public schools has shown is two-fold. First, the nature of the abuse itself is serious, distressing and wicked. We do have the information from a number of legal cases of the kinds of sexual abuse that took place in many of the schools. Where we have very detailed information, as in the examples of Ampleforth and Downside, the evidence is truly shocking. We know that the extent to which historic cases of abuse can be identified and mapped is very challenging, and we cannot say with any certainty that we have a proper, evidenced picture of abuse across our schools. We can say that, as in any part of Catholic society—the parish, the family, the school, the seminary—there was abuse taking place alongside all the committed, dedicated and morally decent teachers, priests, monks and brothers working in the system.

What we can also say with a degree of certainty is that the response of some schools in the recent past to allegations of both historic and contemporary child sexual abuse has been, at the very least, unsatisfactory. An environment where speaking to authority was difficult, where perpetrators were people with religious and temporal authority, where victims were often emotionally vulnerable and isolated, was a product of the schools and their leaders. The fact that up until the last couple of decades that leadership was religious makes those failings all the more reprehensible. The instinct to deny, the instinct to cover up, the tendency

---

[59] *Scottish Child Abuse Inquiry: Case Study No 5: Benedictines* (2021), pp. 11-12.

to move the perpetrator on to another place where he might re-offend, the incessant worry about reputation and public relations rather than righting wrongs, all of these tendencies have come to the fore as the Catholic public schools have confronted the challenge of child sexual abuse.

The 2018–22 IICSA reports on child abuse have underlined how inadequate the response of the Catholic Church has often been. Drawing on the very detailed examination of abuse in a range of environments, the summary findings note a lack of leadership within the Church on safeguarding issues and that "responses to disclosures about sexual abuse have been characterized by a failure to support victims and survivors in stark contrast to the positive action taken to protect alleged perpetrators and the reputation of the Church".[60]

The chronic difficulties of aligning diocesan structures and processes and those of the independent, self-governing religious institutes such as the English Benedictine community remain, and, somewhat depressingly, the complete lack of cooperation from the Vatican that the Inquiry report noted suggests a need to reinforce any progress that has been made.

The tradition of clerical authority, of unquestioned power of control, and of trust, all integral to the nature of Catholic public schools, have all been irreversibly changed by these events. The conjunction of a number of high-profile cases of abuse within a number of Catholic public schools, some dating back to the 1960s and 1970s, when the schools were perhaps at their zenith, coupled with the explicit and forensic reports on Ampleforth and Downside, have meant major reassessments and re-positioning of the Catholic public school in the last two decades or so. The old model, one of an integrated, holistic religious and educational community, has gone. The priests and monastic communities have largely vanished from the schools, and the physical, emotional and spiritual centrality and authority of the priest, monk or brother within schools has gone. The focus today is not on seeking to reproduce those elements which were at the heart of almost all the Catholic public schools in the two or three decades after 1945, but rather on the physical separation of the religious communities that were once at their heart from the daily

---

[60] *The Roman Catholic Church Report*, p. vi.

life of the school and, instead an almost entirely lay school but with a Catholic ethos, supported by a chaplaincy service. Coming on top of the enormous physical transformations in Catholic public schools over the last three decades, it is hardly surprising that, to all intents and purposes, the traditional Catholic public school has gone, to be replaced by a public school with a Catholic ethos. They may sound similar but in character, ethos, structure, staffing and governance the schools are very different.

CONCLUSION

Contemporary perspectives and looking ahead

At the time of Emancipation in 1829, the provision of Catholic secondary education for boys was almost non-existent. The basics of a network of public schools existed but all of the older schools—Stonyhurst, Sedgley Park, St Edmund's, Ampleforth and Downside—were small and often financially challenged. Whilst they were important in securing new recruits for ordination, their impact on the wider Catholic community was limited. The focus of the Church, especially after the Hierarchy was established in 1850, was overwhelmingly on elementary education and these "poor schools", established through donations from Catholic patrons, were at the heart of a strategy of ensuring the growing numbers of Catholic migrants from Ireland had schools for their children. Elementary education, taught to Catholics by Catholics and led by the Hierarchy, was the single-minded focus of the Church.

The political activities of Church leaders, and of some of the converts to Catholicism from the 1840s who lent weight to the strategy, were especially focused on securing equitable treatment for Catholic schools, as the Education Acts of 1870 and 1902 began to provide improved state funding for both elementary and secondary schooling. Resisting any kind of state intervention in the religious focus of the schools, the Hierarchy, sometimes in collaboration with other denominations, gradually achieved an improved funding base for its schools. A similar, single-minded focus characterized their input into the landmark 1944 Education Act which provided for compulsory secondary schooling, and which heralded a huge and costly expansion of Catholic secondary schools in every diocese. The maintenance of independence in teaching, school leadership and governance in Catholic schools was, and has remained, a defining feature of Catholic educational strategy through to the present day.

Examining the history of the Catholic public schools themselves, and, in particular, of the demographic, social and political contexts within which they operated, raises a number of general questions about their role and activities. Three in particular are considered in this conclusion. First, what was the place of these schools within the wider educational and missionary work of the Catholic Church? Second, to what extent did these schools seek to create a nexus of elite, well-educated and well-connected Catholics, able to play an important role in the Establishment, and capture the top jobs in politics and the media. And third, to what extent does the role and ethos of these schools today reflect their past, especially in the extent to which they remain explicitly Catholic in nature and organization?

Public Schools in the Catholic mission

The place of the public school in the wider Catholic educational strategy was not always clear cut. Perhaps a key point to stress again is that by comparison with the huge endeavour, enterprise and resources focused on Catholic elementary and secondary day education over so many decades, the importance of the Catholic public schools could be seen as marginal at best. Whilst school heads, overwhelmingly clerical until recent decades, sought to defend the place of their public schools, it is interesting that the Hierarchy itself often adopted a "hands-off" position, and remained relatively silent, even when the very survival of public schools themselves was under perceived threats. The debates around the 1944 Education Act and the Fleming Report, or the sometimes fervent attacks on the public schools generally in the 1960s and 1970s, brought forth very little in the way of organized action by the Catholic Church to defend the fee-paying sector. The focus of Catholic political activity was on wider educational funding issues and on securing the centrality of Church and diocesan control in the wider educational sector. A key plank of many of the continuing external attacks on public schools—namely the social inequalities that were exacerbated by an independent fee-paying school sector—tended to pass largely without comment. Why should that be so?

It is perhaps not surprising that Catholic leaders seemed reluctant to reflect too closely on some of these issues of equity and social justice. Historically, the focus of Catholic public schools was unashamedly elitist, with a desire to ape the non-Catholic public school, and thereby to create a new Catholic elite. For much of its history, the English Catholic Church has arguably been reasonably comfortable with notions of social hierarchy and stratification and, whilst its work has often sought to mitigate some of the worst aspects of social injustice and poverty, it had largely avoided the kind of political engagement required to fundamentally alter the social and economic conditions they encountered. For much of the twentieth century, the English Catholic Church has been largely conservative in its position on wider social or political change. It is hardly surprising, then, that the nature of the Catholic public-school experience was socially conservative and designed to secure access to the Establishment, rather than questioning the very existence of what was an inherently divisive system.[1]

That may have begun to shift a little with the pace of social and political change from the 1960s onwards, but even then the drive for social justice and "Catholic Action" that produced the liberation theologies and "worker-priests" on the Continent and elsewhere in the 1960s and 1970s was largely absent from the social and educational models and philosophies that underpinned the English Catholic experience. Rather than seeking to reform state and socio-economic structures, the Church seemed largely content at mitigating the worst effects of poverty, and seeking to ensure the state did not interfere in what it saw as the central role of the Church in education and social policy. Hardly surprising,

---

[1] F. Greene and D. Kynaston, *Engines of Privilege: Britain's Private School Problem* (London: Bloomsbury, 2019), pp. 23–53; R. Verkaik, *Posh Boys: How English Public Schools Ruin Britain*, (London: Oneworld, 2018); see also on the general character and issues for Catholic schools as a whole, A. B. Morris, *Fifty Years On: The Case for Catholic Schools* (Chelmsford: Matthew James, 2008), pp. 51–92.

then, that state intervention in education policy, or in growing the welfare state, were seen as, at the very least, potentially inimical to the Catholic mission. Equal funding of Catholic schools, coupled with a public-school group that would train the new, "natural" generation of leaders for a Catholic Establishment, largely defined the boundaries of that mission. For some critics, that conservative mission seemed content to reproduce the existing contours of class, wealth and educational advantage.[2] An acceptance of unequal access to social justice, employment, wealth and power structures sat alongside a wish to ensure that the elite groups holding the keys to economic, cultural and political power had at least their fair share of Catholics who had benefited from education in a Catholic public school. Habits of authority, of hierarchy, of deference, learnt in those establishments would, it was argued, serve those elites, and the Church itself, well in the future.

There can be little doubt that the public schools played a very important part in educating both the wealthier, aristocratic "old recusant" families who were so important in the revival of the faith in the early nineteenth century, and the new generation of well-connected converts who arrived in the Church in the mid-nineteenth century. A number of schools saw themselves as inheriting the mantle of the old continental colleges where aristocratic recusant families educated their sons, and helped to ensure the continued support of the recusant communities. The converts arriving in the Church from the Oxford Movement were also anxious to ensure that their children—habitually attenders of the non-Catholic public schools—were not socially or politically disadvantaged by attending their Catholic equivalents. This "convert class" helped to reshape the curriculum and "tone" of some of our schools. For better or worse, that process, begun in the late nineteenth century, bore fruit in the

---

[2] G. Grace, *Catholic Schools: Mission, Markets and Morality* (Abingdon: Routledge Falmer, 2002), pp. 73–4; M. Fogarty, "Catholics and Public Policy", in M. Hornsby-Smith (ed.), *Catholics in England 1950–2000: Historical and Sociological Perspectives* (London: Cassell, 1999), pp. 122–38. Terry Eagleton, *The Gatekeeper* (Harmondsworth: Penguin, 2003), esp. pp. 30–46 provides an entertaining account of a Catholic upbringing and its political and social underpinnings.

consolidation and expansion of so many of our schools in the inter-war years. Where existing schools were seen as inappropriate, some converts were active in founding new schools, most notably Newman's Oratory School in the 1860s. A further group of schools, catering for the growing Catholic middle class, grew in tandem with that class and consolidated their position and niche by the 1920s. This was the raw material from which a new Catholic elite could be moulded.

Whilst primarily focused on elementary and secondary day education, the leaders of both the seculars and the regulars did clearly understand the role that the public schools might play in the development of a Catholic higher education system. In some European countries (the University of Louvain in Belgium provided perhaps the best example), Catholic universities had been established, and the bishops undoubtedly cast a covetous eye on some of those institutions. As we have seen, alumni of the Catholic public schools were not able to enter Oxford or Cambridge without the permission of their bishop until the end of the nineteenth century and, whilst all of the schools engaged in the external examination schema set up by, for example, the University of London or, at a later date, Oxford and Cambridge, attendance at Oxbridge itself was regarded by the Hierarchy as morally and religiously dangerous. That mindset was an interesting example of an educational strategy that was defensive, seeking to cocoon Catholics within an intellectual and social straitjacket, rather than an outward-looking strategy seeking a place in the wider world and, with it, the potential to convert. The secular authorities, in particular, harboured aspirations from the 1860s to set up a Catholic university; Newman's involvement in creating a Catholic university in Ireland in the 1850s provided an exemplar of both the possibilities and, especially, the problems inherent in such a project.[3]

For the schools themselves, there were perhaps two conflicting responses to the Catholic university project. One was to seek, through pressure on the Hierarchy, to have the ban on Oxbridge entrance

---

[3] See J. Cornwell, *Newman's Unquiet Grave: The Reluctant Saint* (London: Continuum, 2011), pp. 122–37; C. Butler, "Newman and modern education", *Downside Review* 70 (1952), pp. 259–74; Sheridan Gilley, *Newman and His Age* (London: Darton, Longman & Todd, 1990), pp. 284–306.

overturned, which would place the schools on an equal footing with the rest of the public-school sector, and allow them to compete for entry and, especially, the prestigious exhibitions and scholarships which were so central to the public school offer elsewhere. The alternative—pressing for the creation of a Catholic university which had Catholic theology and morals at its heart—was certainly attractive, and the issue was debated, sometimes acrimoniously, by Cardinal Manning and the Hierarchy in the 1860s and 1870s. Manning argued in 1863 that "all the elements for a new Catholic University existed 'in the four great colleges of Stonyhurst, Oscott, Old Hall [St Edmund's] and Ushaw' together with the 'lesser colleges of Sedgley Park, Mount St Mary, St Edward's, Downside, Ratcliffe, St Buenos, Beaumont Lodge and Ampleforth'".[4] Interestingly, Manning does not mention the Oratory School established by John Henry Newman in this list, perhaps a reflection of the sometimes "challenging" relationship between the two men!

A questionnaire circulated to these schools in 1871 showed that most of the schools, with the exception of Ushaw, were broadly supportive of creating a Catholic university. Stonyhurst, in particular, might have had good reason to be nervous because they had for some time established a senior Philosophers class which effectively provided an undergraduate education through the University of London, but their response was positive. In 1874, alongside a reiteration of the ban on enrolling at Oxford or Cambridge, a Catholic university college was created at Kensington. Had the project succeeded, it might have provided a stronger rationale for the continued development of the public schools as primary feeders for a kind of Catholic "closed loop", with the Hierarchy set to control and articulate an integrated system of strong boarding and day schools for the elite, progressing to a strong Catholic university. Newman's "Idea of a University" might have provided a model. It never happened. Newman was excluded from any input into the university (perhaps again, a reflection of his sometimes fractious relationship with Cardinal

---

[4]   H. O. Evennett, "Catholics and the Universities, 1850–1950", in G. A. Beck (ed.), *The English Catholics: Centenary Essays to Commemorate the Restoration of the Hierarchy of England and Wales* (London: Burns & Oates, 1950), p. 296.

Manning), academic autonomy and reputation was lacking, and the project failed within a few years. Public school, followed by Oxford or Cambridge, was firmly established as the route to success for Catholic and non-Catholic public schools alike by the early twentieth century. Henceforth they sank or swam in the same system. The development of Catholic teacher training colleges in the twentieth century was a reflection of the wish of the Hierarchy to maintain tight control over their schools, and those who taught in them, but their overlap with the Catholic public schools was slight. Their emergence as new university colleges and universities from the 1980s helped to provide a form of higher education within a broad Catholic framework, something that had taken over a century to achieve.

Training a Catholic elite

An examination of the history of the Catholic public school over some two centuries has highlighted the extent to which a relatively small number of schools served to both reflect, and to shape, many aspects of the Catholic mission itself. They developed alongside, but distinct from, the numerically much more significant elementary and secondary schools established by the Church to support a growing, often poor, Catholic population in the nineteenth and early twentieth centuries. As the demography and socio-economic status of the Catholic population changed, so the educational mission and priorities of the Church shifted. As we have seen, growing affluence and suburbanization, the emergence of a Catholic middle class, and the increasing confidence of a nascent "Catholic Establishment", helped to shape the size and nature of the Catholic public-school population, and amplified its role in assisting in the formation of the educational mission and socio-political aspirations of the Church.

One of the main aims of this book has been to set the individual histories of Catholic public schools within a wider social, political and educational context. The demographic growth of Catholicism, built from the early nineteenth century on varying combinations of migration and conversion, underpinned the success or otherwise of our schools. Public schools in general were, and remain, about power, money and markets, and the Catholic schools were, and are, no different in that respect. They emerged and grew through a determination by both the seculars and the regulars to exercise power and control over how an educated Catholic elite was to be trained for key positions in the Church or the Establishment. Building a distinctive school environment imbued with high academic standards, a powerful, daily spirituality, and important networks through alumni and supporters into the once-closed corridors of the Establishment were central to their success. That success was essential to a Catholic Church which was seeking to recover and rebuild its place in English society after having been outlawed for some 250 years. Security, acceptance and self-confidence were central to the Hierarchy; the public school was privileged as a means to help achieve this.

The creation of this network of schools demanded significant money and resources from individuals and from those regulars and seculars who staffed and supported the schools. Capital costs of land and buildings had to be found. Uniquely, the Catholic public schools had access to a largely "free" labour force of priests, monks, brothers and nuns to work in the schools. For many of them, there was a "virtuous circle" of pupils moving from their schools to associated seminaries (sometimes at the same place), and then returning to their schools after becoming priests or monks, to teach and begin the process of training the next generation for Catholic service. That virtuous circle was especially important in those schools founded by the Benedictines. The growth of monastic communities at Downside or Ampleforth, for example, was resourced in large part from the monies and potential monks that the school itself provided. The Benedictine Abbey of Belmont established their school in 1924 primarily to help provide new revenue streams which would facilitate the expansion of the monastic community itself. The relationship was symbiotic. As long as the schools continued to generate income, the monastic community could continue to grow and prosper.

The role of the schools in shaping a new elite can perhaps be better understood by considering their contribution in terms of the different forms of capital that are created through the educational process, capital which was, and is, central to social advancement. *Economic capital* was endowed through the elite nature of the public schools,

Catholic or otherwise. Access was privileged and restricted by income and class through the payment of fees. The products of the system were drawn almost entirely from the upper and upper-middle classes, whose attendance at an elite school helped consolidate their economic capital, facilitating their entrance into the Establishment. The clear focus on this particular elite economic group did not chime especially well with the clearly articulated Catholic mission of educating the poorer members of the community.

Alongside economic capital the development of *social* and *cultural capital* within the pupil community was also vital. Such capital was built up through social connections, and through immersion in the literature, music, drama and sporting infrastructure, which school leaders saw as constituting an appropriate upper-class education. As has been shown, it is not surprising that schools were swift to adopt "gentlemanly" pursuits (rugby, fencing, rowing, hosting the local hunt, beagling, cricket) which helped to mark out their pupils for the future. Military service through the cadet or officer training corps served similar functions in equipping pupils with a set of expectations and conventions, often tacit and "invisible", to help them fit well into the mores of higher society. *Spiritual capital* may also be seen as an important fourth element in the educational process. Immersion in a religious culture within the school system, replete with the symbolism, ritual and theatre of the Catholic public school, provided a range of resources of faith and values drawn from a commitment to a particular religious tradition. That capital was most explicitly demonstrated in the priests, monks and brothers who led and staffed the schools for so long, and who sought to pass on to their pupils those resources which, they hoped, would be of lasting value in their future lives. The school, especially the boarding schools, existed to provide a *habitus*, an environment which was, to quote Grace, "comprehensively immersed in cultural teachings and beliefs, rituals, symbols and practices designed to produce deep-seated cultural dispositions in the individual arising out of an intense process of socialization and formation".[5]

---

[5] Grace, *Catholic Schools*, p. 43.

That educational model of the Catholic public school mirrored in some ways the dialectic underpinning the Catholic educational mission up until the recent past: a "retreat from the world" in terms of the enclosed, religious, boarding environment and habitat, alongside a desire to "go out and convert" through the newly opening corridors of power and influence.

As an educational model, the Catholic public schools were able, by and large, to thrive, at least until recent decades. Those elements that have been articulated in the book—the academic environment, models of supervision, sporting, military and cultural activities and an all-embracing religious and spiritual framework for daily life—worked, unless, and until, the seemingly endless supply of potential clerics dried up. At that point, arguably by the mid-1970s, harsher realities began to bite, with rising labour costs for an increasingly lay teaching staff beginning to undermine the ability of schools to continue along the same, well-trodden and familiar path.

The virtuous circle of "pupil—novitiate—monk or priest—teacher—pupil" had largely disappeared by the 1970s. At Downside, for example, not a single post-1970 pupil opted to begin the journey towards becoming a monk, and other Abbey/schools experienced similar patterns.[6] At Belmont, as we noted earlier, only a handful of vocations had come from the school in the 20 years or so before its closure in 1994. Ampleforth was perhaps an exception. The monastic community was over 150 strong in the early 1970s, with many in that community working in the school.

As for markets, they too have shifted. The schools had a captive market and monopoly for a long time in the sense that, compared to the non-Catholic sector, the number of Catholic public schools was relatively small. If a parent wanted a Catholic private education for their children, the choice was limited. Church leaders, in any case, worked very hard to dissuade Catholic parents from educating their children outside the aegis of the church. Almost all the schools were in place by about 1900. Many schools were also increasingly adept at taking advantage of the growing Catholic middle-class market. But Catholics could, and did, choose to send their children to non-Catholic public schools where,

---

[6] G. Mercer, Talk to Old Gregorians at the Travellers Club, London (2021).

by the inter-war years, there was increasing recognition and support for Catholic pupils. Schools such as Eton, for example, made excellent provision for their growing numbers of Catholic boys, with Catholic priests working within the school to provide spiritual support. If the two decades after 1945 marked a period of great confidence and seeming security for our schools, more recent decades have seen much sharper competition, right across the spectrum, for pupils who might traditionally have been destined for Catholic public schools. Equally, competition from the many strong independent Catholic day schools has sharpened. There can also be little doubt that the clerical abuse issues which have emerged in the last decade or so could have a potentially catastrophic impact on those schools most directly affected, and a corrosive effect on confidence in the sector as a whole. How that plays out remains to be seen.

By the 1930s and 1940s, then, the Catholic schools were beginning to make some progress in establishing an elite and making inroads into the Establishment, progress which was accentuated in the decades after 1945. For a number of schools (Ampleforth and Downside are perhaps the best examples), a single-minded focus on the recruitment of pupils from specific sections of society, especially the aristocracy and gentry, did produce results. That pattern was not unique and our evidence from the end of the twentieth century suggests that whilst Ampleforth, Stonyhurst and Downside were of particular significance, all of the Catholic schools were represented in what we might identify as a register of the Catholic elite as Table 5 showed. Medicine, the Law, academia, business and the military all had significant representation of Catholics, amongst which around one-third had been educated by the Catholic public schools. That process of creating an elite was slow and sometimes piecemeal but, by the end of the twentieth century, it had largely been achieved.[7]

Much the same could be said of the historic role of our schools in educating the clerical elite of England. A pattern of Catholic public school followed by seminary and ordination, and then progress up the ranks of the Hierarchy had a sense of inevitability about it. If one examines where

---

[7] D. Sewell, *Catholics: Britain's Largest Minority* (London: Viking, 2001), pp. 2–8.

successive Archbishops of Westminster were educated prior to joining seminaries, the dominance of our schools is clear.

Table 7: Educational background of the Archbishops of Westminster 1850–2009

Archbishop	Dates	School attended
Nicholas Wiseman	1850–65	Ushaw/ Oscott
Henry Manning	1865–92	Harrow
Herbert Vaughan	1892–1903	Stonyhurst
Francis Bourne	1903–35	Ushaw/ St Edmund's
Arthur Hinsley	1935–43	Ushaw
Bernard Griffin	1943–56	Cotton
William Godfrey	1956–63	Ushaw
John Heenan	1963–76	St Ignatius (Jesuit day)
Basil Hume	1976–99	Ampleforth
Cormac Murphy O'Connor	2000–9	Prior Park
Vincent Nicholls	2009–	St Mary's, Crosby (Day)

Similar patterns emerge from examining the background of other senior clergy. Successive Bishops of Birmingham, for example, were educated in our schools—Sedgley Park, Cotton, Prior Park, Downside, Douai dominate; similar patterns apply to the diocese of Liverpool with Ushaw and St Edmund's providing the education of around half of the bishops and archbishops since 1850.

These examples could be multiplied but serve to illustrate the virtuous circle created by the Catholic public schools, and perhaps help to explain why the Hierarchy continued to support the schools with human and other resources, especially at a time of significant educational and missionary pressures elsewhere. The visits of archbishops and bishops to their old *alma mater* for annual celebratory events has remained a constant theme in school histories through to the present. Whether that will continue into the future is unlikely. Certainly the Hierarchy in 2024 has a much more diverse educational background than previous ones, with the dominance of the old Catholic public schools weakening significantly.

The success in creating and sustaining a new Catholic elite was clearly a source of pride for so many schools, but it can perhaps obscure a question that has become paramount in recent decades. What justification can there be for the Church maintaining an educational model which is fundamentally elitist, given the huge advantages that can be obtained through paying for a private education? The debate over public schools has continued over recent decades with issues over university entrance, access to the professions, and the continuance of old-boy networks within both the public and private sector, leading to strong critiques of the continued role, not to say existence, of public schools.

At times, as we have seen, critics have advocated a range of options from reforming bursary and scholarship support within schools to diversifying intake, the abolition of charitable status, greater state control over admissions through to outright abolition and closure. Whilst the arguments over public schools have been rehearsed in recent literature, what is perhaps noteworthy has been the lack of any clear position from the Catholic public schools. It might be argued that, for at least a couple of decades, the Catholic Hierarchy no longer plays a part in the governance of many of our schools. But does that absolve them from any responsibility for the social inequalities resulting from helping to maintain a public-school system?

Catholic public schools are now much more closely aligned with the public-school sector as a whole, and there may be little to distinguish their respective positions on the ethics, or otherwise, of public-school provision. That position, powerfully articulated through bodies such as the Independent Schools Council, applies to Catholic and non-Catholic public schools alike. Historically, the drive to create an elite, educated through a privileged public-school system, was seen as entirely appropriate, necessary and ethically unproblematic by the Church. At a time when the Catholic Church was only beginning to grow in numbers, confidence and representation, that position might be seen as justified. But holding to that position is much less justifiable today. The nature of a dual education system is not seen as problematic but rather advantageous. Does that matter? Arguably, Catholic educational policies have been consistently successful, and the Catholic public school has contributed to that success in its own way. Nevertheless, political and social winds do change. The public-school sector largely survived the political challenges of the 1960s and 1970s by being flexible, well organized and politically astute, and Catholic schools were content to be carried along with that new organizational dynamism. Moves to shift terminology from "public schools" to "independent schools" for example was part of a wider public relations effort by the public schools as a whole in the early 1970s.[8] How well they adapt to changing political and social attitudes and environments will be an important marker for the future. Catholic and non-Catholic public schools now sit within a largely uniform political and organizational lobby; it may prove difficult to discern a distinctive and credible voice for them outside of that monolith. They will face the same political and social criticism. Debates about charitable status and the tax benefits they provide will affect all public schools, Catholic or otherwise.

Religious and educational change in the Catholic school

Dealing with change has been a constant within the Catholic public school sector. Demographic and religious changes in the nineteenth century shaped early school development. Curriculum changes—the growth of science education, the decline of the classics, the creation of new forms of organization within schools—all initiated major changes in the structure and character of the school. The use of sport or the military to stimulate leadership and help create a social elite marked all of our schools. The religious triumphalism of the 1940s and 1950s gave way to the significant changes in staffing, management and leadership by the end of the century. Schools have always sought to both shape and reflect the Catholic *zeitgeist*; how then are they positioned to adapt to contemporary

---

[8] On the PR efforts of the public schools in the 1960s and 1970s see J. Rae, *The Public School Revolution: Britain's Independent Schools 1964–1979* (London: Faber & Faber, 1981), pp. 58–90.

social and religious change? And is a Catholic infrastructure, spirituality and ethos still central to the work of the schools?

There is a sizeable literature dealing with contemporary Catholic educational issues from a number of perspectives—curriculum, staffing and leadership, the nature of the pupil intake, academic performance, parental input, socio-economic impact—and some of these issues have arisen in the course of the book. A particular focus here has been on the nature of Catholic spirituality as a key unifying, perhaps defining, element, underpinning so many other aspects of the school—its curriculum, staffing, leadership and academic performance have historically been seen as integral to a holistic view of what constituted the core of the Catholic public school. To what extent has that changed and, if it has, what is it that might now characterize the unique selling point of these schools?

The schools are now much bigger, more diverse, staffed, led and governed by lay rather than clerical staff, and part of an intensely competitive school system driven by individual academic results and league table position. They increasingly work in an environment where the *visible* markers of Catholicism may be difficult to discern and where significant numbers of both staff and pupils do not define themselves as Catholics. Interestingly, in 2021, in the Catholic independent sector, the proportion of Catholic staff and pupils is lower than that to be found in the Catholic maintained sector as a whole.[9]

Most obvious is the absence of priests, monks or lay brothers within the school environment. Whilst a few schools are able to maintain a small presence of priests or monks within the school community (Ampleforth, for example, still has a sizeable monastic community but only a small number involved with the school), elsewhere numbers range from small to tiny. A chaplaincy service, staffed perhaps on a part-time basis, has replaced the large religious community of 30 or 40 years ago. It is also evident that the number and frequency of religious services and functions delivered as part of school life has inevitably reduced significantly. A school calendar, once dominated by daily religious observance, and imbued with a strong sense of Catholic religiosity, has significantly

---

[9] Data from *Catholic Education Service 2022.*

altered. With the growth in pupil numbers and diversity over the last two decades, and with the enormous pressures of a full curriculum, whole school events have become logistically difficult because of the lack of church space; amidst the frenzy of building work in the last two or three decades it is noticeable that new church space has not featured highly if at all. Whilst not denying their continued role in school life, communal and corporate religious events are now less frequent and largely form- or house-, rather than school-based. As Glackin notes, school heads have had to reflect at length on how to maintain the spiritual capital or charism that underpinned their schools when they were founded.[10]

Does this matter? Certainly, it would be hard to argue that the schools are no longer Catholic because of these changes. All of our schools continue to emphasize the importance of a Catholic religious and moral core to their work, despite their overwhelmingly lay character. Religious observance today is in any case arguably much more personal. That collective, corporate sense of Catholicity, so fundamental in the schools in the past, is arguably less relevant to the practice of worship and religious reflection today. For Hornsby-Smith, "religion has largely become a purely private affair" with personal morality and religious affiliation "much less likely to be dictated by some religious or authority figure".[11]

The Catholic character of the schools perhaps now resides much less in observance reinforced by a priestly presence in the chapel, classroom and corridors of the school, and rather more in a mix of religiously informed teaching and facilitation of individual reflection, prayer and pastoral support, alongside some elements of collective worship. For Arthur, writing in the mid-1990s, these shifts presaged what he regarded as an "ebbing tide" within Catholic schools, in which pluralism of intake and teachers, and a utilitarianism focused on individual academic

---

[10] M. Glackin, "Maintaining the Charism: Leadership Matters in Catholic Independent Schools", in S. Whittle (ed.), *Leadership Matters in Catholic Education* (Singapore: Springer, forthcoming, 2024).

[11] M. Hornsby-Smith, *An Introduction to Catholic Social Thought* (Cambridge: Cambridge University Press, 2006), pp. 21, 34.

performance and league tables, threatened the distinctive nature and mission of the Catholic school.[12]

The extent to which contemporary Catholic public schools articulate this rather different religious emphasis is hard to judge and the conclusions of Arthur were disputed. An examination of the marketing presence of Catholic public schools, for example, highlights the importance they continue to attach to the religious origins of the schools and continue to emphasize the importance of their strong Catholic and Christian ethos without necessarily reflecting on the differences between those two. As Glackin suggested in her survey of independent heads, "the charism, defined centuries before, speaks to the heart of schools today and continues to benefit them pedagogically, pastorally, spiritually and even commercially".[13] But is that more a matter of celebrating a particular history and heritage, and the patina of tradition that it gives a school, rather than something at the heart of everything the school does? The clerical abuse crisis has undoubtedly led some schools to seek to distance themselves physically and managerially from any interaction with religious orders or communities. It is impossible to judge but is clearly a matter of some debate.

One feature that does mark out the Catholic education sector in general is that there is a body of documents and papers drawn up in particular by the Vatican (especially through the Sacred Congregation for Catholic Education), seeking to articulate what it is that is distinctive about education in a Catholic school, independent or otherwise. Table 8 highlights some of these key documents.

Table 8: Key contemporary Catholic Education documents

Vatican documents
Divini Illius Magistri ("The Christian Education of Youth", 1929).
Gravissimum Educationis (Declaration on Christian Education, 1965).

---

[12] J. Arthur, *The Ebbing Tide: Policy and Principles of Catholic Education* (Leominster: Gracewing, 1995).

[13] Glackin, "Maintaining the Charism".

Sacred Congregation for Catholic Education
The Catholic School (1977).
Lay Catholics in School: Witnesses to Faith (1982).
The Religious Dimension of Education in a Catholic School (1988).
The Catholic School on the Threshold of the Third Millenium (1998).

Source: A. B. Morris, *Fifty Years On: The Case for Catholic Schools* (Chelmsford: Matthew James, 2008).

What might such documents reveal about the issues around the nature of public-school education? *Gravissimum Educationis* articulated a new openness in Catholic schools with a special concern for the poorer members of the community, together with a renewal of a missionary focus towards those who were not Catholic. In *The Catholic School* (1977), a special concern for the less well-off was noted and it argued that "knowledge is not to be considered as a means of material prosperity but as a call to serve and be responsible for others".[14]

Recognizing the decline in the numbers of priests and members of religious orders, *Lay Catholics* (1982) emphasized how important the laity was in leading and inspiring schools through "the best possible qualifications, with an apostolic intention inspired by faith".[15] Finally, the 1998 document was both realistic, and pessimistic, about the apathy and indifference to religious studies facing many Catholic schools. Concerns about the social exclusivity of the independent sector, about the way in which educational models sometimes sought to prioritize individual accumulation of capital (especially those intangibles aimed at securing access to the higher echelons of society) and about the importance of the laity, resonate with a number of contemporary aspects of the sector.

There are a number of contemporary member organizations seeking to explore these issues in a collective and collaborative way. The most important, the Catholic Independent Schools' Conference (CISC), established in 1990, has helped to coordinate and disseminate information, training and leadership work in relation to the nature of a

---

[14] Grace, *Catholic Schools*, p. 19.
[15] Grace, *Catholic Schools*, p. 20.

Catholic education in independent schools. Some 120 schools were in membership in the CISC in 2022 with around 40,000 pupils enrolled in their schools ranging between ages 3 and 18.[16] The central importance of values informing a holistic view of education, coupled with a visible demonstration of Catholic worship through assemblies, retreats and religious education seems to underpin much of the material. Pastoral care and interaction with the Catholic community as a whole, and traditions of charitable and social engagement feature as well. The extent to which such characteristics are equally applicable to the term "Christian" as to the term "Catholic" is a moot point. Unsurprisingly, both terms feature in many schools, independent or otherwise. The cynic might argue that the term "Catholic" is most useful at a time when the academic performance of the Catholic sector as a whole is higher than the average, but that any change in that position might produce a predominance of the term "Christian".

Certainly the Catholic independent sector is engaged in such fierce competition with other schools that it is sometimes hard to identify a unity or sense of cohesion, although Raymond Friel has looked at pragmatic and practical ways in which this might be achieved in the Catholic school, independent or otherwise.[17] Cohesion and collaboration might also be the product of aligning different schools within a particular group. The Catholic public schools have made some efforts to develop such frameworks. Some schools, as with their non-Catholic rivals, have developed an overseas campus such as Stonyhurst in Malaysia. Others, Prior Park College for example, have made tentative efforts to develop relations both overseas (a Gibraltar college) and with neighbouring schools in the state sector. Whilst the Catholic Hierarchy has not always favoured the creation of formal Academy Trusts embracing a range of schools as a response to the market (grouping "failing" schools with "successful" ones *pour encourager les autres*), more collaborative relations would seem to be a way to mitigate some of the consequences

---

[16] *Catholic Independent Schools' Conference* at <https://www.catholicindependentschools.com/>, accessed 23 August 2023.

[17] R. Friel, *Gospel Values for Catholic Schools: A Practical Guide for Today* (Chawton: Redemptorist Publications, 2017), pp. 120–7.

of the underlying elitism evident in the public schools. For some, such collaboration was seen as a way of justifying the continuation of their charitable status.

The Jesuits have arguably moved some way in this direction. As we have noted, the Jesuit intervention in education in nineteenth-century England was often structured and logical; they established a range of schools—public schools, distinguished day schools, elementary urban schools—reflecting, at least in part, their understanding of social structures and of the wide educational remit the Church required at that time. A similar logic perhaps underpins Jesuit schools today. The 11 Jesuit schools in England (including Stonyhurst and Mount St Mary's alongside publicly funded schools)) sit within an educational framework developed by the Jesuit Institute which emphasizes the distinctive nature of a Jesuit education common to all its schools. That framework recognizes the importance of helping its students to "reason reflectively, logically and critically and to promote education as an apostolic instrument".[18] The emphasis is on an intellectual formation and reasoning, coupled with promoting dialogue and reflection and serving the common good. Collaboration, exchange and collective meetings and engagement are some of the features the Jesuit Institute seeks to grow within its schools.

Such attempts to define a cohesive framework within which the public schools might work alongside other parts of the Catholic educational system are interesting. They may well provide one of the ways in which the "offer" of the Catholic public school may be distinguished from the rest of the public-school system in England. What is distinctive about the Catholic public school? Has the Catholic public school ceased to exist as a recognizable entity within the public-school group as a whole? Why would parents—Catholic or otherwise—choose to send their children there? If one considers the rich history and heritage of these schools, distinctiveness and identity is rather easier to recognize in the past, than in the present. Whether these schools are able to mark out a clear and distinctive path may well prove to be the key to their survival in the future.

---

[18] *The characteristics of Jesuit Education*, <http://www.sjweb.info/documents/education/characteristics_en.pdf>, accessed 23 August 2023.

Bibliography

Almond, C., *The History of Ampleforth Abbey* (London: Longman, 1903).
Almond, L., *Downside Abbey and School, 1814–1914* (Exeter: Wheaton, 1914).
Archer, R. L., *Secondary Education in the Nineteenth Century* (London: Frank Cass, 1966).
Arthur, J., *The Ebbing Tide: Policy and Principles of Catholic Education* (Leominster: Gracewing, 1995).
Aspden, K., "The English Roman Catholic Bishops and the Social Order 1918-1926", *Recusant History* 25:3 (2001), pp. 543–64.
Aspden, K., *Fortress Church: The English Roman Catholic Bishops and Politics, 1903–1963* (Leominster: Gracewing, 2002).
Aspinall, B., "Towards an English Catholic Social Conscience 1829-1920", *British Catholic History* 25:1 (2000), pp. 106–19.
Atherton, D. and Peyton, M., *St Joseph's College, Upholland: One of the glories of Catholicism in England. Its rise and fall.* Unpublished (2013), <https://www.academia.edu/48825759/St_Joseph_s_College_Upholland_One_of_the_glories_of_Catholicism_in_England_Its_rise_and_fall_Revised_and_Updated>, accessed on 17 August 2023.
Badhern, J. R., "The symbolic landscapes of nineteenth and early-twentieth century English Catholic Public Schools", unpublished MA Thesis, Faculty of Environment and Leisure, University of Gloucestershire, 2004.
Bamford, T., "Public Schools and social class 1801–1851", *British Journal of Sociology* 12:5 (1961), pp. 224–33.
Bamford, T., *The Rise of the Public Schools: A Study of Boys' Public Boarding Schools in England and Wales from 1837 to the Present Day* (London: Nelson, 1967).

Barnes, A. S., *The Catholic Schools of England* (London: Williams & Norgate, 1926).

Battersby, W. J., "Secondary Education for Boys", in G. A. Beck (ed.), *The English Catholics: Centenary Essays to Commemorate the Restoration of the Hierarchy of England and Wales* (London: Burns & Oates, 1950), pp. 322–6.

Beales, A. C., "The Struggle for the Schools", in G. A. Beck (ed.), *The English Catholics: Centenary Essays to Commemorate the Restoration of the Hierarchy of England and Wales* (London: Burns & Oates, 1950), pp. 365–409.

Beattie, M., *Portrait of our College: Mount St Mary and Barlborough Hall, 1842–2017* (London: Society of Jesus, 2017).

Beck, G. A. (ed.), *The English Catholics: Centenary Essays to Commemorate the Restoration of the Hierarchy of England and Wales* (London: Burns & Oates, 1950).

Bellenger, D. A., *Downside: A Pictorial History* (Downside Abbey, 1998).

Bellenger, D. A., "Religious Life for Men", in V. A. McClelland and M. Hodgetts (eds), *From Without the Flaminian Gate: 150 Years of Roman Catholicism in England and Wales, 1850–2000* (London: Darton, Longman & Todd, 1999), pp. 142–66.

Bellenger, D. A., *Benedictine Education: A Historical Perspective* (Downside Abbey, 2009).

Bellenger, D. A. (ed.), *Downside Abbey: An Architectural History* (London: Merrell, 2011).

Birt, D. N., *Downside: The History of St. Gregory's School from its Commencement at Douay to the Present Time* (London: Kegan Paul & Co., 1902).

Bossy, J., *The English Catholic Community 1570–1850* (London: Darton, Longman & Todd, 1975).

Bright, L. and Clements, S. (eds), *The Committed Church* (London: Darton, Longman & Todd, 1966).

Broadley, M. J., *Bishop Vaughan and the Jesuits: Education and Authority* (London: Boydell, 2010).

Brothers, J., *Church and School. A Study of the Image of Education on Religion* (Liverpool: Liverpool University Press, 1964).

Brown, C., *The Death of Christian Britain: Understanding Secularisation 1800–2000* (London: Routledge, 2001).

Brown, C., "What was the religious crisis of the 1960s?", *Journal of Religious History* 34:4 (2010), pp. 468–79.

Bruce, S., "Secularisation, Church and Popular Religion", *Journal of Ecclesiastical History* 62:3 (2011), pp. 543–61.

Burton-Ware, E., *St Edmund's College, Old Hall* (Ware: St Edmund's College, 1925).

Buscot, Canon W.., *A History of Cotton College* (London: Burns, Oates & Washbourne, 1940).

Butler, C., "Newman and modern education", *Downside Review* 70 (1952), pp. 259–74.

Campbell, W. J. (ed.), *Ushaw College 1808–2008: A Celebration* (Keighley: PKP Publishing, 2008).

Caparrini, B. R., "A Catholic School in the making: Beaumont College during the Rectorate of the Rev. Joseph Bampton", *Paedagogica Historica* 39:6 (2003), pp. 737–57.

Cashmann, J., "Old Prior Park—the Final Years, 1843–1856", *Recusant History* 23:1 (1996), pp. 79–106.

Chadwick, O., *The Victorian Church:1829–1901, 2 vols,* (London: SCM Press, 1997).

Champ, J., *Oscott* (Birmingham: Archdiocese of Birmingham Historical Commission, 1987).

Champ, J. (ed.), *Oscott College, 1838–1988: A Volume of Commemorative Essays* (Oscott: Oscott Publishing, 1988).

Champ, J., *William Bernard Ullathorne 1806–1889: A Different Kind of Monk,* (Leominster: Gracewing, 2006).

Cleary, J. M., *Catholic Social Action in Britain, 1909–1959* (Oxford: Catholic Social Guild, 1961).

Connolly, G., "The transubstantiation of myth: towards a new popular history of nineteenth-century Catholicism in England", *Journal of Ecclesiastical History* 35 (1984), pp. 78–104.

Cornwell, J., *Seminary Boy* (London: Harper, 2007).

Cornwell, J., *Newman's Unquiet Grave: The Reluctant Saint* (London: Continuum, 2011).

Cornwell, J., *The Dark Box: A Secret History of Confession* (London: Profile Books, 2014).

Cornwell, P., *Prior Park College: The Phoenix* (Tiverton: Halsgrove Press, 2005, revised with additional material by D. Clarke, 2018).

Cramer, A., *Ampleforth: The Story of St Laurence's Abbey and College* (Ampleforth Abbey, 2001).

Crichton, J. D., "1920–1940 The Dawn of a Liturgical Movement", in J. D. Crichton, H. Winstone and J. Ainslie (eds), *English Catholic Worship* (London: Chapman, 1979), pp. 17–47.

Curtis, S. J. and Boultwood, M., *An Introductory History of English Education since 1800* (London: University Tutorial Press, 1964).

Davie, G., *Religion in Britain since 1945* (Oxford: Blackwell, 1996).

Davies, J., "'L'Art du Possible': The Board of Education, the Catholic Church and negotiations over the White Paper and the Education Bill, 1943–4", *Recusant History* 22:2 (1994), pp. 231–50.

de la Bedoyere, M., *The Future of Catholic Christianity* (Harmondsworth: Penguin, 1968).

Doyle, P., "The Education and Training of Roman Catholic Priests in nineteenth-century England", *Journal of Ecclesiastical History* 35:2 (1984), pp. 208–19.

Doyle, P., "Charles Plater SJ and the Origins of the Catholic Social Guild", *British Catholic History* 21:3 (1993), pp. 401–17.

Doyle, P., *Mitres and Missions in Lancashire: The Roman Catholic Diocese of Liverpool 1850–2005* (Liverpool: Bluecoat Press, 2005).

Duffy, E., *The Stripping of the Altars: Traditional Religion in England 1400–1580* (London: Yale University Press, 1992).

Duffy, E., *Faith of Our Fathers* (London: Continuum, 2004).

Eagleton, T., *The Gatekeeper* (Harmondsworth: Penguin 2001).

Elliot, B., "Mount St Bernard's Reformatory, Leicestershire, 1856–1881", *British Catholic History* 15:1 (1979), pp. 15–22.

Evennett, H. O., *The Catholic Schools of England and Wales* (Cambridge: Cambridge University Press, 1944).

Evennett, H. O., "Catholics and the Universities, 1850–1950", in G. A. Beck (ed.), *The English Catholics: Centenary Essays to Commemorate the Restoration of the Hierarchy of England and Wales* (London: Burns & Oates, 1950), pp. 293–302.

Fielding, S., *Class and Ethnicity: Irish Catholics in England, 1880–1939* (Buckingham: Open University, 1993).

Fogarty, M., "Catholics and Public Policy", in M. Hornsby-Smith (ed.), *Catholics in England 1950–2000: Historical and Sociological Perspectives* (London: Cassell, 1999), pp. 122–38.

Foster, S., "Monseigneur Lord William Joseph Petre (1847–1883): A Pillar of Downside", *Recusant History* 22:1 (1994), pp. 88–101.

Friel, R., *Gospel Values for Catholic Schools: A Practical Guide for Today* (Chawton: Redemptorist Publications, 2017).

Gabriel Communications, *Who's Who in Catholic Life 1997* (Manchester: Gabriel Communications Ltd., 1997).

Galliver, P., "The Early Ampleforth College", *Recusant History* 8:4 (2007), pp. 511–28.

Galliver, P., *Ampleforth College: The Emergence of Ampleforth College as the 'Catholic Eton'* (Leominster: Gracewing, 2019).

Gathorne-Hardy, J., *The Public School Phenomenon* (London: Hodder & Stoughton, 1977).

Gerard, J., *Stonyhurst Centenary Record* (Belfast: Marcus Ward, 1894).

Gilbert, J., "The Catholic Church and Education", in *100 years of Catholic Emancipation 1829–1929* (London: Longmans Green, 1929), pp. 47–76.

Gilley, S., "The Age of Equipoise, 1892–1943", in V. A. McClelland and M. Hodgetts (eds), *From Without the Flaminian Gate: 150 Years of Roman Catholicism in England and Wales, 1850–2000* (London: Darton, Longman & Todd, 1999), pp. 21–46.

Gilley, S., "The Roman Catholic Church and the Nineteenth Century Irish Diaspora", *Journal of Ecclesiastical History* 35:2 (1984), pp. 188–207.

Gilley, S, *Newman and his Age* (London: Darton, Longman & Todd, 1990).

Glackin, M., "Maintaining the Charism: Leadership Matters in Catholic Independent Schools", in S. Whittle (ed.), *Leadership Matters in Catholic Education* (Singapore: Springer, forthcoming, 2024).

Grace, G., *Catholic Schools: Mission, Markets and Morality* (Abingdon: Routledge Falmer, 2002).

Green, B., *The English Benedictine Congregation* (London: Catholic Truth Society, 1979).

Greene, F. and Kynaston, D., *Engines of Privilege: Britain's Private School Problem* (London: Bloomsbury, 2019).

Greene, G. (ed.), *The Old School Tie: Essays by Divers Hands* (London: Jonathan Cape, 1934).

Gwynn, D., "Growth of the Catholic Community", in G. A. Beck (ed.), *The English Catholics: Centenary Essays to Commemorate the Restoration of the Hierarchy of England and Wales* (London: Burns & Oates, 1950), pp. 410–30.

Hagerty, J., *The Catenian Association: A Centenary History* (Coventry: Catenian Association, 2008).

Harding, J. A., *The Diocese of Clifton 1850–2000* (Clifton: Clifton Catholic Diocesan Trustees, 1999).

Harris, A., *Faith in the Family. A Lived Religious History of English Catholicism, 1945–82* (Manchester: Manchester University Press, 2013).

Hastings, A. (ed.), *Modern Catholicism: Vatican II and after* (London: SPCK, 1991).

Hastings, A., *A History of English Christianity 1920–2000* (London: SPCK, 2001).

Hattersley, R., *The Catholics* (London: Vintage, 2018).

Heinmann, C., *Catholic Devotion in Victorian England* (Oxford: Clarendon Press, 1995).

Heward, C., *Making a Man of Him: Parents and their Sons' Education at an English Public School, 1929–1950* (London: Routledge, 1988).

Hickey, J., *Urban Catholics: Urban Catholicism in England and Wales from 1829 to the present day* (London: Catholic Book Club, 1967).

Hickman, M., *Religion, Class and Identity: The State, the Catholic Church and the Education of the Irish in Britain* (London: Avebury, 1995).

Hill, J. M., *The Rosminian Mission* (Leominster: Gracewing, 2017).

Hill, J. M., *Angelo Rinolfi: The Preacher* (Leominster: Gracewing, 2021).

Hill, R., *God's Architect: Pugin and the Building of Romantic Britain* (London: Penguin, 2008).

Holmes, J. D., *More Roman than Rome: English Catholicism in the Nineteenth Century* (London: Burns & Oates, 1978).
Honey, J. de S., *Tom Brown's Universe: The Development of the Victorian Public School* (London: Millington, 1977).
Hornsby-Smith, M., *Catholic Education: The Unobtrusive Partner* (London: Sheed & Ward, 1978).
Hornsby-Smith, M., *Roman Catholic Beliefs in England: Customary Catholicism and Transformations of Religious Authority* (Cambridge: Cambridge University Press, 1991).
Hornsby-Smith, M. (ed.), *Catholics in England 1950–2000: Historical and Sociological Perspectives* (London: Cassell, 1999).
Hornsby-Smith, M., *An Introduction to Catholic Social Thought* (Cambridge: Cambridge University Press, 2006).
Howell, P. A., "The School Buildings at Downside", *The Raven*, 62/63 (1971–3).
Husenbeth, F. C., *The Life of the Right Reverend Monsignor Weedall, DD, Domestic Prelate of His Holiness Pope Pius IX and President of St Mary's College, Oscott* (London: Longmans Green, 1860).
Kay-Ware, D., *People of St Edmund's* (Ware: Edmundian Association, 2003).
Keating, J., "Faith and Community Threatened: Roman Catholic responses to the Welfare State, Materialism and social mobility, 1945–1962", *Twentieth-century British History* 9:1 (1998), pp. 86–108.
Kenny, A., *A Path from Rome* (Oxford: Oxford University Press, 1986).
Lambert, R. and Millham, S., *The Hothouse Society* (Harmondsworth: Penguin, 1974).
Lane, P., *The Catenian Association 1908–1983: A Microcosm of the Development of the Catholic Middle Class* (London: Catenian Association, 1982).
Lawson, J. and Silver, H., *A Social History of Education in England* (London: Methuen, 1973).
Leetham, C. R., *Ratcliffe College 1847–1947* (Leicester: Ratcliffian Association, 1950).
Leinster-Mackay, D., *The Rise of the English Prep School* (London: Falmer Press, 1984).

Levi, P., *Beaumont 1861–1961* (London: André Deutsch, 1961).
Levi, P., *The Flutes of Autumn* (London: Arena, 1985).
Leys, M., *Catholics in England 1559–1829* (London: Catholic Book Club, 1961).
Little, B., *Prior Park: Its History and Description* (Bath: Prior Park College, 1975).
Mangan, J. A., *Athleticism and the Victorian and Edwardian Public School* (London: Cass, 1981).
Marrett-Crosby, A., *A School of the Lord's Service: A History of Ampleforth* (London: James & James, 2002).
Marshall, J., "Catholic Family Life", in M. Hornsby-Smith (ed.), *Catholics in England 1950–2000: Historical and Sociological Perspectives* (London: Cassell, 1999), pp. 67–77.
Mathew, D., "Old Catholics and Converts", in G. A. Beck (ed.), *The English Catholics: Centenary Essays to Commemorate the Restoration of the Hierarchy of England and Wales* (London: Burns & Oates, 1950), pp. 223–42.
McCann, J. and Cary-Elwes, C. (eds), *Ampleforth and its Origins* (London: Burns, Oates & Washbourne, 1952).
McClelland, V. A., *Cardinal Manning: His Public Life and Influence 1865–1892* (London: Oxford University Press, 1962).
McClelland, V. A., *English Roman Catholics and Higher Education 1830–1903* (Oxford: Clarendon, 1973).
McClelland, V. A., "A Catholic Eton by hook or by crook: John Henry Newman and the establishment of the Oratory School", *Aspects of Education* 22 (1980), pp. 3–17.
McClelland, V. A., "Great Britain and Ireland", in A. Hastings (ed.), *Modern Catholicism: Vatican II and after* (London: SPCK, 1991), pp. 365–76.
McClelland, V. A., "Bourne, Norfolk and the Irish Parliamentarians: Roman Catholics and the Education Bill of 1906", *Recusant History* 23:2 (1996), pp. 228–56.
McClelland, V. A. and Hodgetts, M. (eds), *From Without the Flaminian Gate: 150 Years of Roman Catholicism in England and Wales, 1850–2000* (London: Darton, Longman & Todd, 1999).

McLaughlin, T., O'Keefe, J. and O'Keeffe, B. (eds), *The Contemporary Catholic School: Context, Identity and Diversity* (London: Falmer, 1996).

McLeod, H., "Building the Catholic Ghetto: Catholic organisations, 1870–1914", in W. Sheils and D. Wood (eds), *Voluntary Religion* (London: Studies in Church History: Blackwell, 1986), pp. 411–44.

McLeod, H., "The religious crisis of the 1960s", *Journal of Modern European History* 3:2 (2005), pp. 205–30.

Milburn, D., *A History of Ushaw College* (Durham: Ushaw College, 1964).

Morris, A. B., *Fifty Years On: The Case for Catholic Schools* (Chelmsford: Matthew James, 2008).

Muir, T. E., *Stonyhurst College 1593–1993* (Cirencester: St Omers Press, revised edition, 2006).

Norman, E., *Roman Catholicism in England* (Oxford: Oxford University Press, 1985).

O'Brien, S., "Religious Life for Women", in V. A. McClelland and M. Hodgetts (eds), *From Without the Flaminian Gate: 150 Years of Roman Catholicism in England and Wales, 1850–2000* (London: Darton, Longman & Todd, 1999), pp. 108–41.

Ogilvie, V., *The English Public School* (London: Batsford, 1957).

O'Keeffe, B., "Reordering perspectives in Catholic schools", in M. Hornsby-Smith (ed.), *Catholics in England 1950–2000: Historical and Sociological Perspectives* (London: Cassell, 1999), pp. 242–65.

O'Neill, C., *Catholics of Consequence: Transnational Education, Social Mobility and the Irish Catholic Elite, 1850–1900* (Oxford: Oxford University Press, 2014).

Peel, M., *The New Meritocracy: A History of UK Independent Schools, 1979–2015* (London: Elliot & Thompson, 2015).

Pepinster, C., *The Keys of the Kingdom: The British State and the Papacy from John Paul to Francis* (London: Bloomsbury, 2017).

Rae, J., *The Public School Revolution: Britain's Independent Schools 1964–1979* (London: Faber & Faber, 1981).

Rausch, T., *Catholicism in the Third Millenium* (Collegeville, MN: Liturgical Press, 2003).

Roberts, F. (with Henshaw, N.), *A History of Sedgley Park and Cotton College* (Privately published, 1985).

Roberts, I. D., "Jesuit Collegiate Education in England, 1794–1914", MEd Thesis, University of Durham (1986).

Roche, J. S., *A History of Prior Park and its founder Bishop Baines* (London: Burns, Oates & Washbourne, 1931).

Rosman, D., *The Evolution of the English Churches 1500–2000* (Cambridge: Cambridge University Press, 2003).

Scally, D., *The Best Catholics in the World: The Irish, the Church and the End of a Special Relationship* (London: Sandycove/Penguin, 2021).

Scarisbrick, J. J. (ed.), *History of the Diocese of Birmingham, 1850–2000* (Strasbourg: Editions du Signe, 2008).

Schofield, N., *William Lockhart: First Fruits of the Oxford Movement* (Leominster: Gracewing, 2011).

Schofield, N., *The History of St Edmund's College* (Ware: The Edmundian Association, 2013).

Scott, G. (ed.), *The English Benedictine Community of St Edmund, King and Martyr: Paris 1615/Douai 1818/Woolhampton 1903–2003* (Worcester: Stanbrook Abbey Press, 2003).

Sewell, D., *Catholics: Britain's Largest Minority* (London: Viking, 2001).

Shrimpton, P., *A Catholic Eton? Newman's Oratory School* (Leominster: Gracewing, 2005).

Shrosbee, C., *Public Schools and Private Education: The Clarendon Commission 1861–4 and the Public Schools Act* (Manchester: Manchester University Press, 1988).

Simon, B., *Education and the Social Order: British Education since 1944* (London: Lawrence & Wishart, 1999).

Smith, J. T., "The Priest and the Elementary School in the second half of the nineteenth century", *Recusant History* 25:3 (2001), pp. 530–41.

Snell, K. and Ell, P., *Rival Jerusalems: The Geography of Victorian Religion* (Cambridge: Cambridge University Press, 2000).

Snow, Abbot, *Sketches of Old Downside* (London: Sands & Co., 1903).

Stanford, P., *Cardinal Hume and the Changing Face of English Catholicism* (London: G. Chapman, 1993).
Stourton, E., *Absolute Truth: The Catholic Church Today* (Harmondsworth: Penguin, 1999).
Stourton, E., *Confessions: Life Re-Examined* (London: Doubleday, 2023).
Tenbus, E., *English Catholics and the Education of the Poor, 1847–1902* (London: Pickering Chatto, 2010).
Thompson, J., *History of Oscott* (The Oscotian, 1932–1937).
Tinkell, T., *Cardinal Newman's School: 150 Years of the Oratory School* (London: Third Millenium Publishing, 2009).
Turnbull, M., *Abbey Boys: Fort Augustus Abbey Schools* (Perth: corbie.com, 2000).
Turner, D., *The Old Boys: The Decline and Rise of the Public School* (London: Yale University Press, 2016).
Van Zeller, H., *Downside By and Large* (London: Sheed & Ward, 1954).
Verkaik, R., *Posh Boys: How English Public Schools Ruin Britain* (London: Oneworld, 2018).
Ward, C. K., *Priest and People: A Study in the Sociology of Religion* (Liverpool: Liverpool University Press, 1961).
Williams, M., "Seminaries and Priestly Formation", in V. A. McClelland and M. Hodgetts (eds), *From Without the Flaminian Gate: 150 Years of Roman Catholicism in England and Wales, 1850–2000* (London: Darton, Longman & Todd, 1999), pp. 62–83.
Williams, M., *Oscott College in the Twentieth Century* (Leominster: Gracewing, 2001).
Wills, C., *The Best are Leaving: Emigration and Post-war Irish Culture* (Cambridge: Cambridge University Press, 2015).
Wills, C., *Lovers and Strangers: An Immigrant History of Post-War Britain* (London: Penguin, 2017).
Winch, J., "The role and impact of athleticism at 'two outposts of the Vatican' during the 1850s–1950s", *Sport in History* 40:2 (2020), pp. 179–206.

Index

Allen, William   8, 43
alumni associations   14, 82–4
Ampleforth College   iv, 11, 12, 30, 36–9, 71, 75, 79–90, 81, 95, 99, 100, 104–5, 108, 112, 114, 124, 125–7, 163, 178, 195, 197–200, 206
assisted places scheme   122

Baines, Bishop   37, 41, 52, 121
Beaumont College   iv, 12, 57–8, 66, 71, 75, 92, 96, 100, 105, 108, 109–11, 112, 114, 130, 149–50, 172
Belmont Abbey School   iv, 12, 73, 75, 174–5, 217
Benedictines   4, 8–9, 27–8, 35-36, 41–80, 68, 79, 91–2, 131, 135, 144, 152, 168–9, 176, 188, 208, 217
Benet House, Cambridge   95
Birmingham Diocese   19, 24–5, 69, 121
Board Schools   24–5
Bourne, Cardinal   106–7, 112–13
Bullivant Report   184

Campion Hall, Oxford   93
Catenians   117, 137, 140
Catholic
  converts   20–1, 53, 213
  Emancipation Act   iv, v, 11
  Establishment   27, 124–26, 211, 212–13, 216, 220
  Catholic Evidence Guild   90
  Hierarchy   11–12, 23, 210, 220–1
  Catholic Independent Schools' Conference   227
  Catholic Poor Schools Committee   22–3
  population   18, 67–8, 118–19, 151

Catholic Relief Act   10, 20
Catholic Safeguarding Standards Agency   189
Catholic university   214–15, 216
Challoner, Richard   44, 47
Charity Commission   200, 205
Christian Brothers of Ireland   8, 41, 70, 74, 145
Clarendon Commission   2–3, 33, 37
Clifton Diocese   19, 121, 202, 204
co-education   166–8
Conference of Catholic Colleges   113–14
convent schools   iv, 69–70, 119–20, 160
Corpus Christi celebrations   87, 135
Cotton College   iv, 12, 47–8, 78, 103, 109, 112, 141–3, 173, 191
Cumberledge Report   188–9
curriculum   5, 40, 47, 57, 96–9, 123

day pupils   132, 165–6
Dominicans   8, 13
Douai, English College   8, 30, 43–4
Douai School   iv, 12, 57, 61–2, 73, 75, 90–1, 100, 114, 133–6, 162, 175–6, 191–2
Downside School   iv, 11, 12, 30, 36, 37, 40, 71, 79–80, 81, 95, 100, 108, 112, 114, 116, 124, 130–2, 163, 167, 178, 194, 200–5, 219

Education Acts   v–vi, 23–4, 69, 120, 187, 210, 211
education
  elementary   vi, 4, 21–6, 85
  secondary   25–6, 69–70, 85, 120–1, 154, 210–11

equity issues–6, 29, 212–13, 222–3
external examinations and boards 34, 35, 40, 48, 92, 96, 122–3

female religious communities 13, 24, 25, 28, 70, 119–20, 159–60, 166
Fleming Report 4, 100, 121–2, 211
Fort Augustus School (Scotland) 62, 202, 206–7
Franciscans 8, 12, 173
Free Place System 26

governance and leadership issues 168–9, 171, 187, 208
grammar schools 25
Gravissimum Educationis 226–7
Guild of the Blessed Sacrament 90

Headmasters' Conference (HMC) 4–5, 99–100, 152, 169
house system 101–4, 126

Independent Inquiry into Child Sexual Abuse 16, 183–5, 194–7
Independent Schools Inspectorate 152, 187, 193, 200, 205
international pupils 177–8
inspection schemes 123, 152, 157, 169
Irish immigration vi, 18–20, 118–19
Irish pupils 40, 63–4

Jesuits 4, 8, 9, 27, 30, 33, 54, 68, 89, 92, 105, 172, 190, 229

Labour Party 121, 122
Lamspringe, Hanover 36
Laxton School 13, 73, 113
lay teaching and management v, viii, 15, 79, 89, 98–9, 126, 134, 138, 140–1, 147, 162
league tables 178–9
liturgy 89–90, 155–6

Manning, Cardinal 27, 215
Maryvale, Birmingham 48
military training 111–13

Mount St Benedict, Ireland 62
Mount St Mary's College 12, 54–7, 65, 66, 78, 81, 84, 96, 103, 105, 109, 112, 137–8, 170, 177, 180

Newman, St John Henry vii, 20, 48, 58, 66, 86–7, 101, 215
Nolan Report 187, 188, 198, 203
Northampton Diocese 69, 138
Nottingham Diocese 69, 140

Office for Standards in Education (OFSTED) 200, 204–5
Old Hall Green Academy 44
Oratory Fathers 48
Oratory School vii, 12, 58–62, 65, 66, 73–4, 86–7, 101, 109–11, 145–7, 191
Oscott College iv, 12, 13, 48–50, 143, 174
Oxbridge entrance 14, 35, 84, 93–6, 123, 126, 179, 214

parishes 19, 85–6, 91, 133
Passionists 8
preparatory schools 5, 80–2, 185–6
Prior Park College iv, 39, 41–3, 57–8, 74–5, 144–5, 171–2
Princethorpe College 177
Public Schools Commission 153
Pugin, Augustus Welby 21, 40, 45, 46, 48, 52

Ratcliffe College 12, 41, 52–4, 65, 66, 71, 81, 96, 103, 108, 109, 138–41, 162, 170, 177, 192–3
Recusancy Laws 6–7, 10, 20–1
Reformation and Catholic schools 6–7
regulars 8–9
Religious Census (1851) 18
Restoration of the Catholic hierarchy 9, 11
Rosminians 8, 41, 52, 99, 162, 192–3

Sacred Congregation for Catholic Education 227
safeguarding legislation 186–7
St Benet's Hall, Oxford 95

St Bernadine's College   12, 57, 73, 173
St Edmund's College, Ware   11–12, 13, 29, 43–4, 45, 46, 71, 78, 80, 95, 105–7, 112–13, 132–3, 165, 169, 170, 177
St Edmund's House, Cambridge   93–5
St Gregory's, Douai   36
Sts Hadrian and Dionysius   36, 37
St Laurence, Dieulouard   36
St Omers, France   30–2
school spirituality 12, 85–92, 126–7, 131, 143, 156–7, 179–80, 218, 224–5
seculars   9–10, 27, 28
secularization   157–8
Sedgley Park   iv, 12, 47–8
seminaries   8, 13, 29–30, 53, 174
Society of St Vincent de Paul   117
sports   65–6, 107–12, 179, 180–1
Stonyhurst College   iv, 11, 12, 30, 32–5, 64, 66, 75, 87, 92, 95, 100, 103–4, 105, 112, 114, 127–30, 177, 189–90, 215

university expansion   123, 216
University of London examinations   35, 41, 92
Upholland   12, 51, 174, 190
Ushaw College   12, 13, 29, 44–5, 78, 112, 174, 190

vocations   vii, 68, 86, 118, 140–1, 148, 158–61, 163–4, 219
Vatican II   vii, 15, 117, 148, 155–6, 160–1, 170, 172

Wiseman, Cardinal   27, 53
Woburn Park School   41
Woodard Schools   56
Worth Abbey and School   81

EU GPSR Authorized Representative:

LOGOS EUROPE, 9 rue Nicolas Poussin, 17000 La Rochelle, France

contact@logoseurope.eu